AF305237

today is tomorrow's yesterday

RUBÉN SÁNCHEZ

slanted

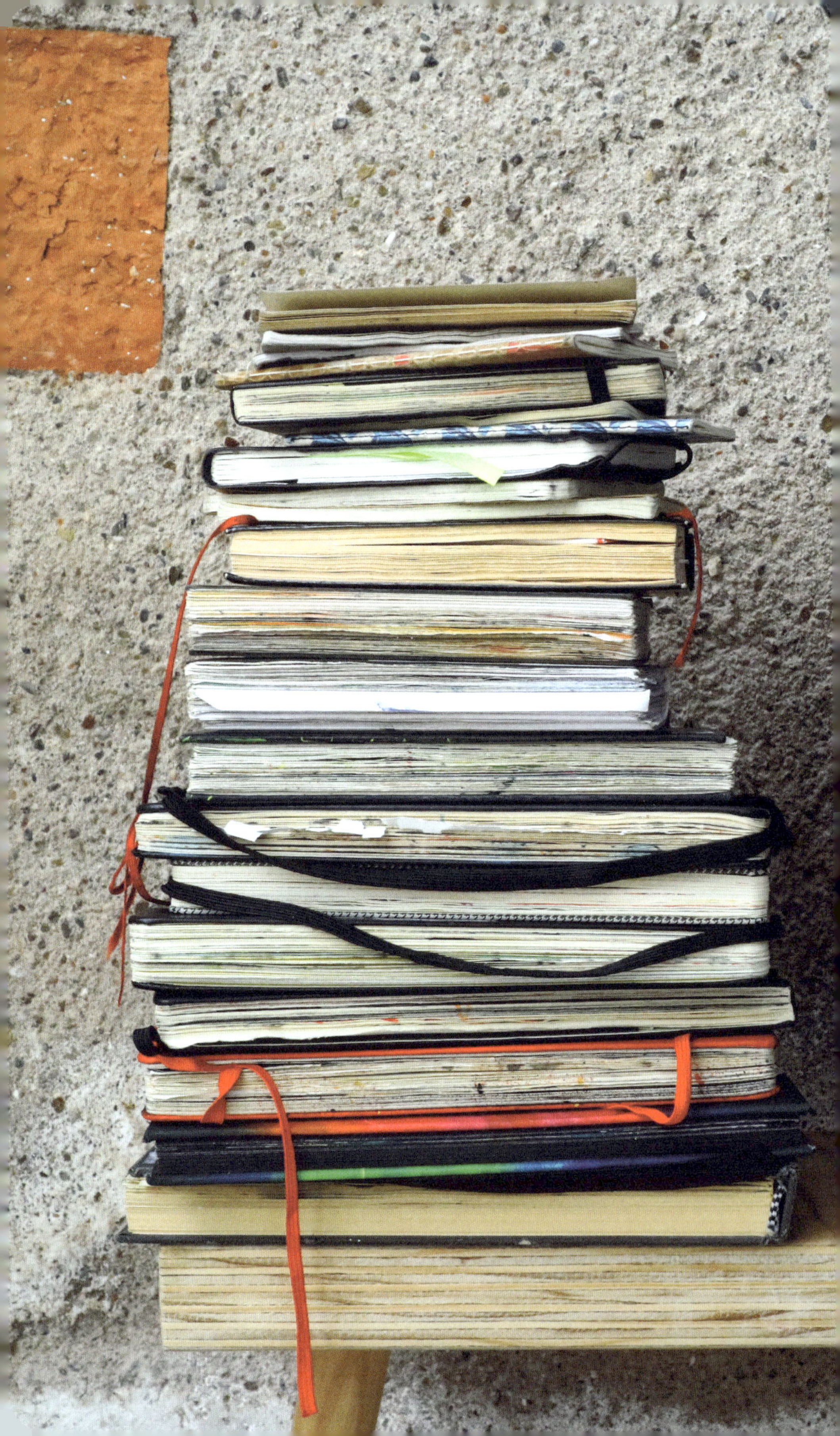

I feel like an explorer in a foreign terrain.

First time I make a book but I'm not a writer. I don't even know if I have the requirements to be an artist, if there are any.

In order to avoid any misunderstanding, I'm just a human being with lots of sketchbooks that were never intended to be public, but for some reason I'm sharing with you.

These notebooks have been my closest friends in different countries and stages of my life, don't expect much sense nor cleanness. They are shown as raw as they are.

They are showing today's from many yesterday's, but there are many tomorrow's to come.

Enjoy this journey with no destination.

Rubén.

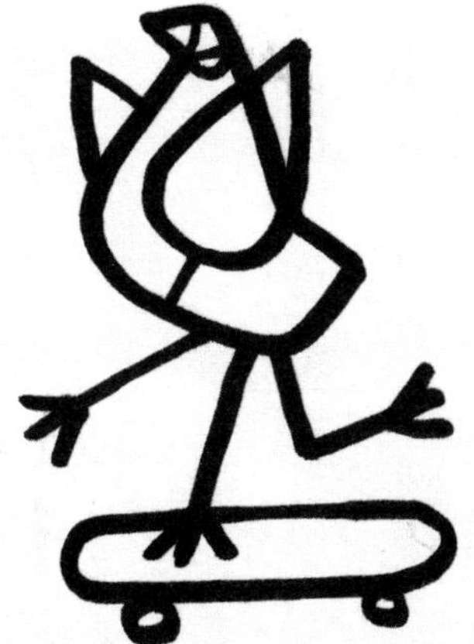

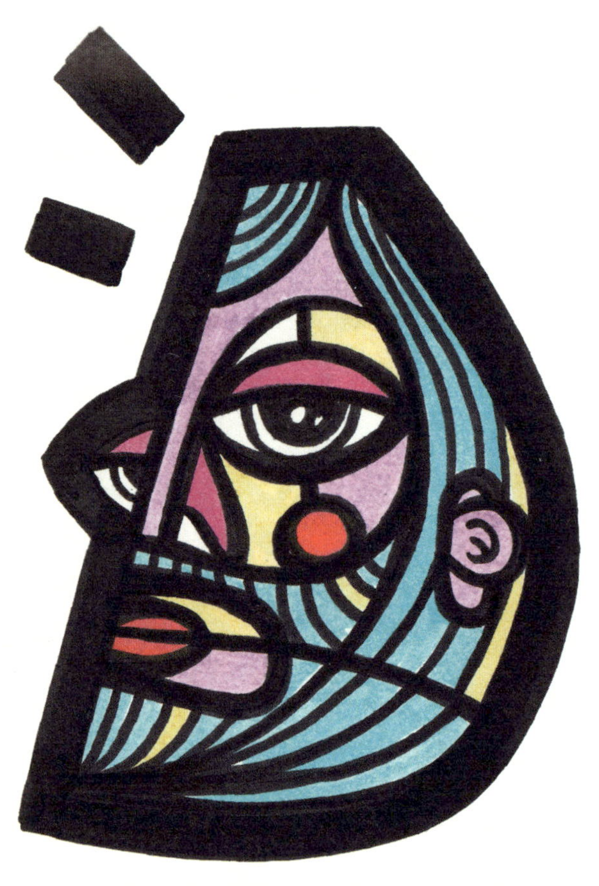

THE BOOK NOT MANY PEOPLE WAS WAITING FOR

ΕΚΘΕΣΙΣ

ΠΕΡΙ ΤΩΝ

ΕΝ ΤΩι ΘΕΑΤΡΩι ΤΗΣ ΕΠΙΔΑΥΡΟΥ

ΑΝΑΣΚΑΦΩΝ.

Α΄.

Μετὰ τὰς ἐν Ὀλυμπίᾳ καὶ ἐν Δήλῳ ἀνασκαφὰς οἱ ἀρχαιο-
λογοῦντες ἔπρεπε νὰ ἀποβλέψωσι μάλιστα πάντων εἰς τὸ
ἐν τῇ Ἐπιδαυρίᾳ ἱερὸν τοῦ Ἀσκληπιοῦ, τὴν χώραν ἐκείνην,
ἥτις πολλὰ καὶ σπουδαῖα εὑρήματα ὑπέσχετο τῇ ἡμετέρᾳ
ἐπιστήμῃ. Τὴν φορὰν δὲ ταύτην ἐπεφυλάσσετο ἡ τιμὴ
τῆς πρωτοβουλίας καὶ ___ ὐλάχιστον ἐκτελέ-
σεως τῶν ἀνασκαφῶν ___ τέραν Ἀρχαιο-
λογικὴν Ἑταιρίαν, ___ ἀπεστάλην
ἐκεῖσε ὑπὸ τοῦ ὑπο___ ῆς ἀπο-
στολῆς μου ταύτ___ ρίας
κ. Εὐθ. Καστόρχη ___ 3)
τάδε· «Εἰς τὸ παρ___ ,
»ἐνεκρίθη νὰ καθαρισθῇ α___ τῶν
»καλυπτόντων αὐτὸ θάμνων καὶ χωμάτων, ἐφεξῆς δὲ νὰ
»ἐκτελεσθῶσιν ἀνασκαφαὶ ἐν τῷ ἱερῷ. Ἀπεστάλη δ᾽ ἐκεῖσε
»ὁ ἔφορος κ. Π. Καββαδίας ἵνα καθαρίσῃ ἐν πρώτοις τὸ
»θέατρον καὶ περιγράψῃ αὐτό, καὶ προτείνῃ τῇ Ἑταιρίᾳ
»ὅ,τι δυνατὸν ἀμέσως γενέσθαι πρὸς ἐπιχείρησιν τῆς τοῦ
»ἱεροῦ ἀνασκαφῆς.»

Τοιαύτην λοιπὸν ἐντολὴν ἔχων μετέβην εἰς Ἐπίδαυρον
τῇ 15 Μαρτίου λήγοντος ἔτους 1881, καὶ αὐθημερὸν ἐπε-
σκέφθην τὸ μίαν ὥραν ἀπέχον τοῦ Λιγουρίου [1]), πρωτευού-

---

[1]) Ἡ ὁδὸς διέρχεται διὰ μικροῦ τινος χω___ ον περίπου
ἀπέχοντος τοῦ ἱεροῦ, καλουμένου Κορ___ ωνυμία

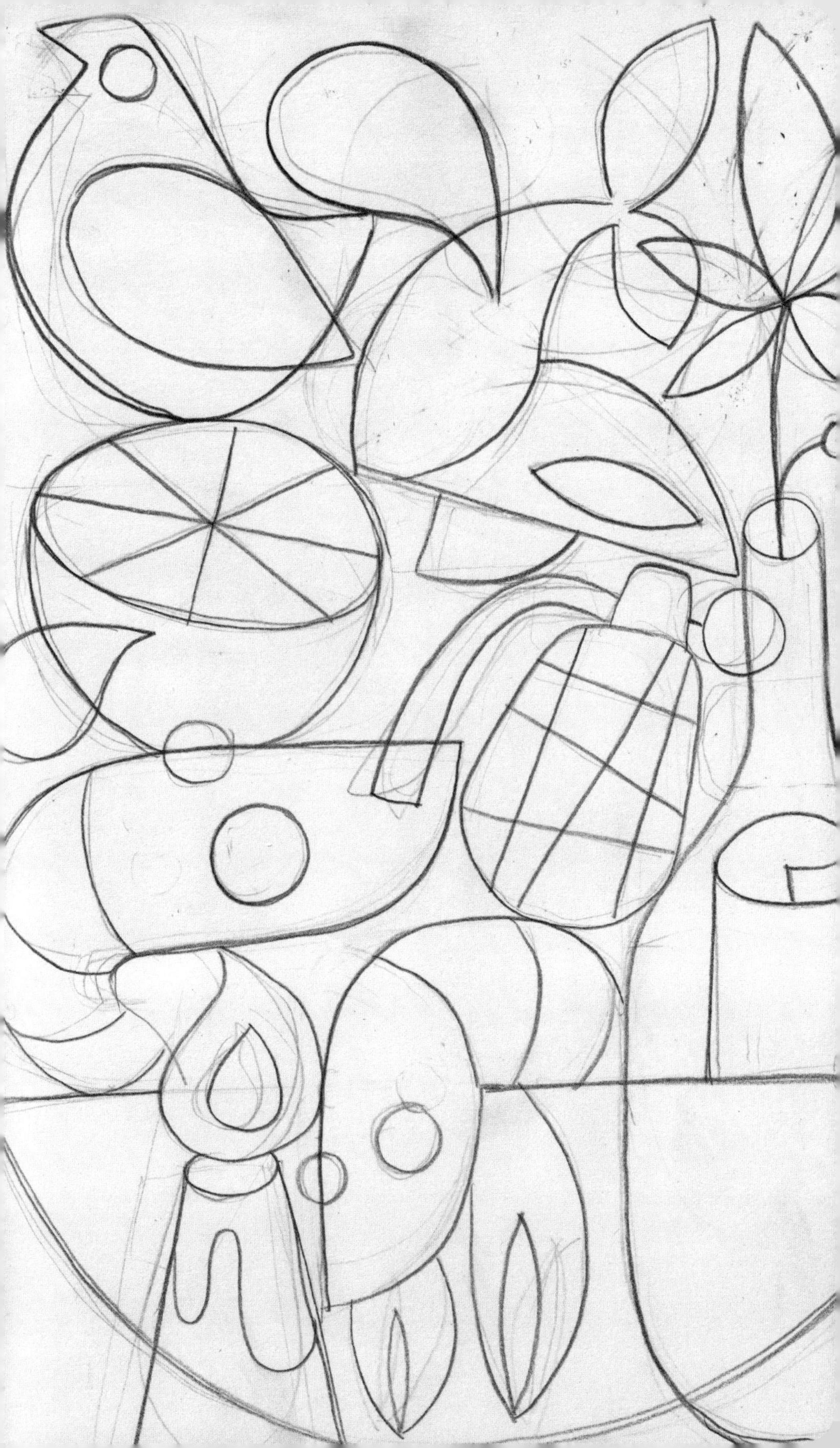

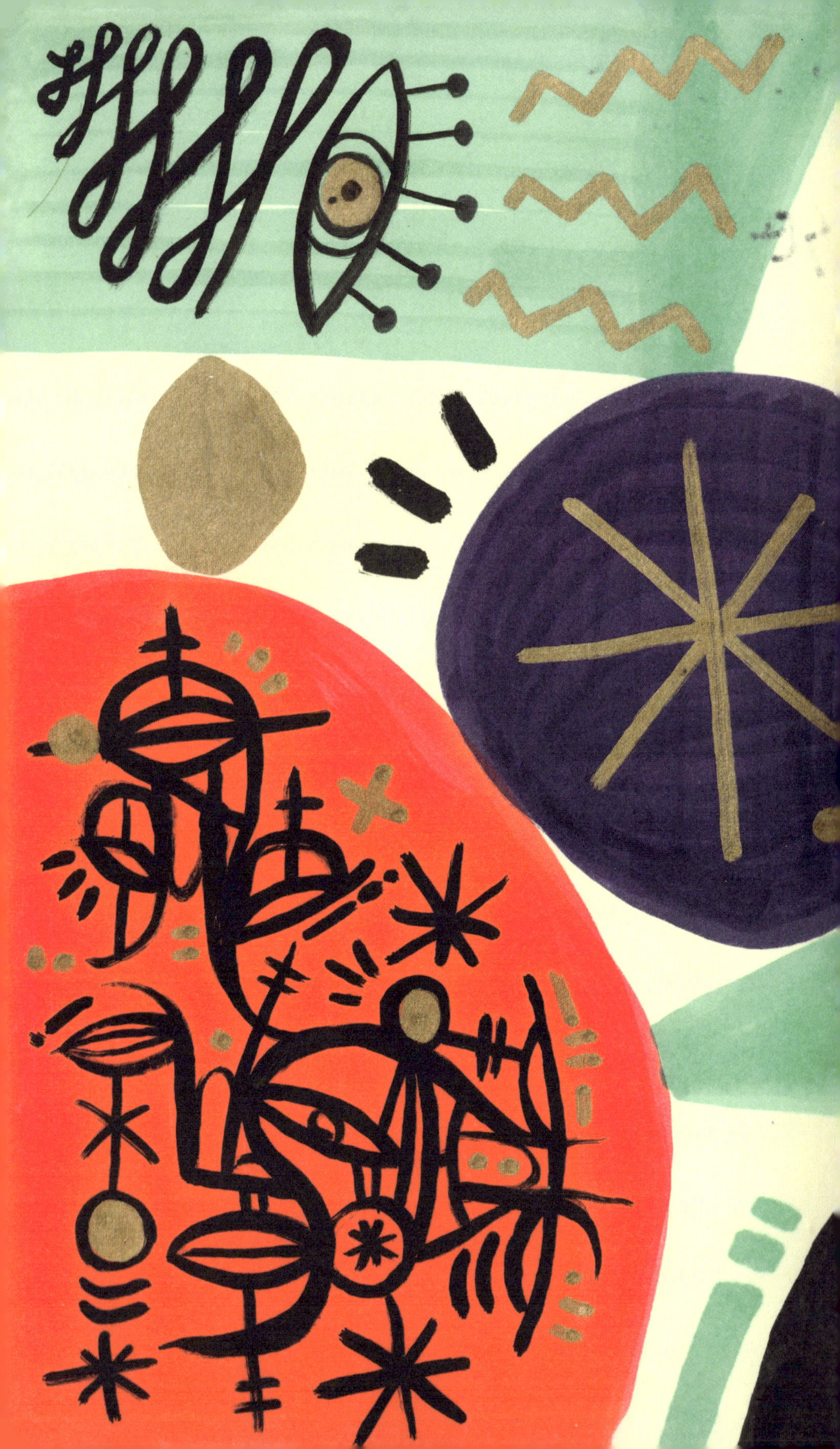

Nothing is a
mistake
There's no win & no fail
There is only
make!

Poetry is a lonely pleasure, a solitary art. The way to make poetry ridiculous and effete is to read it in public...

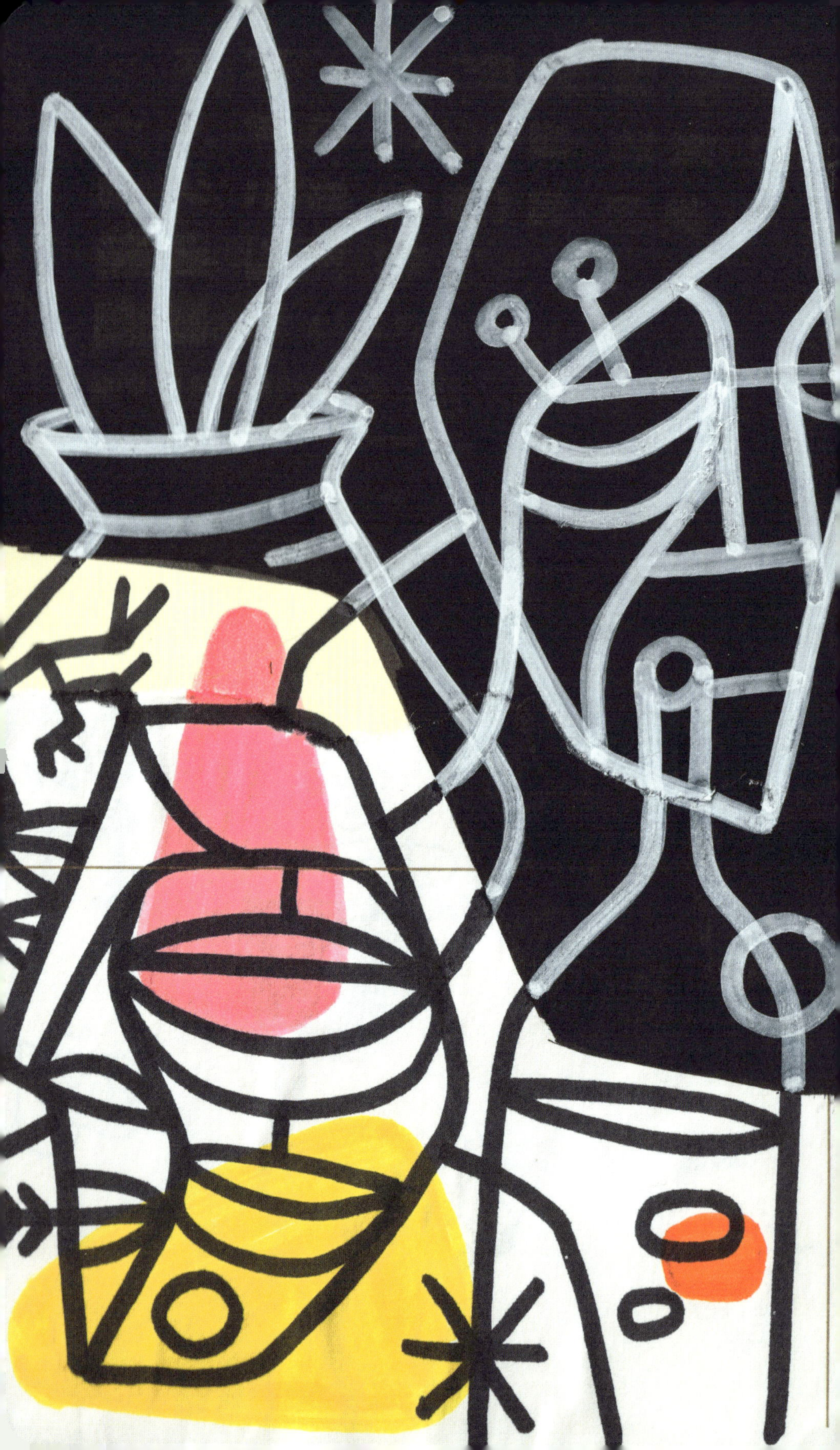

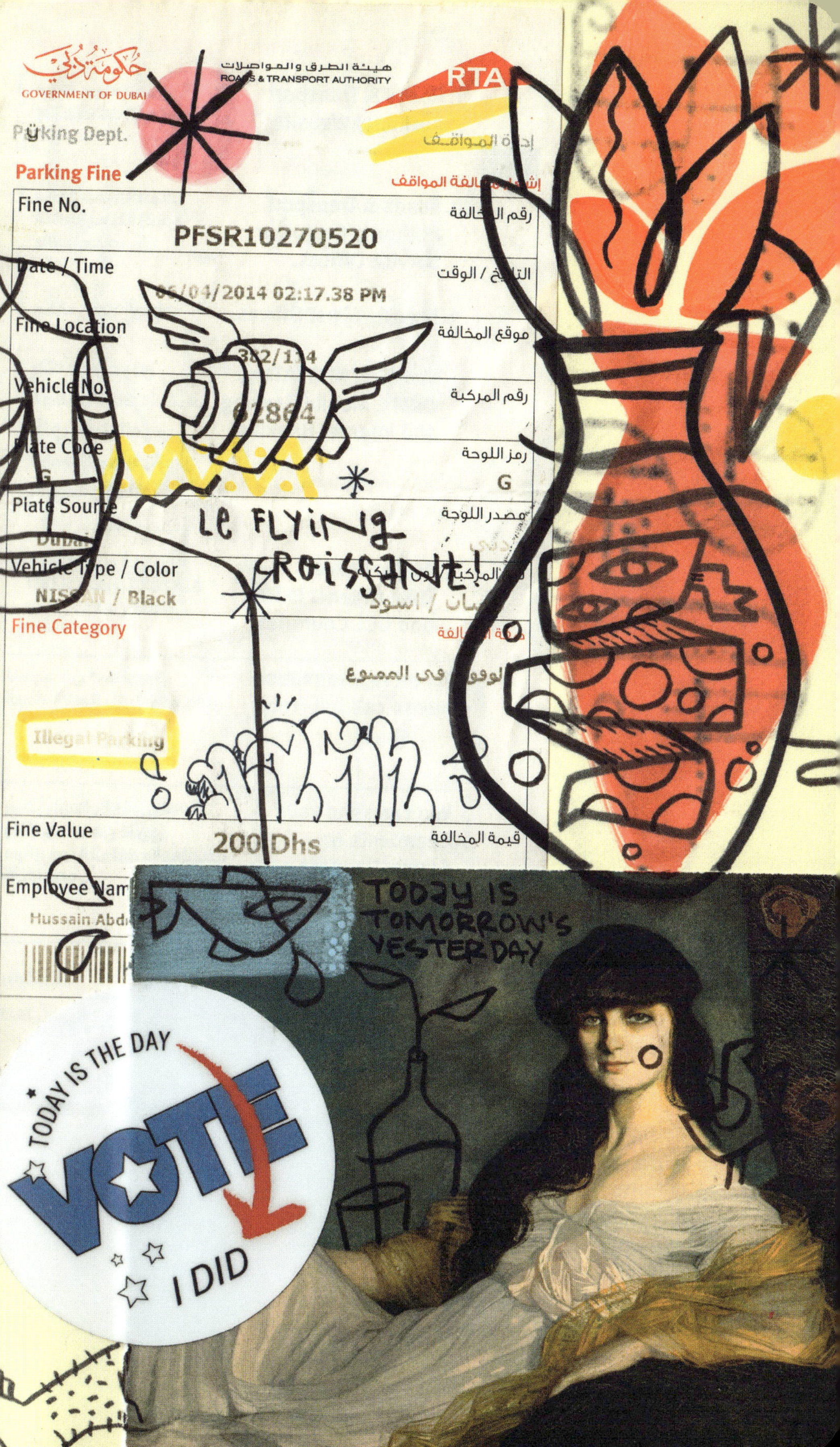
GOVERNMENT OF DUBAI
حكومة دبي
هيئة الطرق والمواصلات
ROADS & TRANSPORT AUTHORITY
RTA
إدارة المواقف
Parking Dept.
Parking Fine
إشعار بمخالفة المواقف
Fine No.
رقم المخالفة
PFSR10270520
Date / Time
التاريخ / الوقت
06/04/2014 02:17.38 PM
Fine Location
موقع المخالفة
362/154
Vehicle No.
رقم المركبة
62864
Plate Code
رمز اللوحة
G
G
Plate Source
مصدر اللوحة
Dubai
Vehicle Type / Color
نوع المركبة / اللون
NISSAN / Black
نيسان / اسود
Fine Category
نوع المخالفة
الوقوف فى الممنوع
Illegal Parking
Fine Value
قيمة المخالفة
200 Dhs
Employee Name
Hussain Abdul
LE FLYING
CROISSANT!
TODAY IS
TOMORROW'S
YESTERDAY
TODAY IS THE DAY
VOTE
I DID

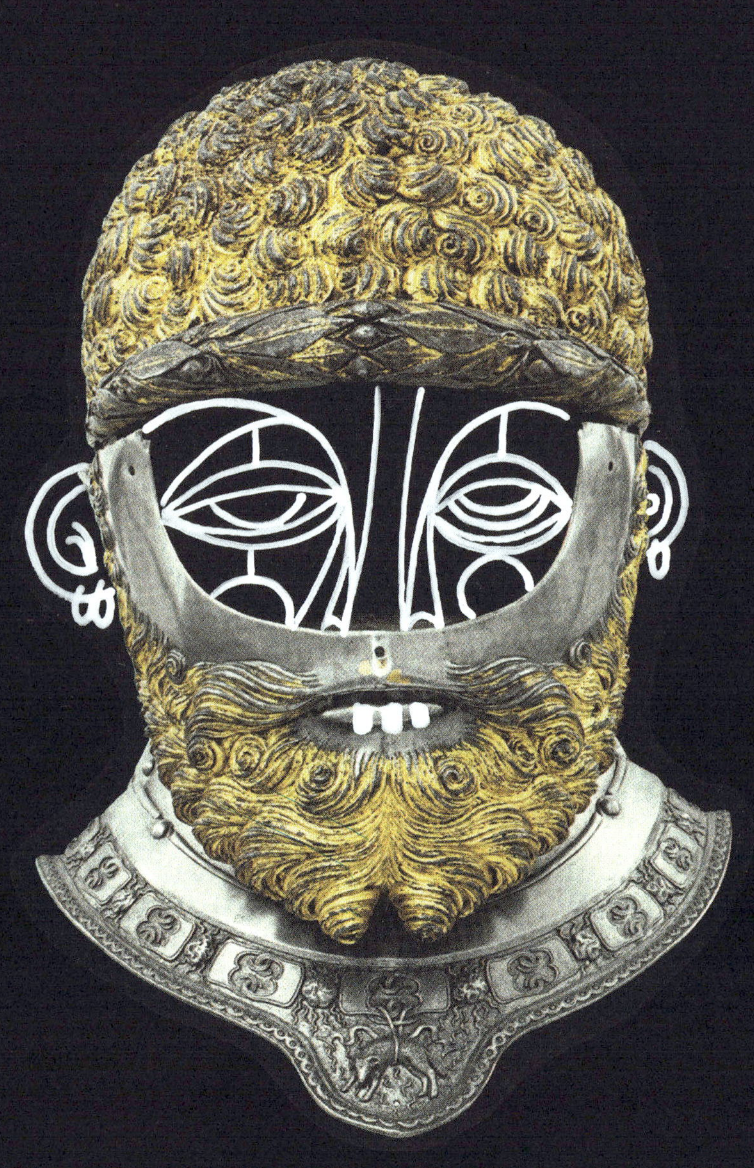

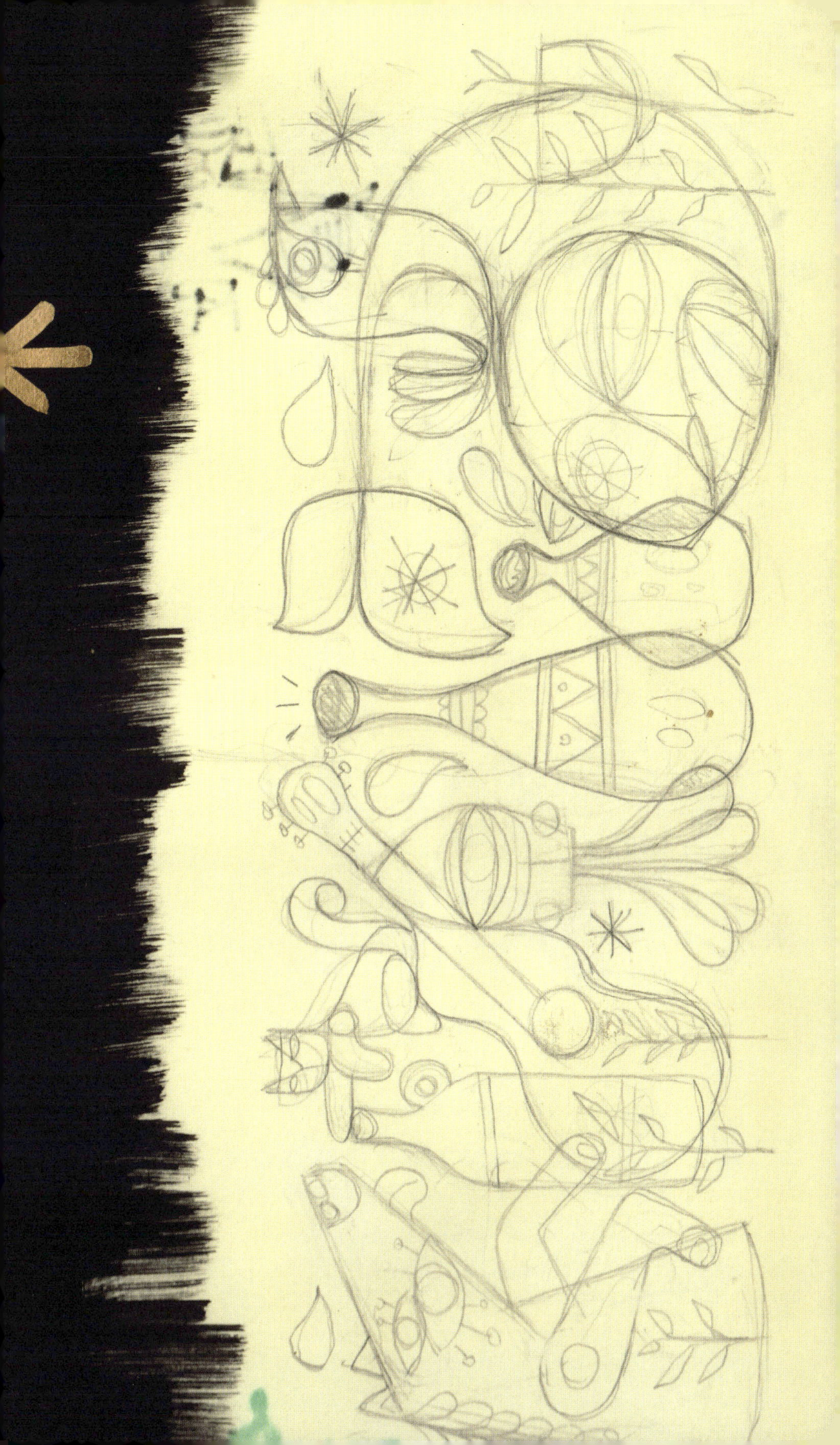

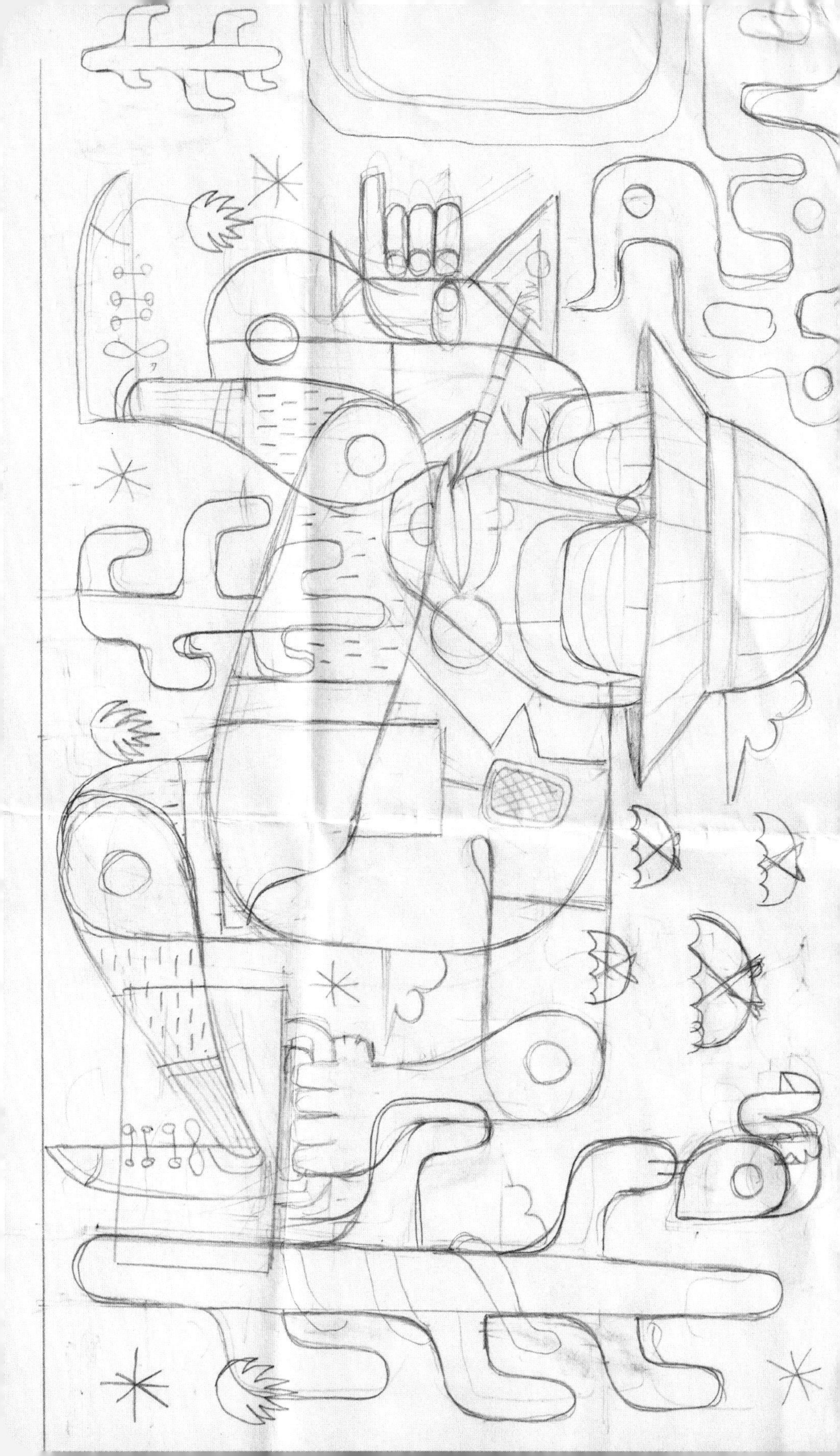

PANTONE®
319 C
PANTONE®
320 C
Diazepam mg/ml
Morphine mg/ml
NITROglycerine mg/ml
PANTONE®
374 C 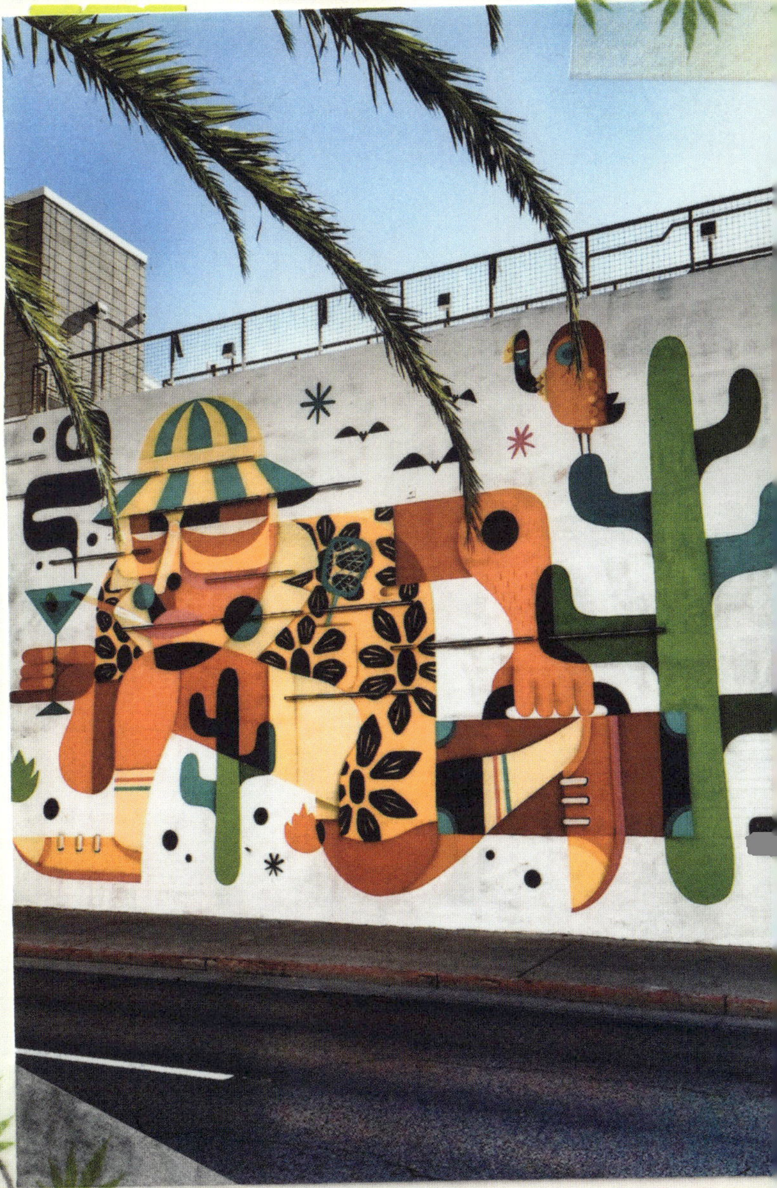
PANTONE®
376 C 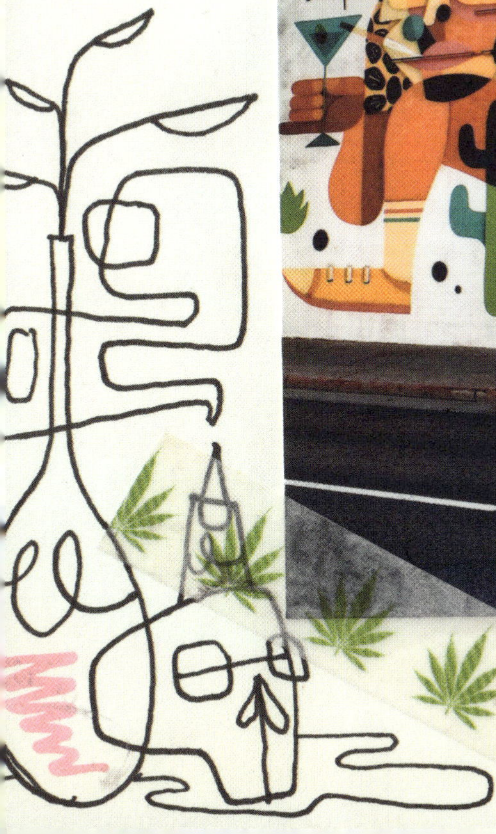
DOPAmine mg/ml

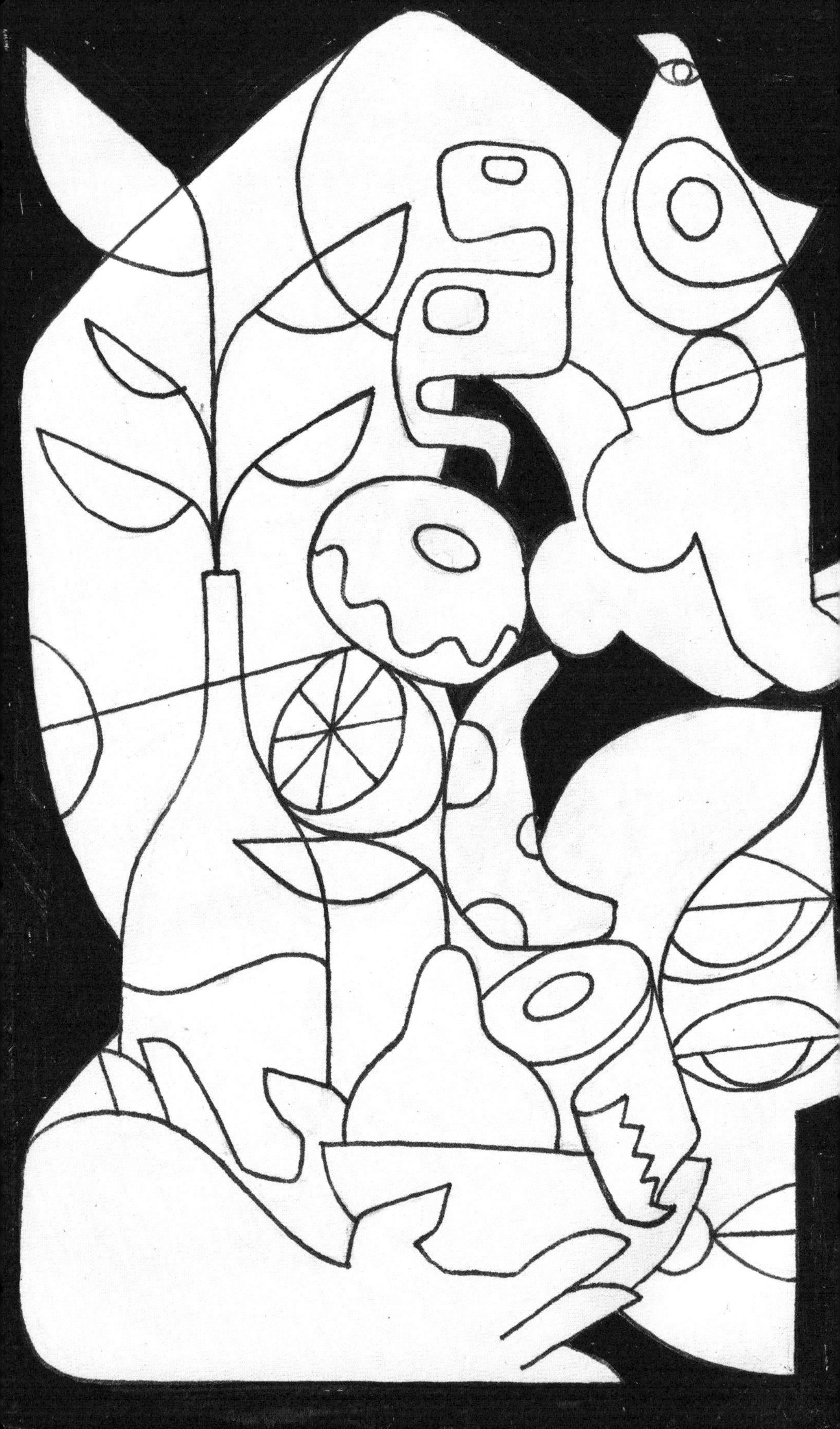

MARZO 2020

DISTANCIAMI
ENTO SOCIAL X
LTO CONTAGIO...
HIPERACTI
VO PASIVO *
ESTADO DE ALAR
MA. STOP

*

ONELA
IAS DE CONOCIM
ENTO PERDI
IO CON NUES
TROS VIEJITOS
MONGO-
LOS DE
MERCADO
MA. TE CO
MO LA BOCA *
PERO A 2 MTS.

CUARENTENA
POR CORONAVI
RUS *
ENCERRONA
MUESTRAS FÍ
SICAS DE AFECTO
IGUAL A CERO-
MANOS PUR
SE

IND
EPENDIENTE
MENTE
JUNTOS
*
REFLEXIÓN
RECETAS &
FALSETAS
INMUNOLÓGI
A TUNNING
SEMANA 1

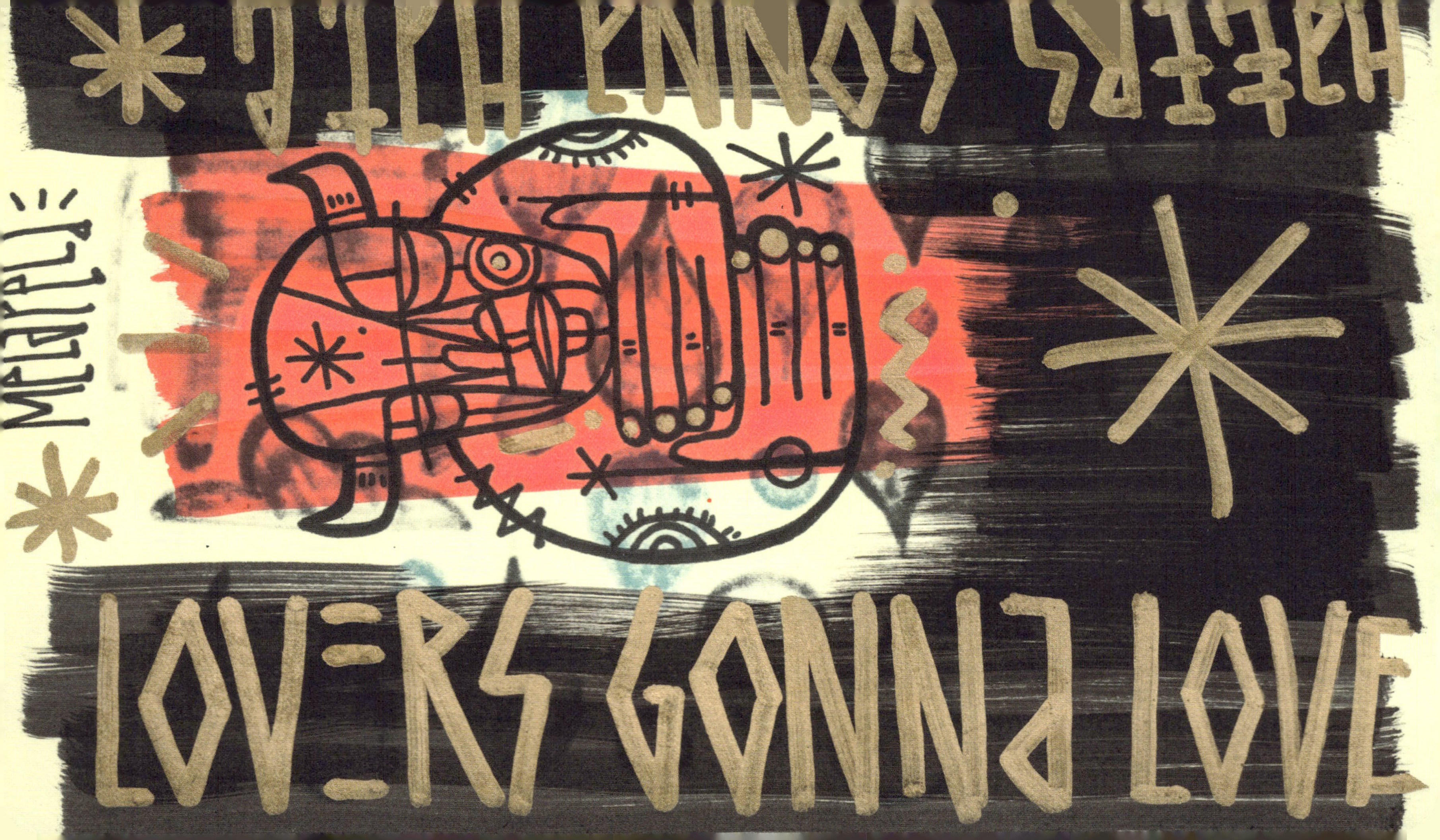
LOVERS GONNA LOVE
HATERS GONNA HATE
MELAPELI

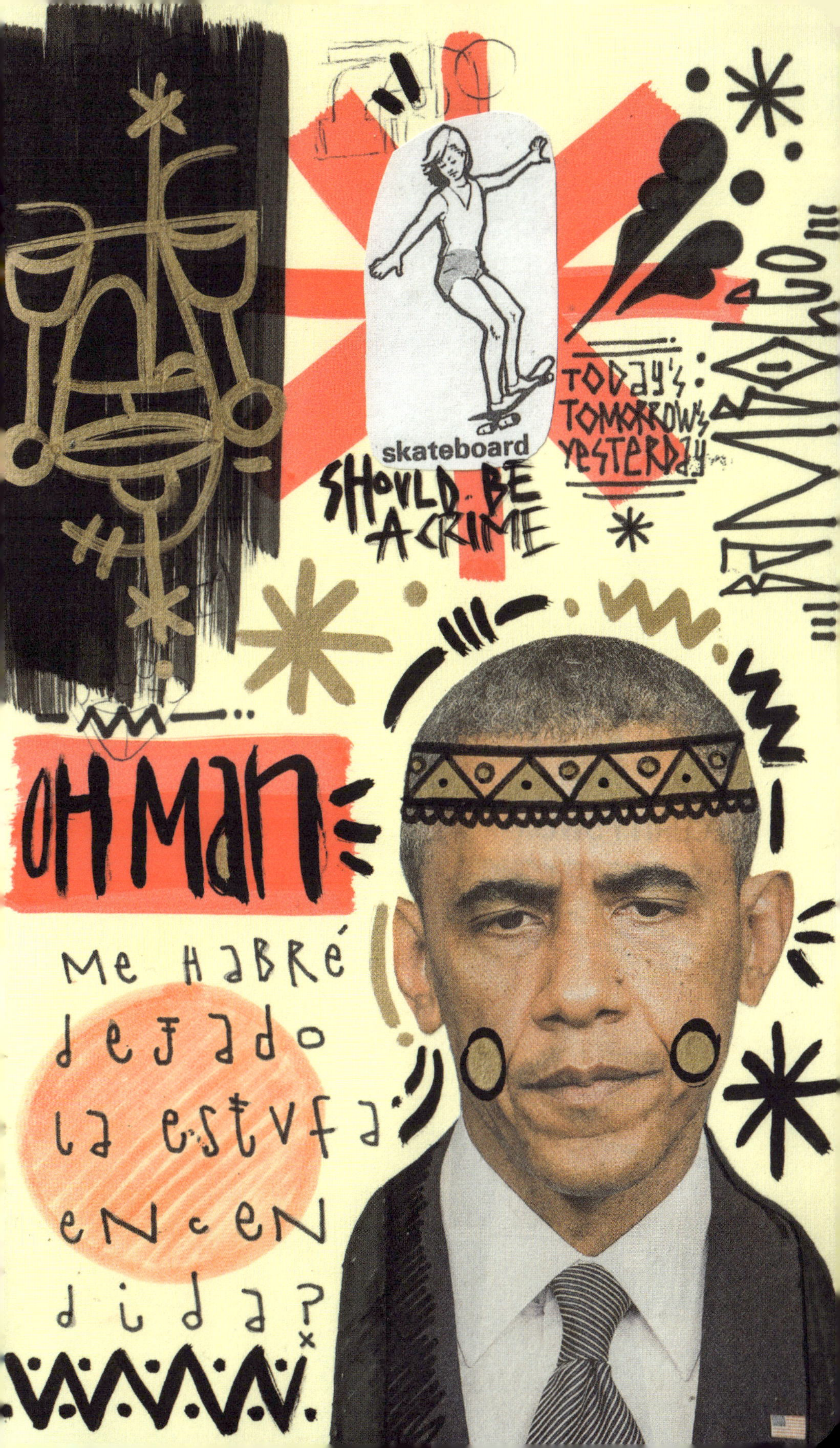

skateboard
TODAY's:
TOMORROW;
YESTERDAY
SHOULD BE
A CRIME
OH MAN
ME HABRÉ
dejado
La estufa
encen
dida?

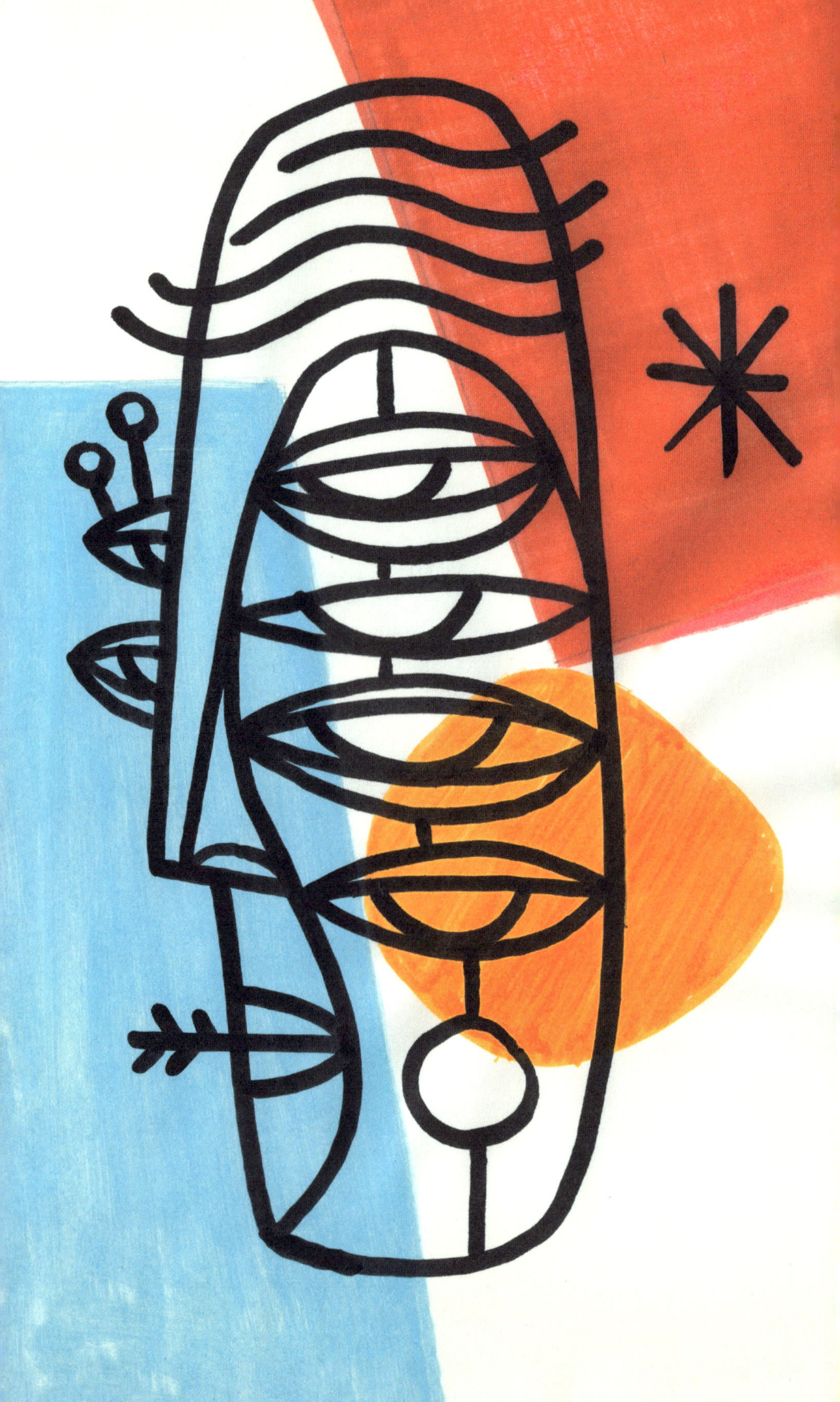

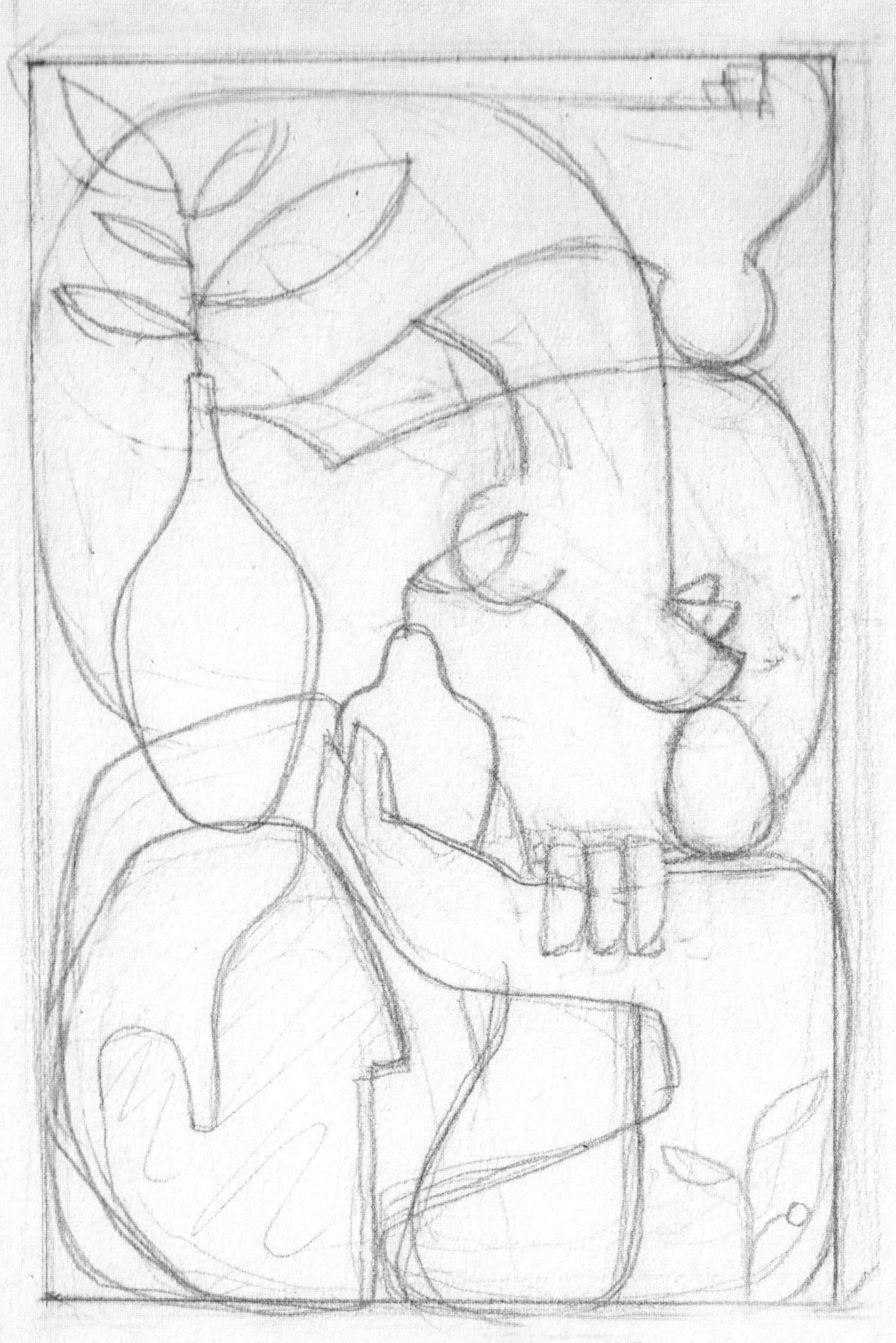

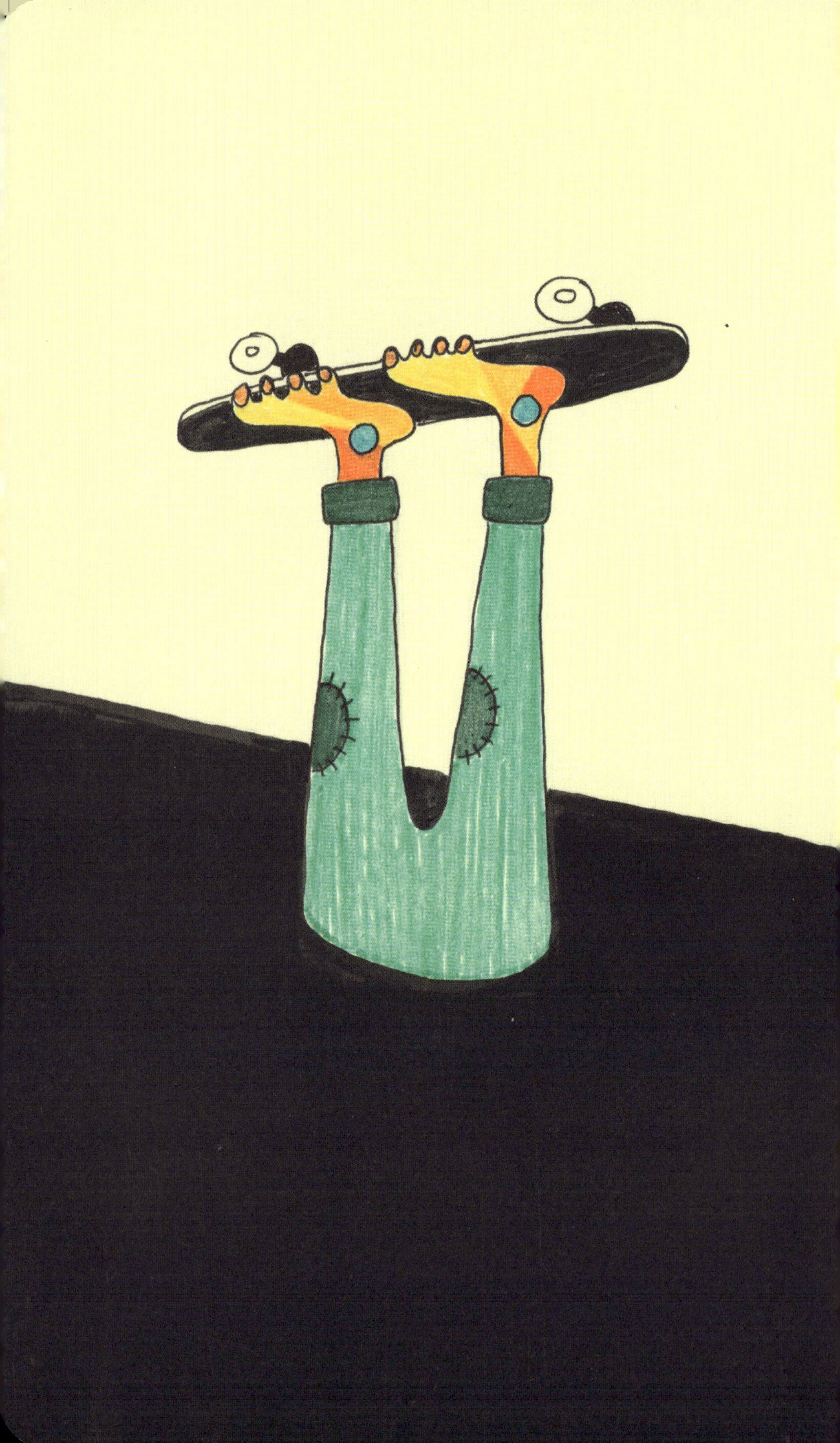

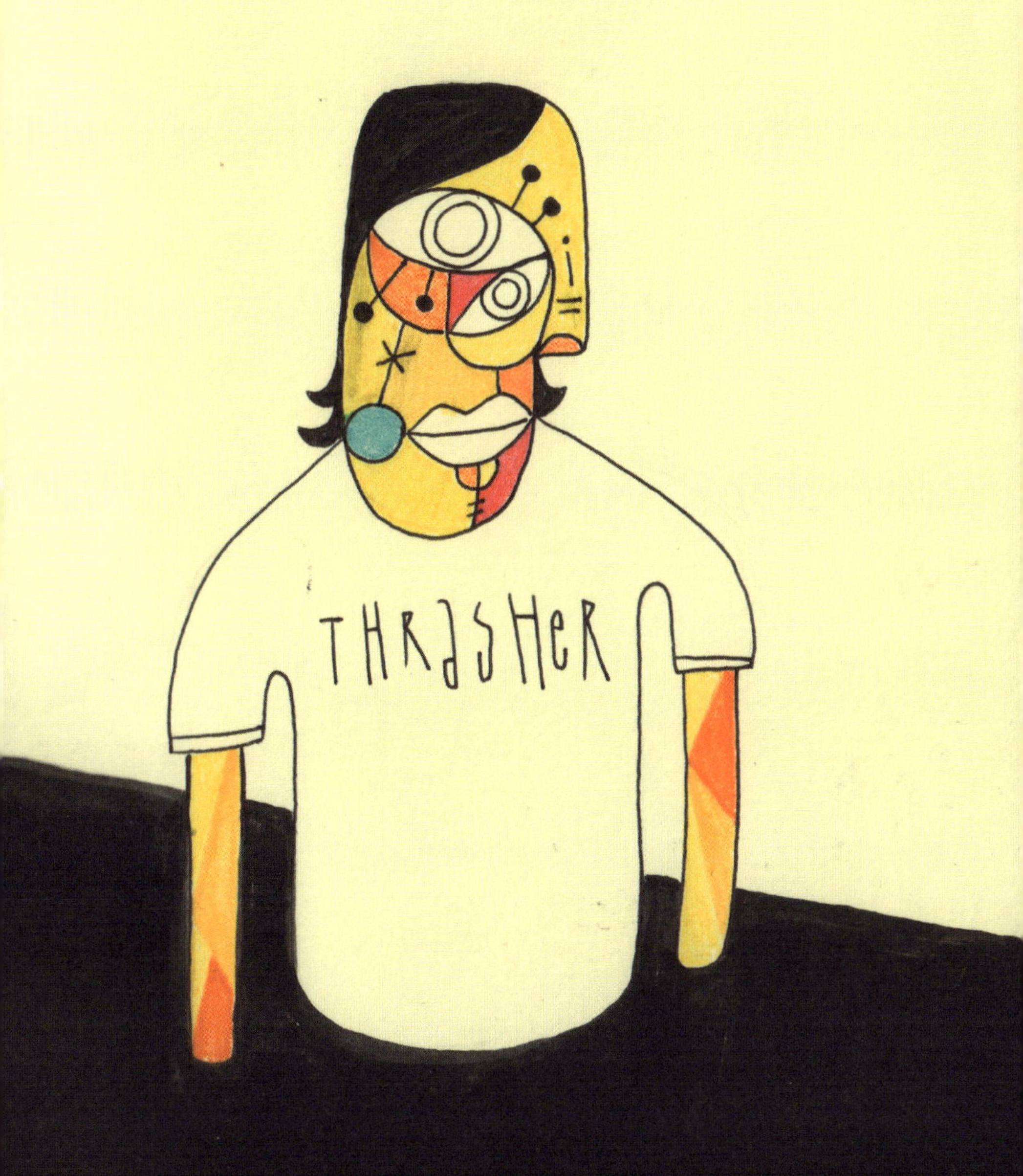

THRASHER

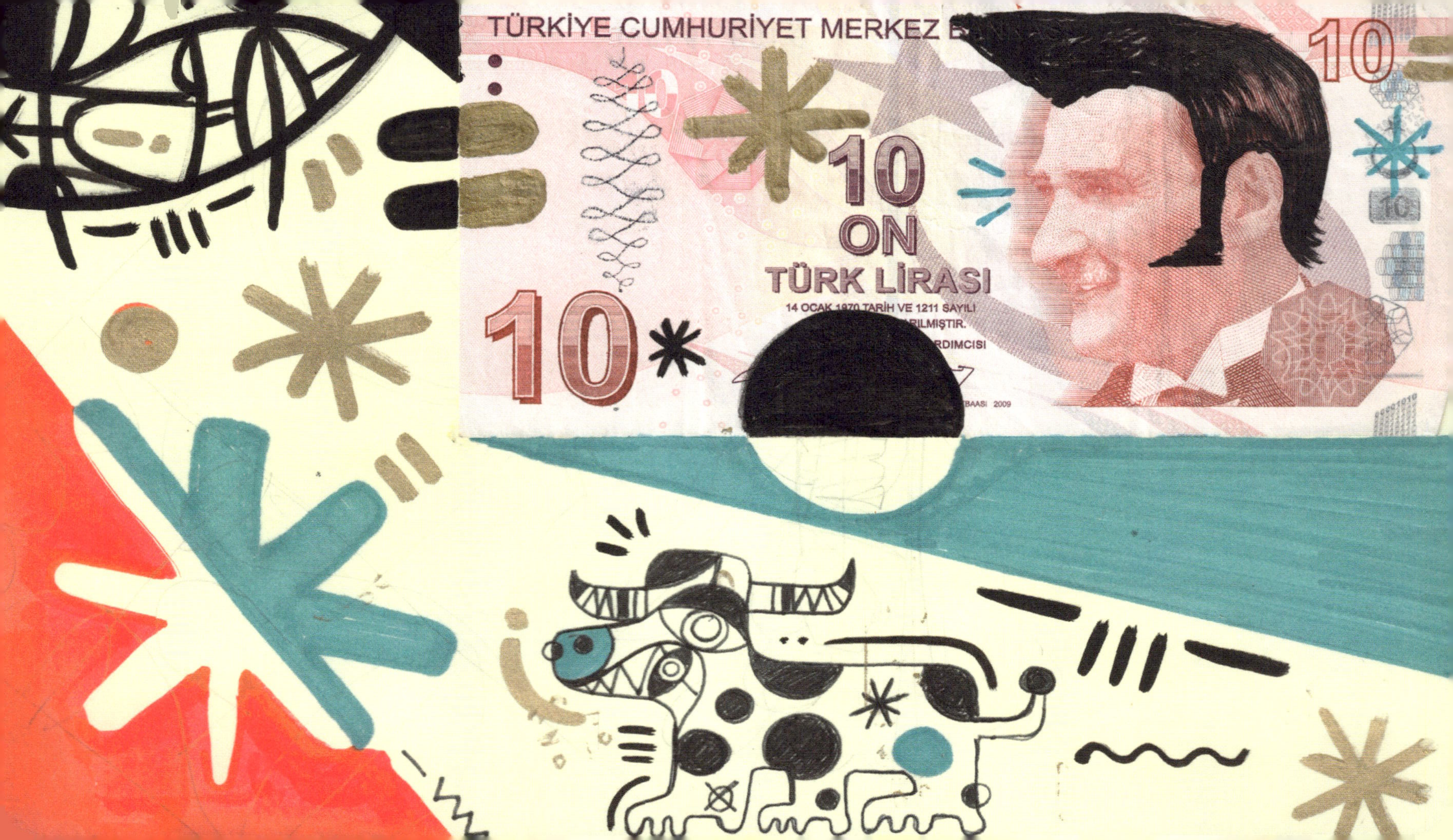

TÜRKİYE CUMHURİYET MERKEZ B
10
10
ON
TÜRK LİRASI
14 OCAK 1970 TARİH VE 1211 SAYILI
RILMIŞTIR.
RDIMCISI
BAASI 2009
10
10

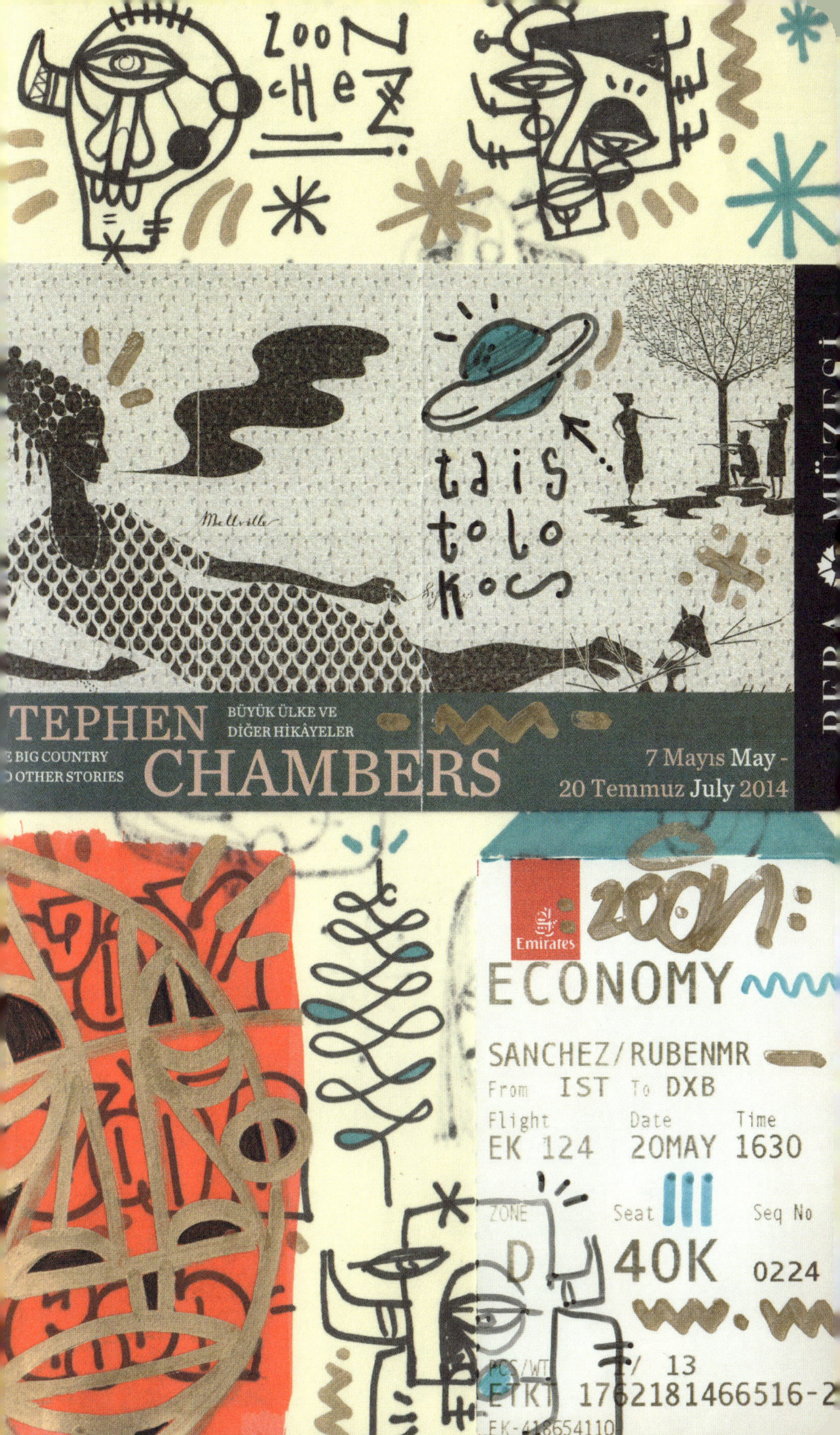

ZOON
CHEZ
Mellville
tais
tolo
Kocs
PERA MÜZESİ
TEPHEN
BÜYÜK ÜLKE VE
DİĞER HİKÂYELER
E BIG COUNTRY
O OTHER STORIES
CHAMBERS
7 Mayıs May -
20 Temmuz July 2014
Emirates
ZOON:
ECONOMY
SANCHEZ/RUBENMR
From IST To DXB
Flight EK 124
Date 20MAY
Time 1630
ZONE D
Seat 40K
Seq No 0224
PCS/WT / 13
ETKT 1762181466516-2
EK-418654110

el amor
es una
fiesta
donde
baila el
corazón

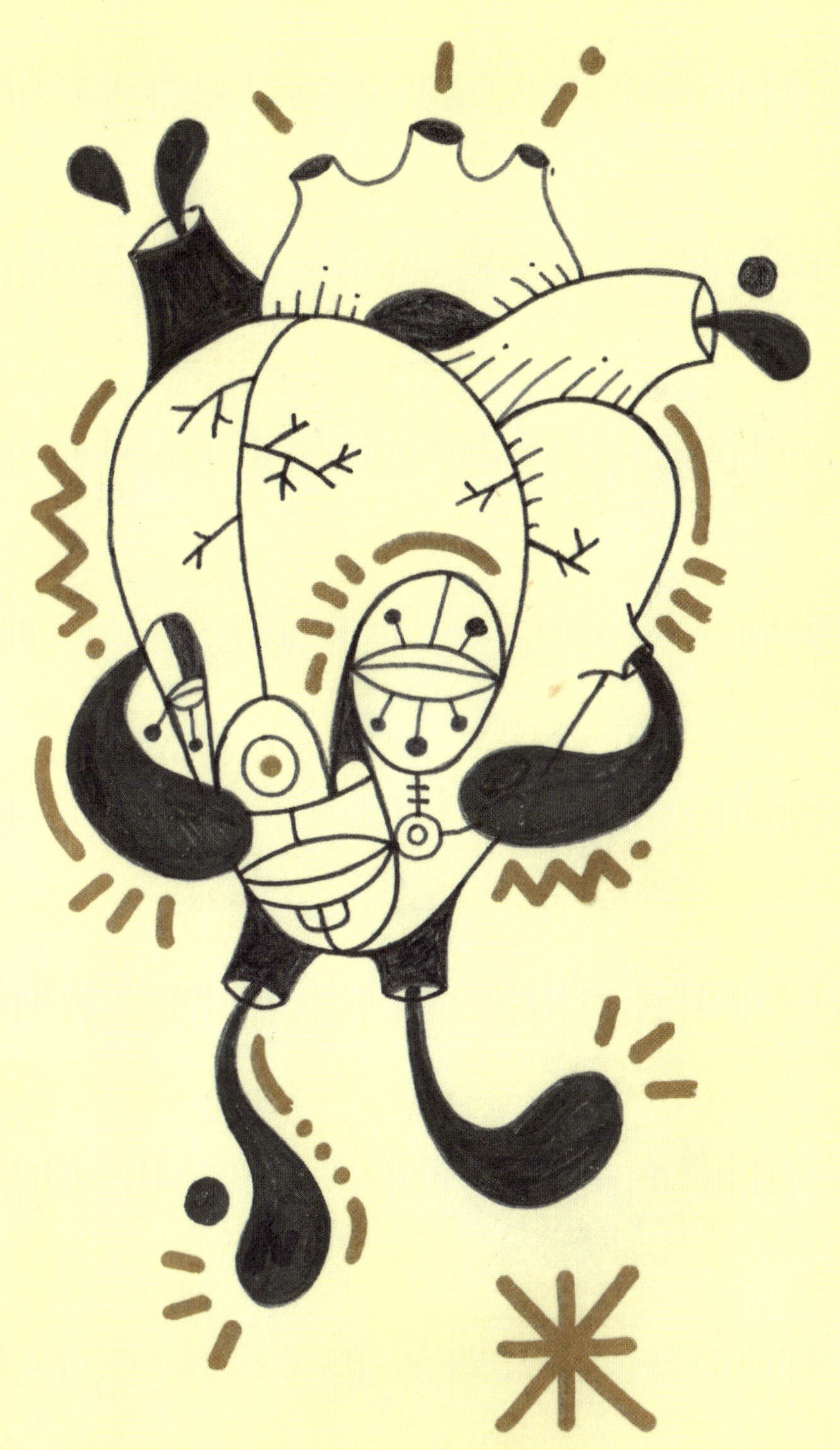

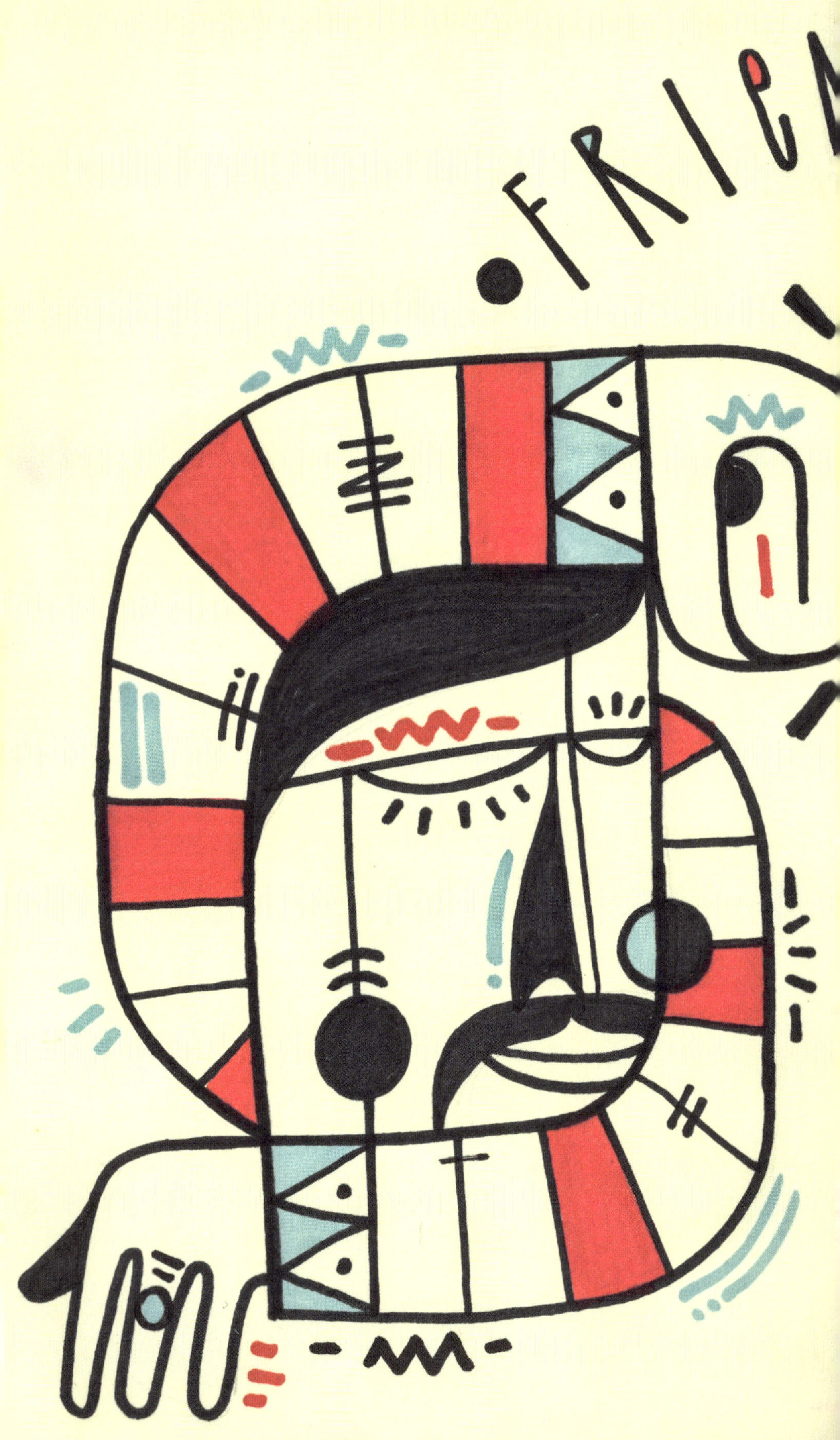

FRICA

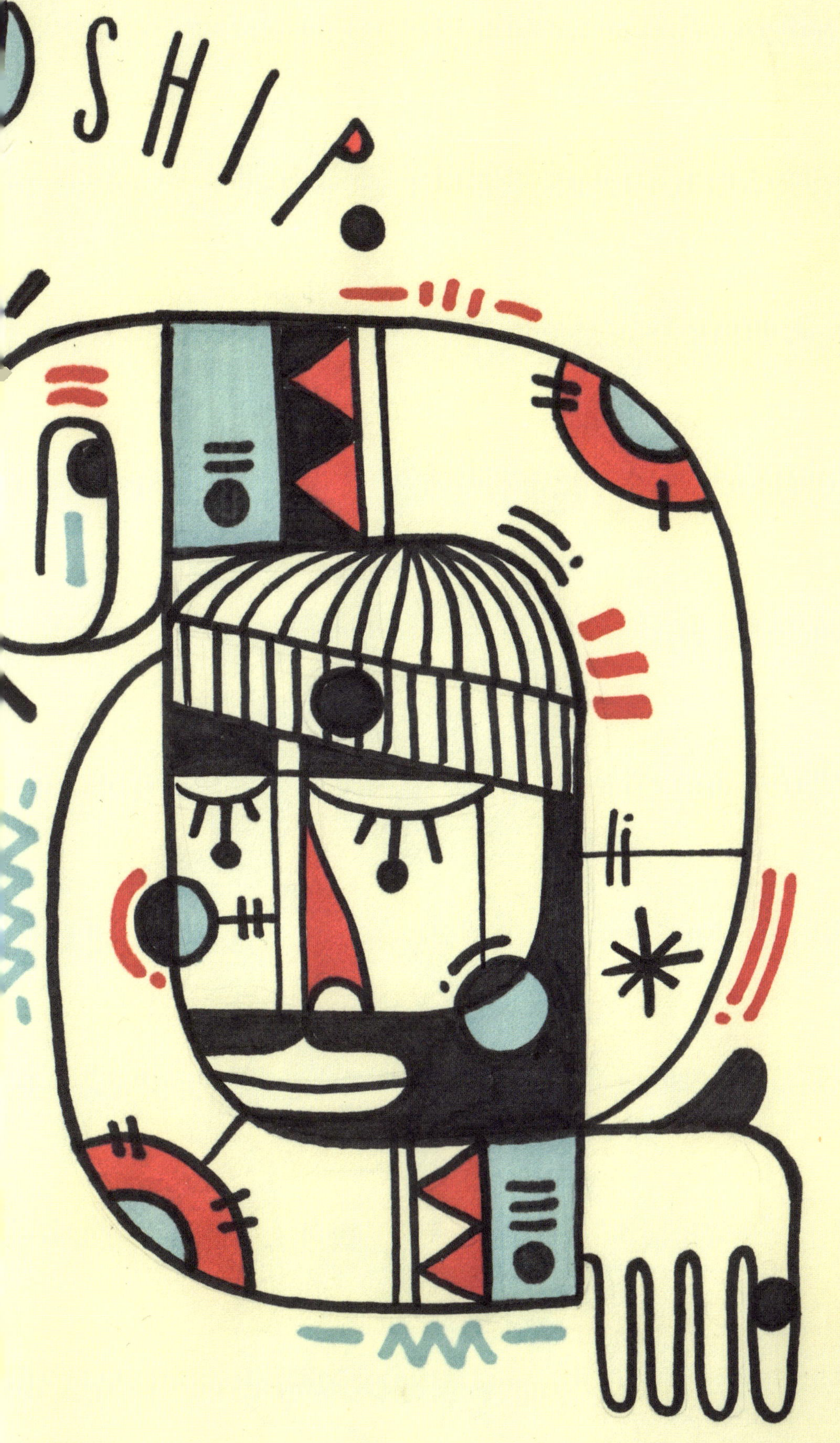

SHIP.

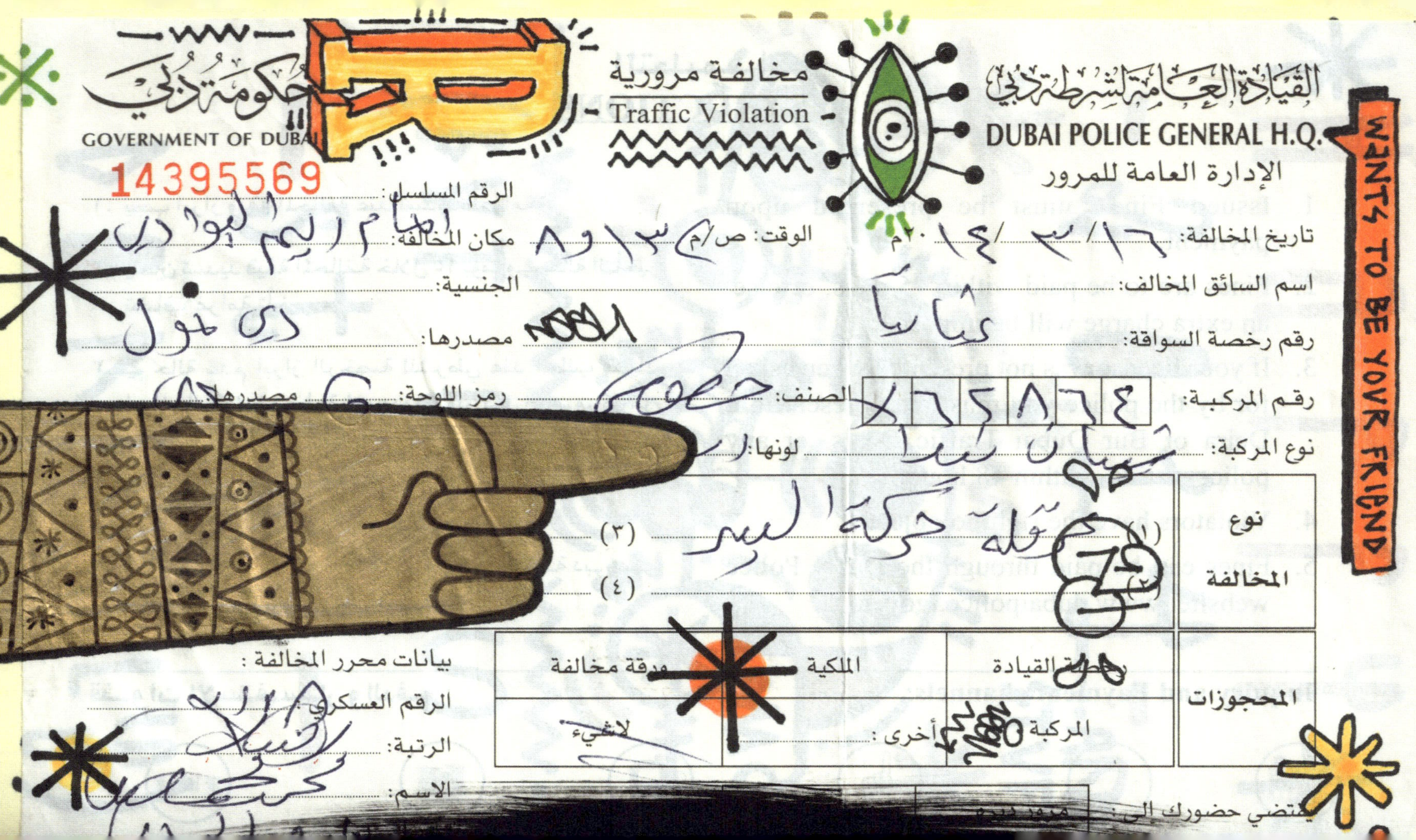
القيادة العامة لشرطة دبي
DUBAI POLICE GENERAL H.Q.
الإدارة العامة للمرور
مخالفة مرورية
Traffic Violation
GOVERNMENT OF DUBAI
14395569
WANTS TO BE YOUR FRIEND
الرقم المسلسل :
تاريخ المخالفة :   الوقت : ص/م   مكان المخالفة :
اسم السائق المخالف :
الجنسية :
رقم رخصة السواقة :   مصدرها :
رقم المركبة :   الصنف :
رمز اللوحة :   مصدرها :
نوع المركبة :
لونها :
نوع المخالفة
(٣)
(٤)
المحجوزات
رخصة القيادة
الملكية
دقة مخالفة
المركبة   أخرى :   لاشيء
بيانات محرر المخالفة :
الرقم العسكري :
الرتبة :
الاسم :
يقتضي حضورك إلى :

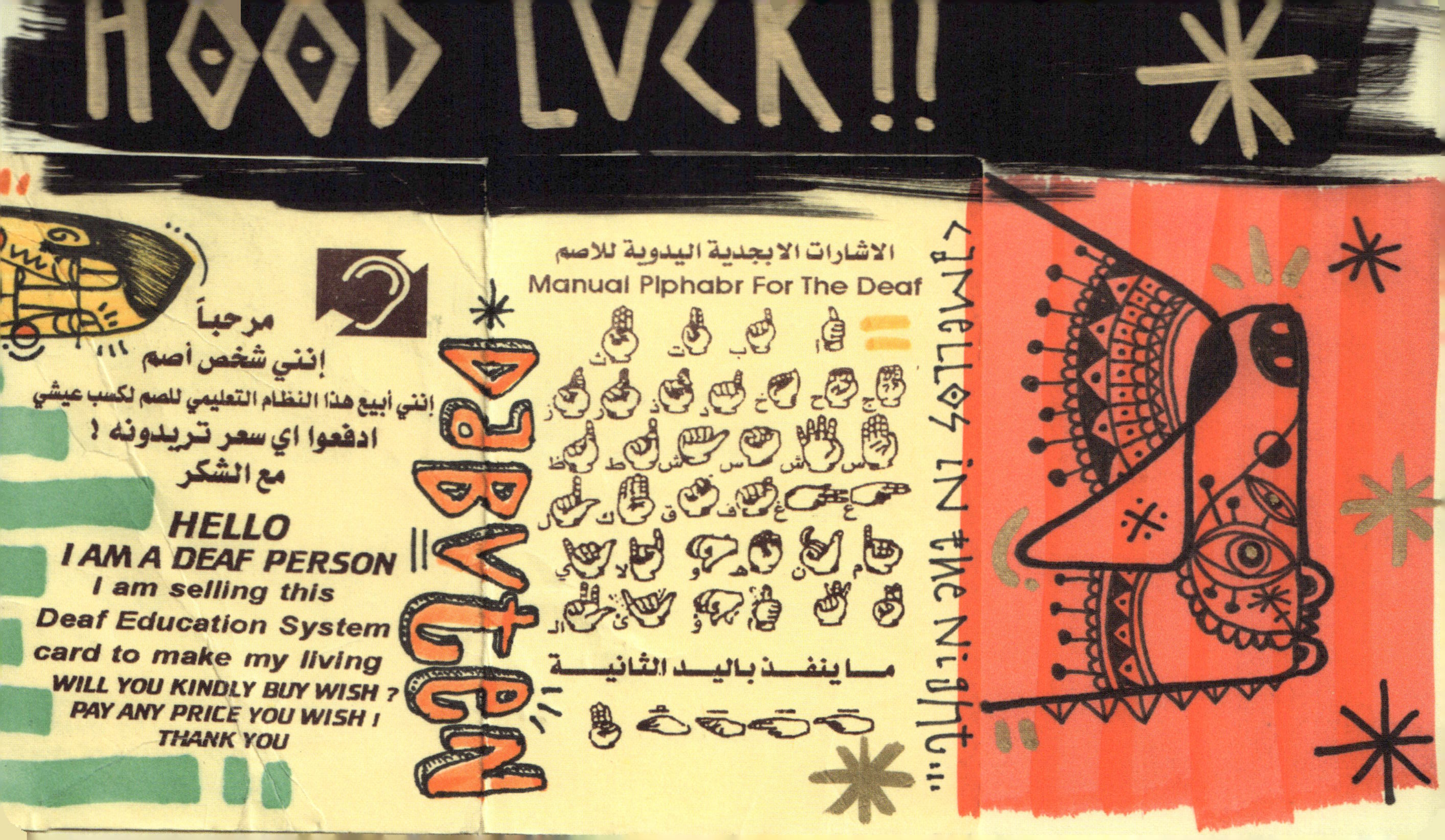
HOOD LVCK!!
الاشارات الابجدية اليدوية للاصم
Manual Plphabr For The Deaf
مرحباً
إنني شخص أصم
إنني أبيع هذا النظام التعليمي للصم لكسب عيشي
ادفعوا اي سعر تريدونه ا
مع الشكر
HELLO
I AM A DEAF PERSON
I am selling this
Deaf Education System
card to make my living
WILL YOU KINDLY BUY WISH ?
PAY ANY PRICE YOU WISH !
THANK YOU
ما ينفذ باليد الثانية
DABVTEN
CAMELLOS IN the NIGHT...

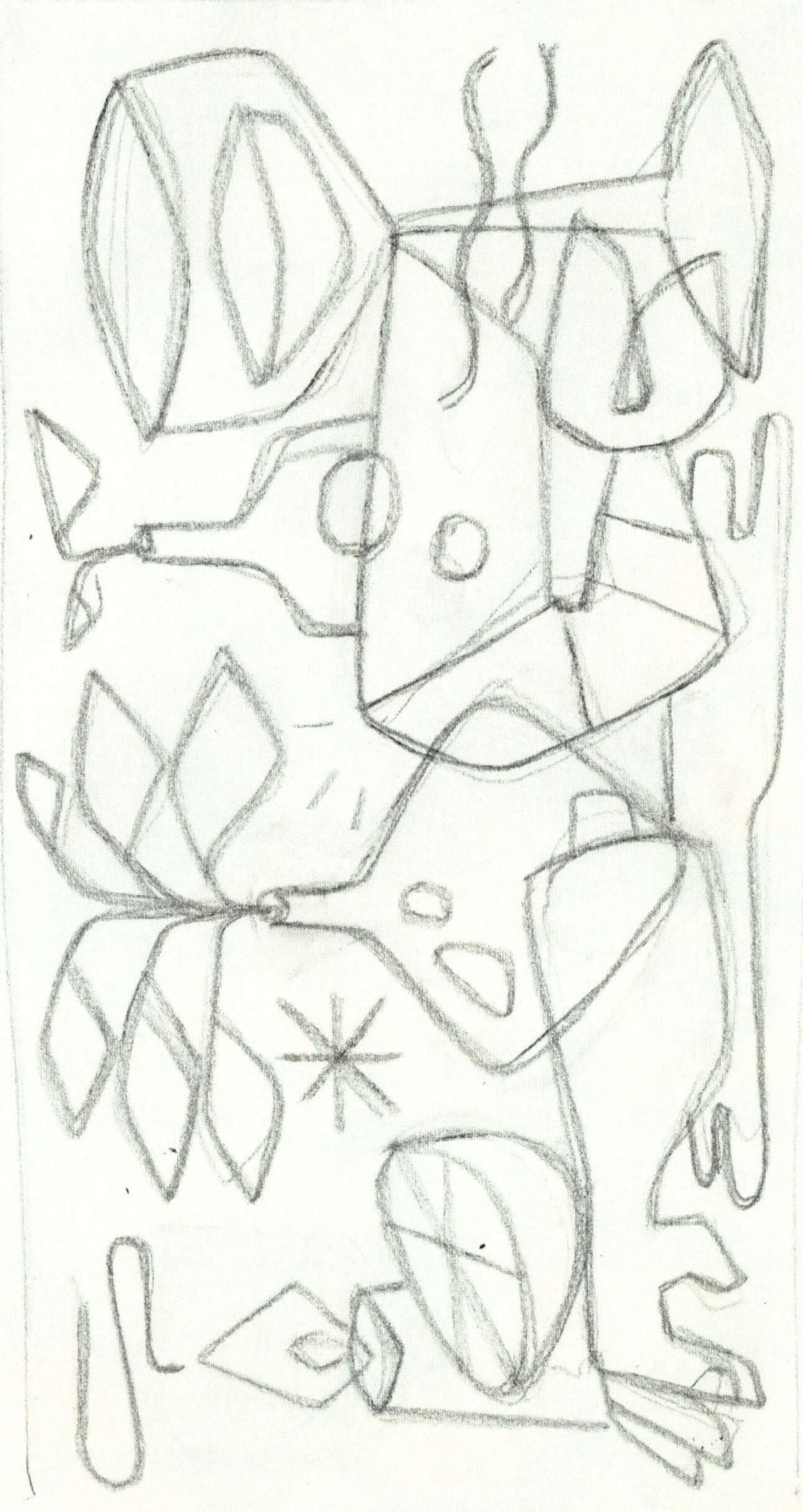

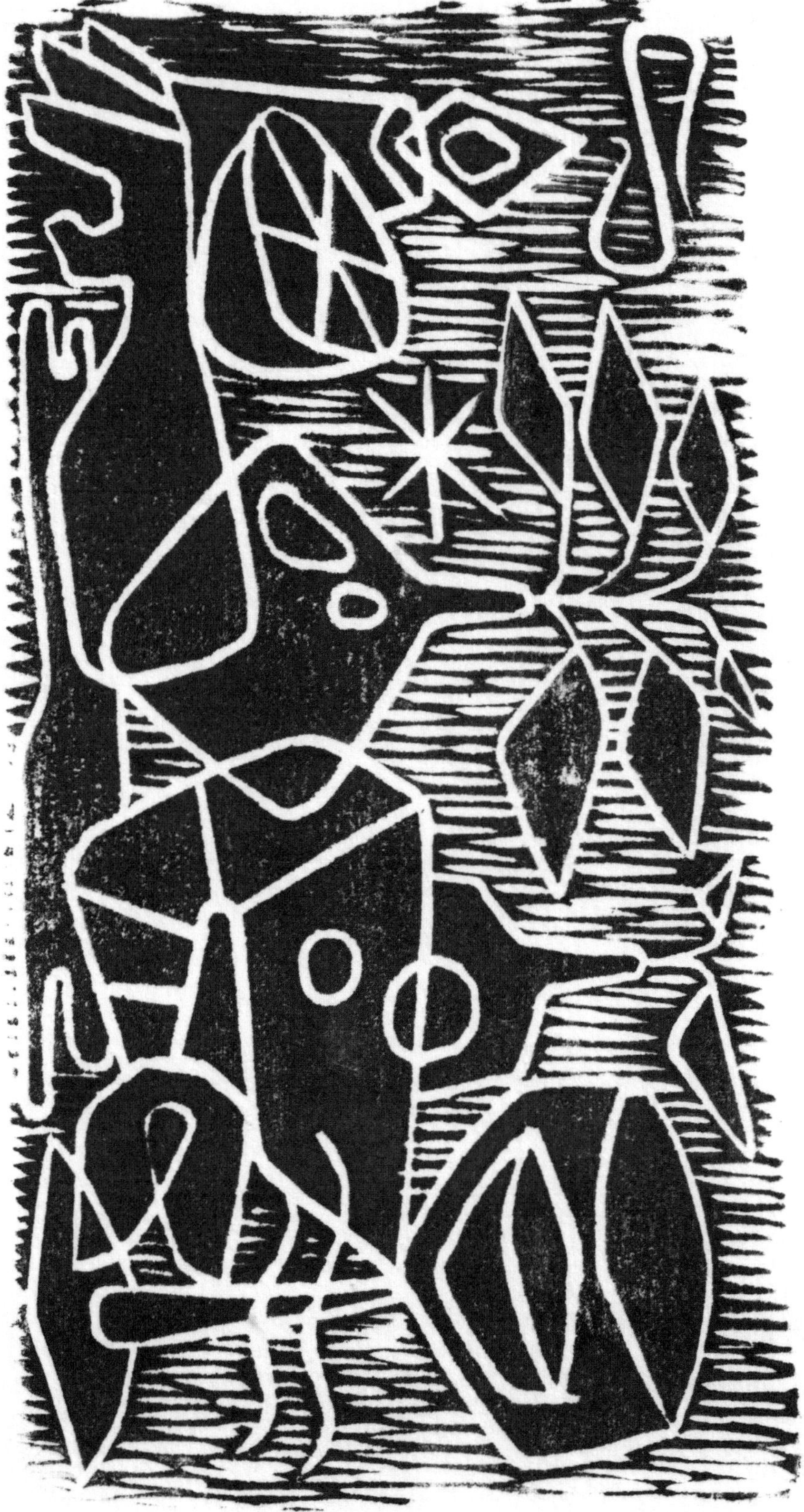

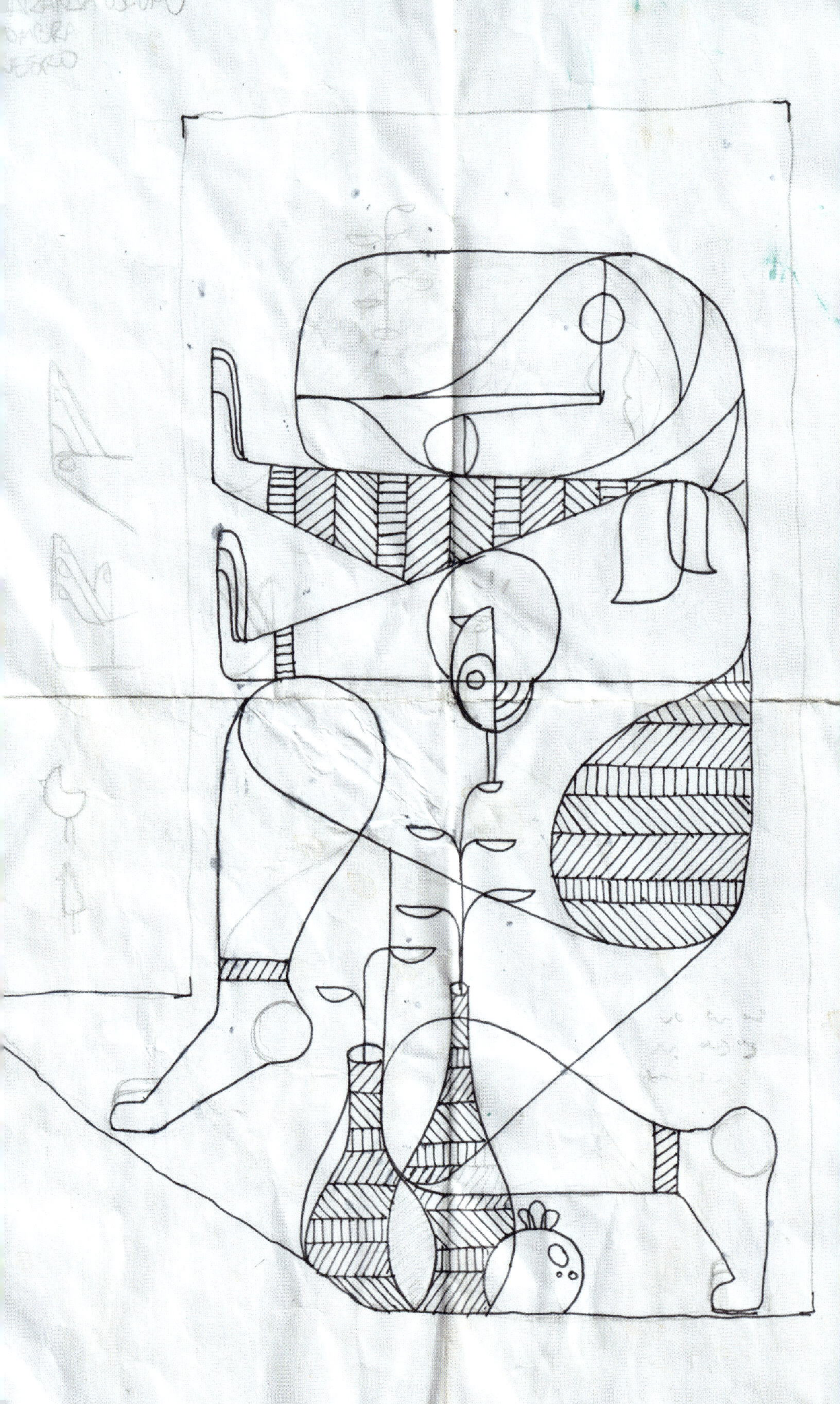
MANZANA OSCURO
OMBRA
NEGRO

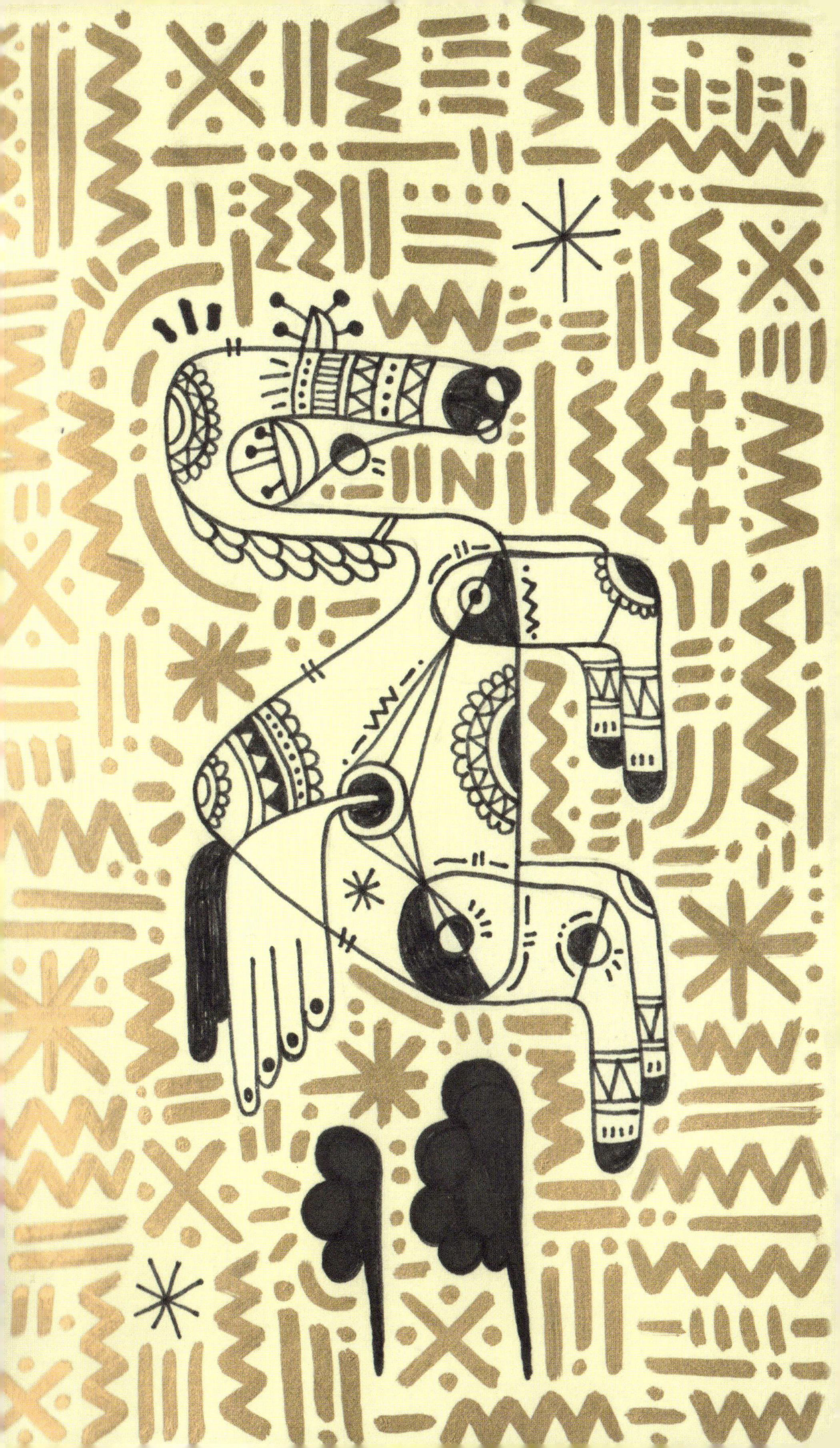

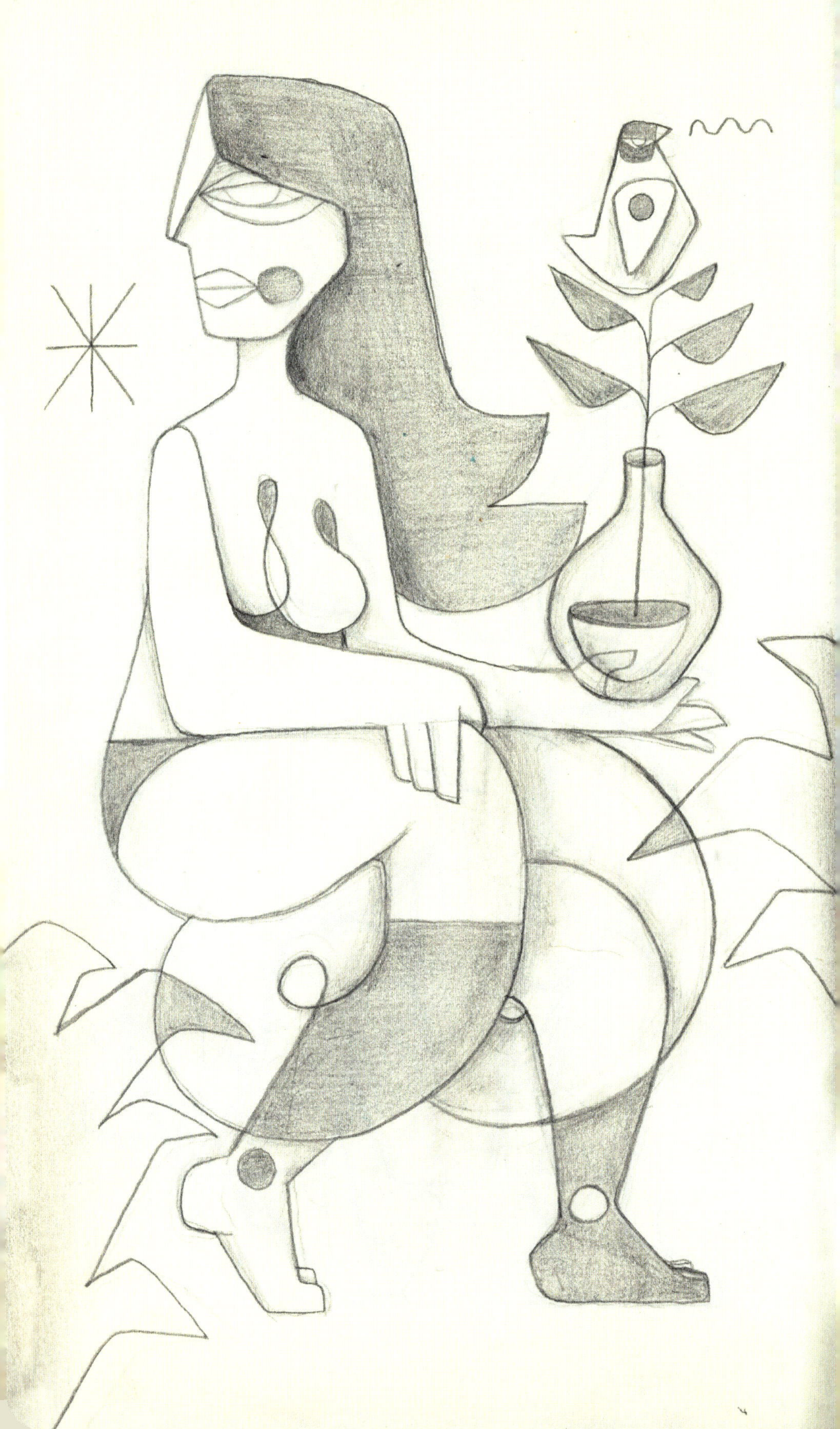

PIERNAS INFINITAS

sabor total

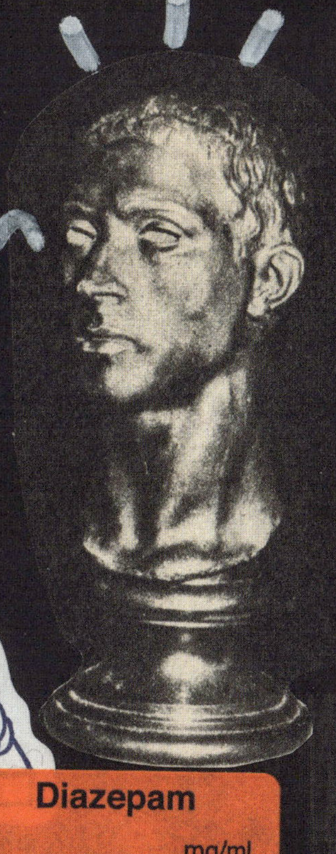

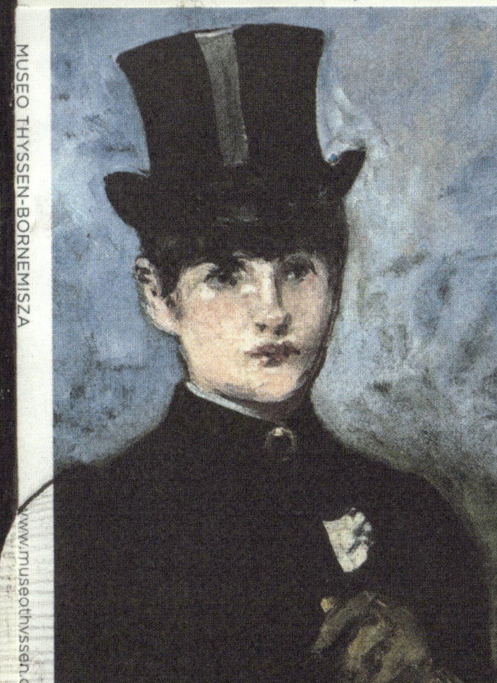

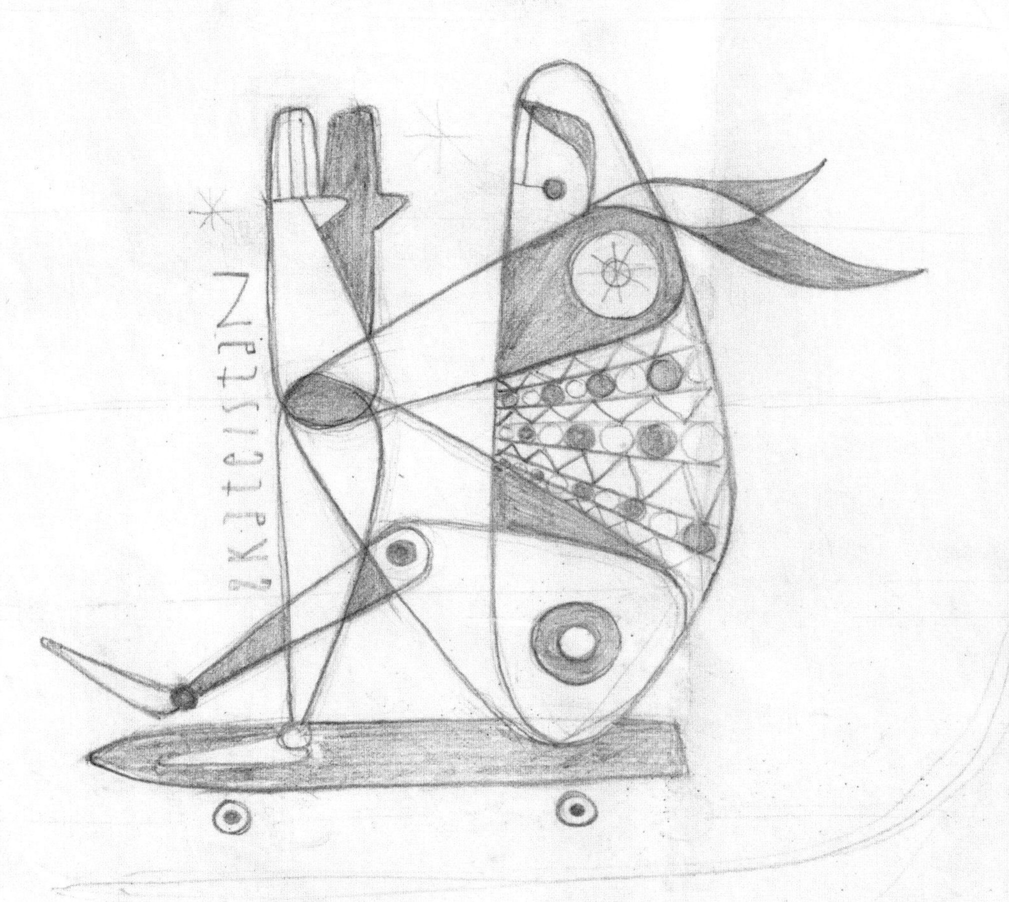

KRISTIN

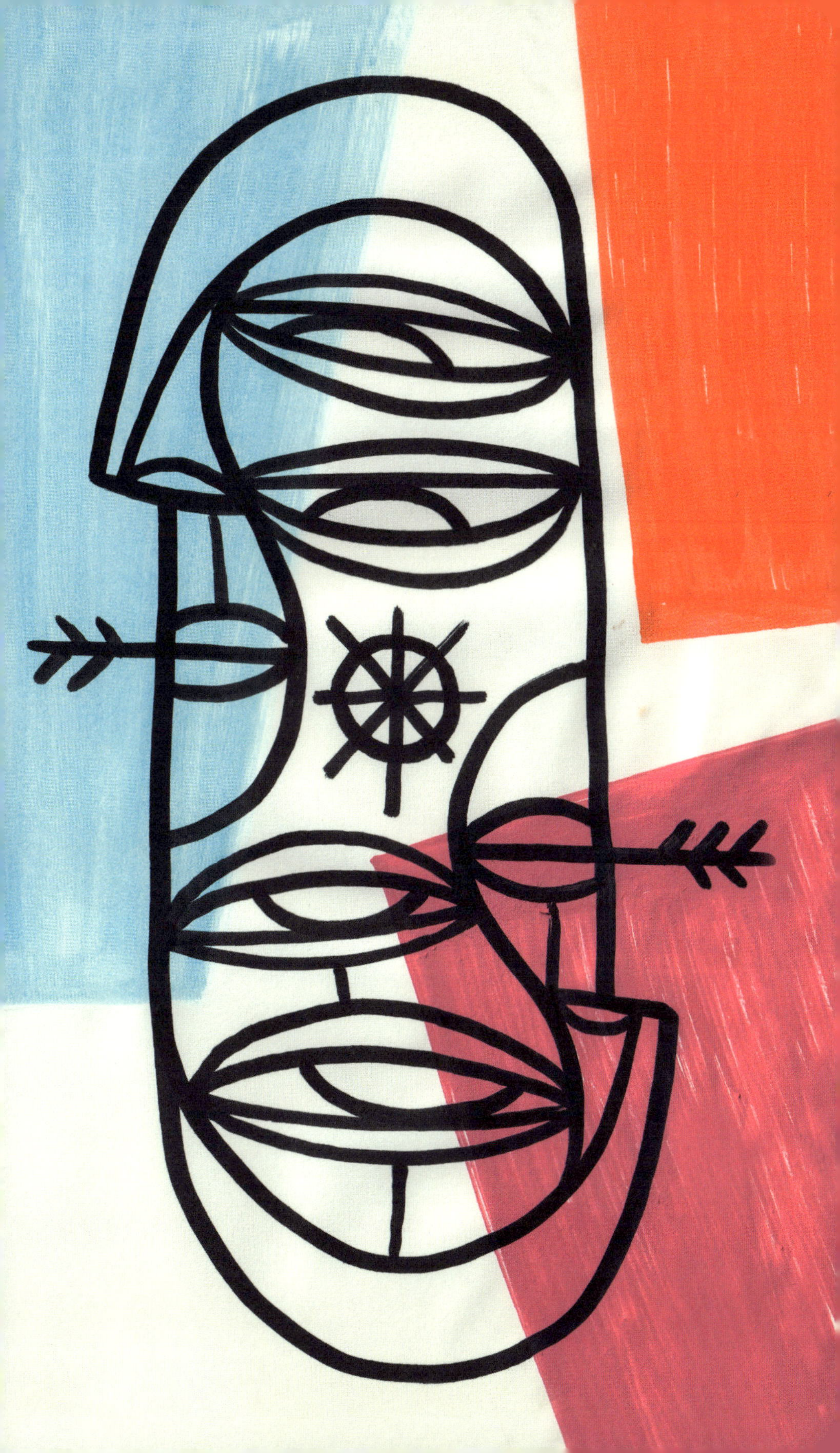

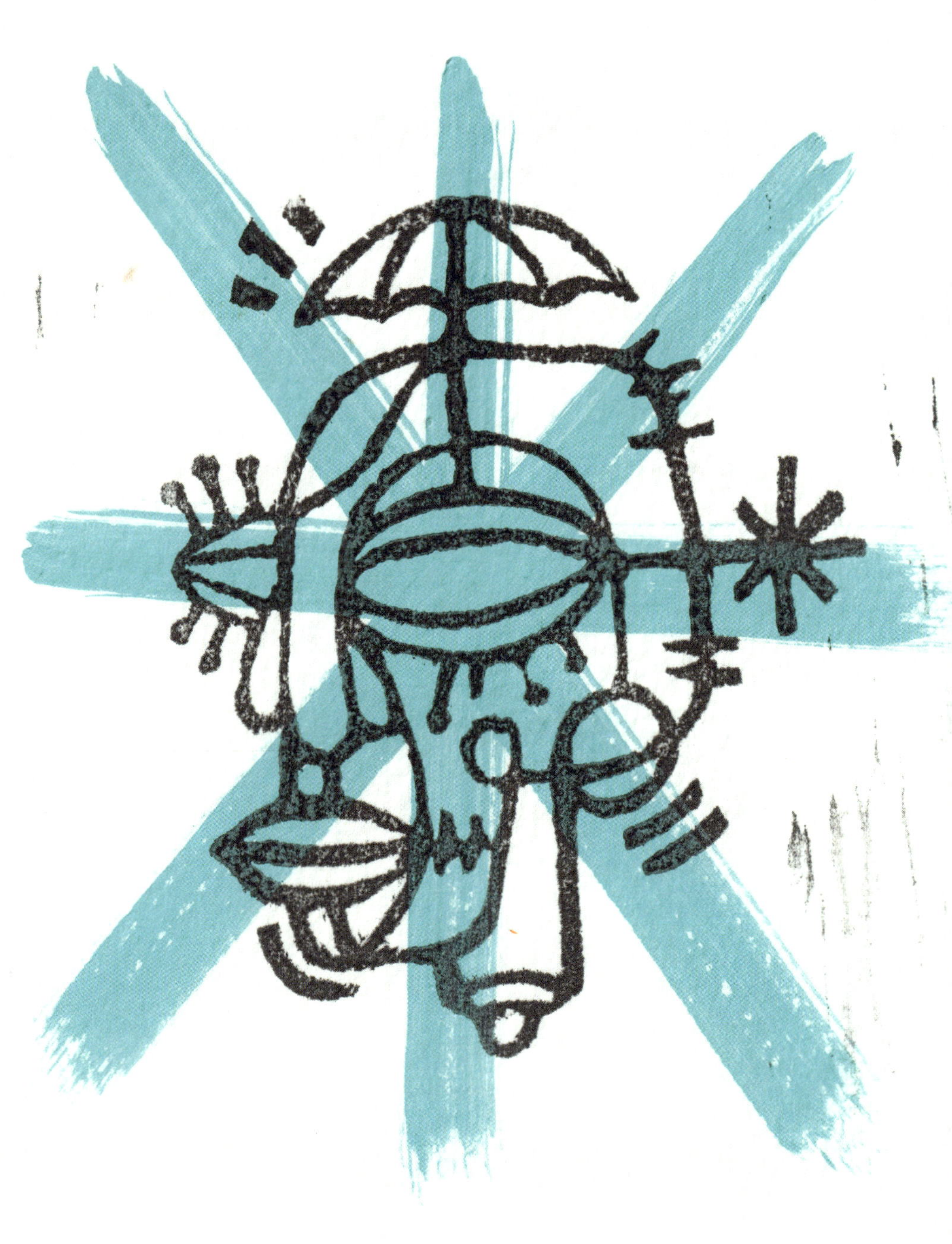

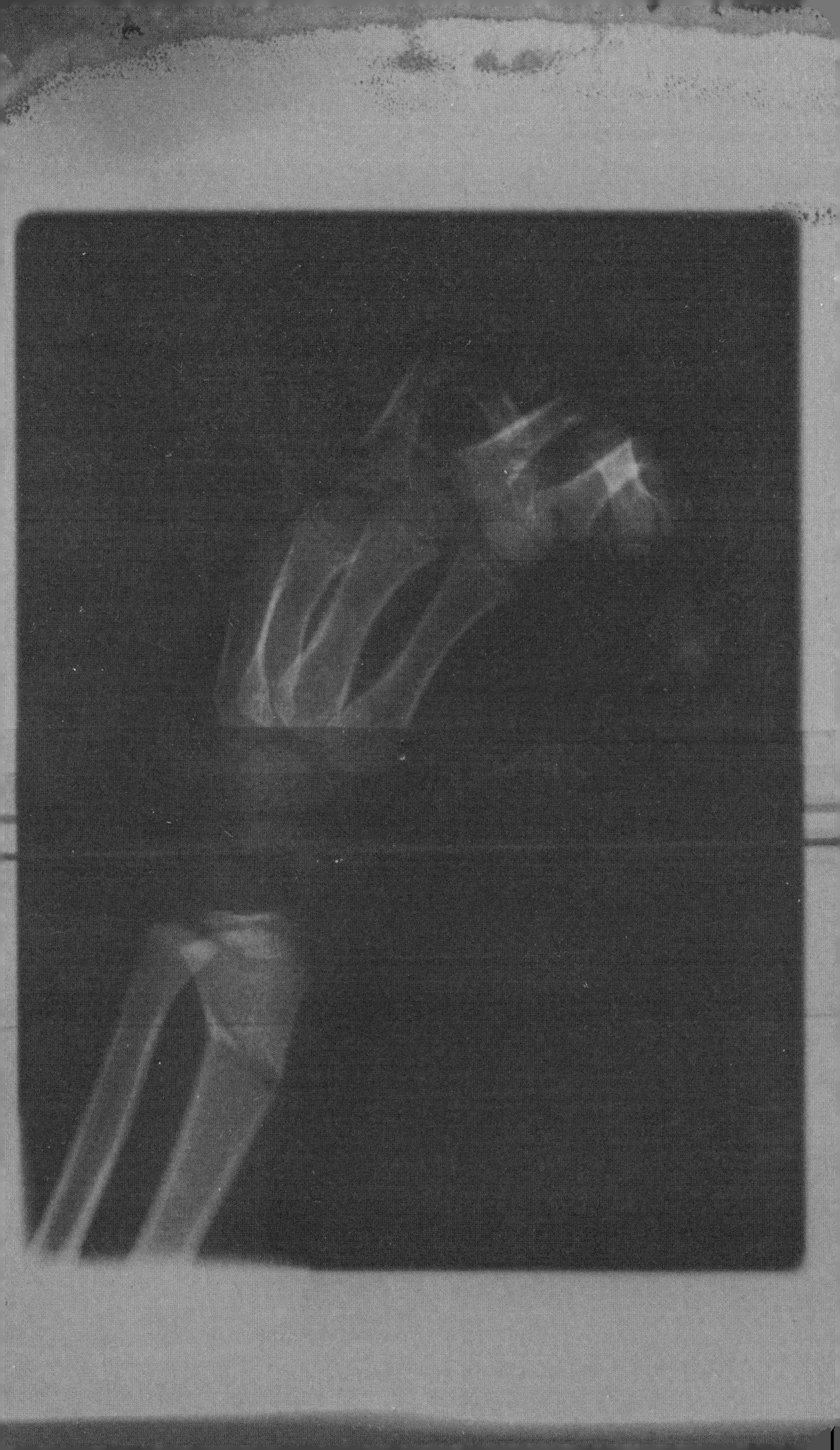

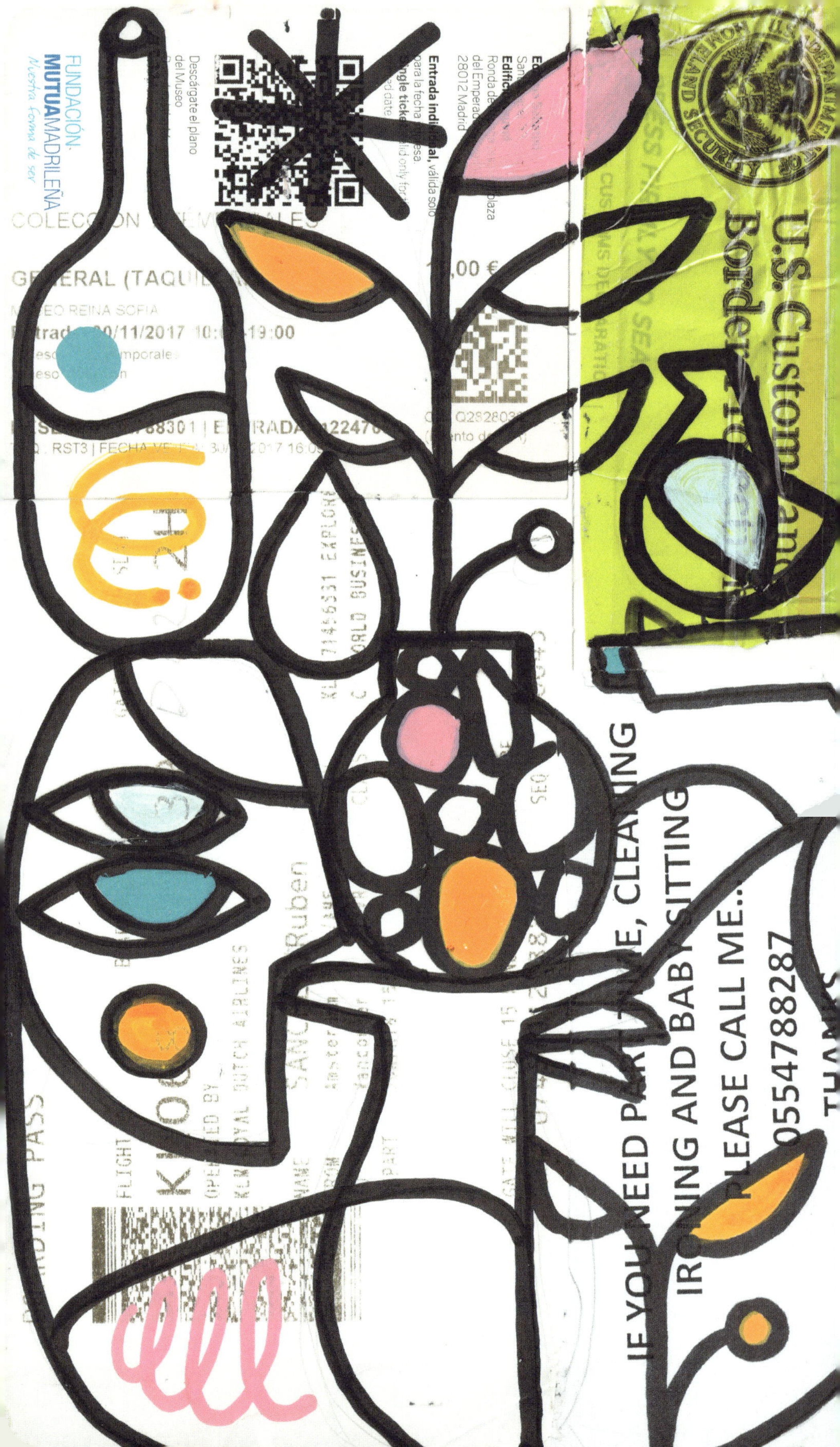

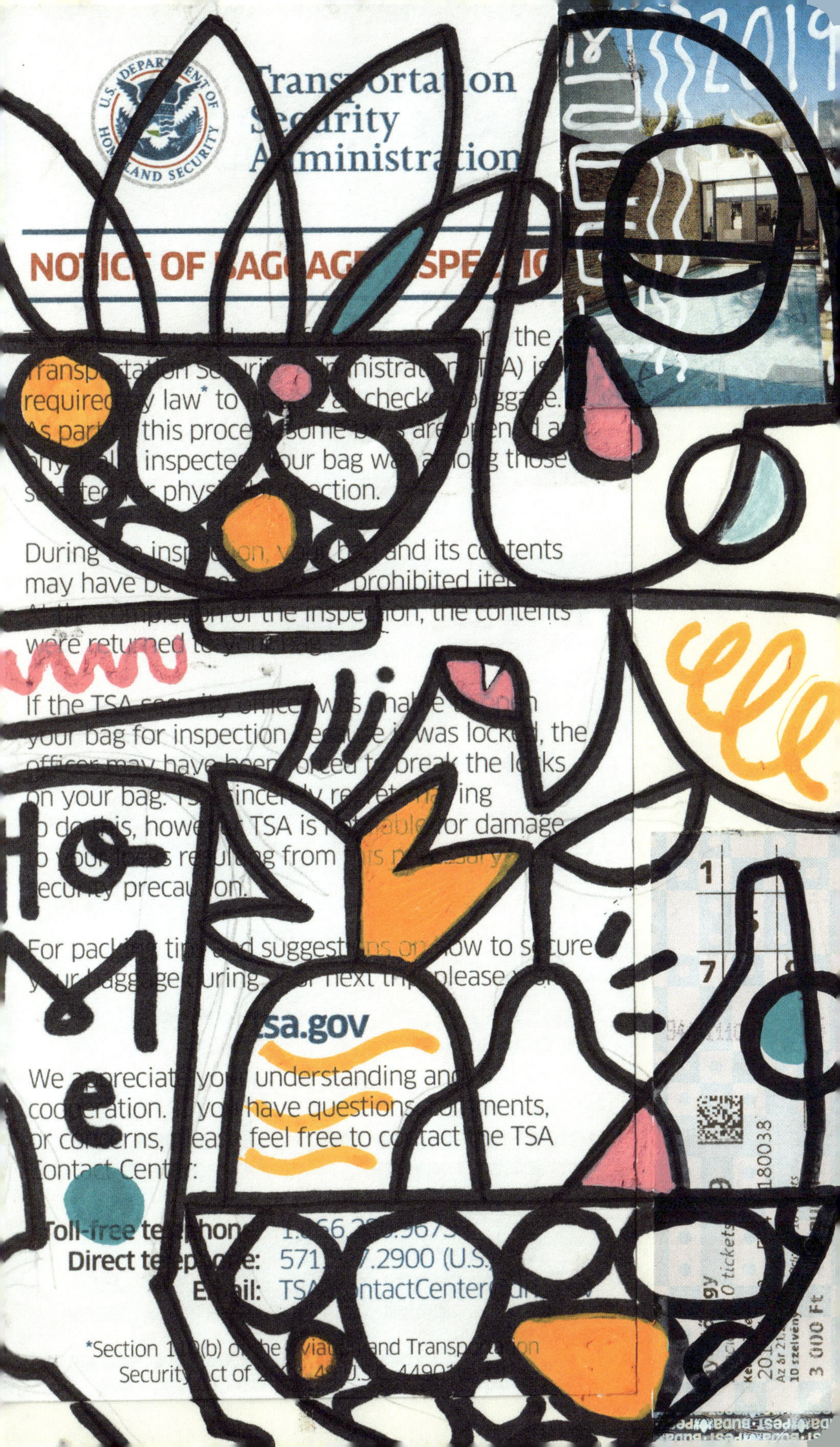

Transportation Security Administration

NOTICE OF BAGGAGE INSPECTION

To protect you and your fellow passengers, the Transportation Security Administration (TSA) is required by law* to inspect all checked baggage. As part of this process, some bags are opened and physically inspected. Your bag was among those selected for physical inspection.

During the inspection, your bag and its contents may have been searched for prohibited items. At the completion of the inspection, the contents were returned to your bag.

If the TSA security officer was unable to open your bag for inspection because it was locked, the officer may have been forced to break the locks on your bag. TSA sincerely regrets having to do this, however TSA is not liable for damage to your locks resulting from this necessary security precaution.

For packing tips and suggestions on how to secure your baggage during your next trip, please visit:

tsa.gov

We appreciate your understanding and cooperation. If you have questions, comments, or concerns, please feel free to contact the TSA Contact Center:

Toll-free telephone: 1.866.289.9673
Direct telephone: 571.227.2900 (U.S.)
Email: TSA-ContactCenter@dhs.gov

*Section 110(b) of the Aviation and Transportation Security Act of 2001 49 U.S.C. 44901

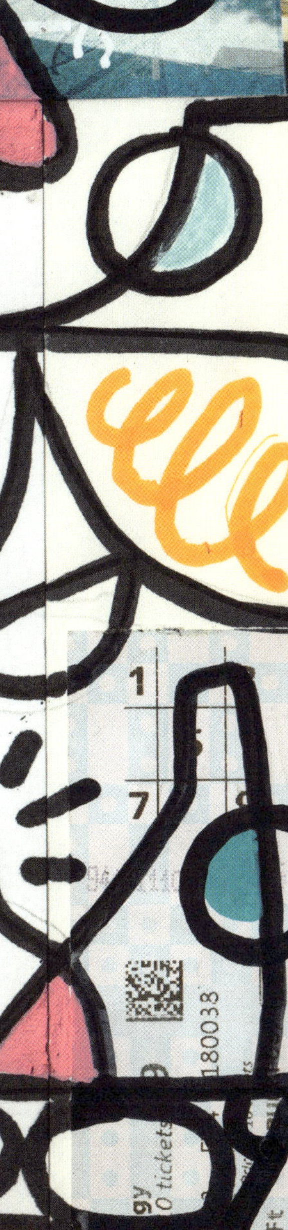

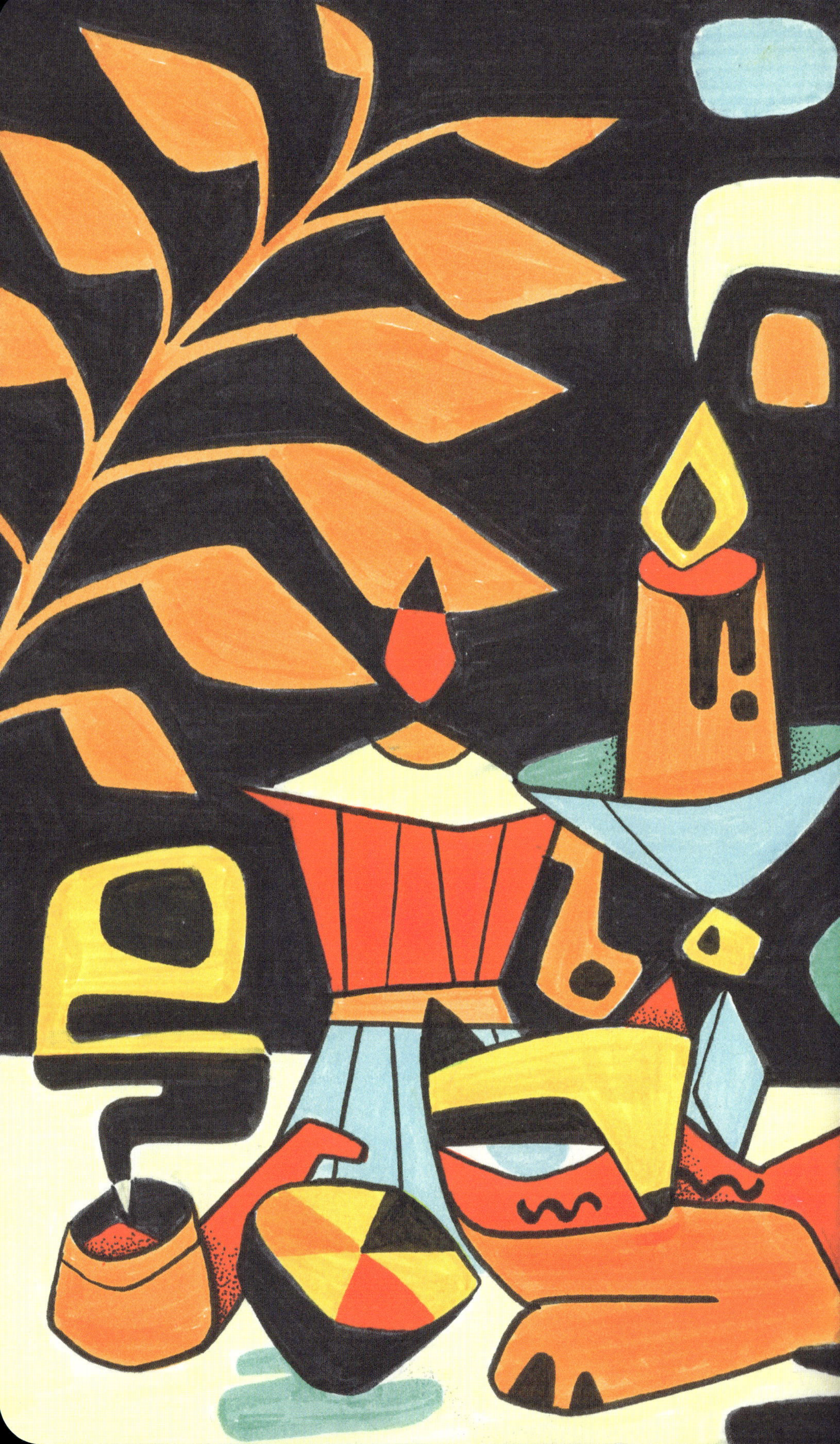

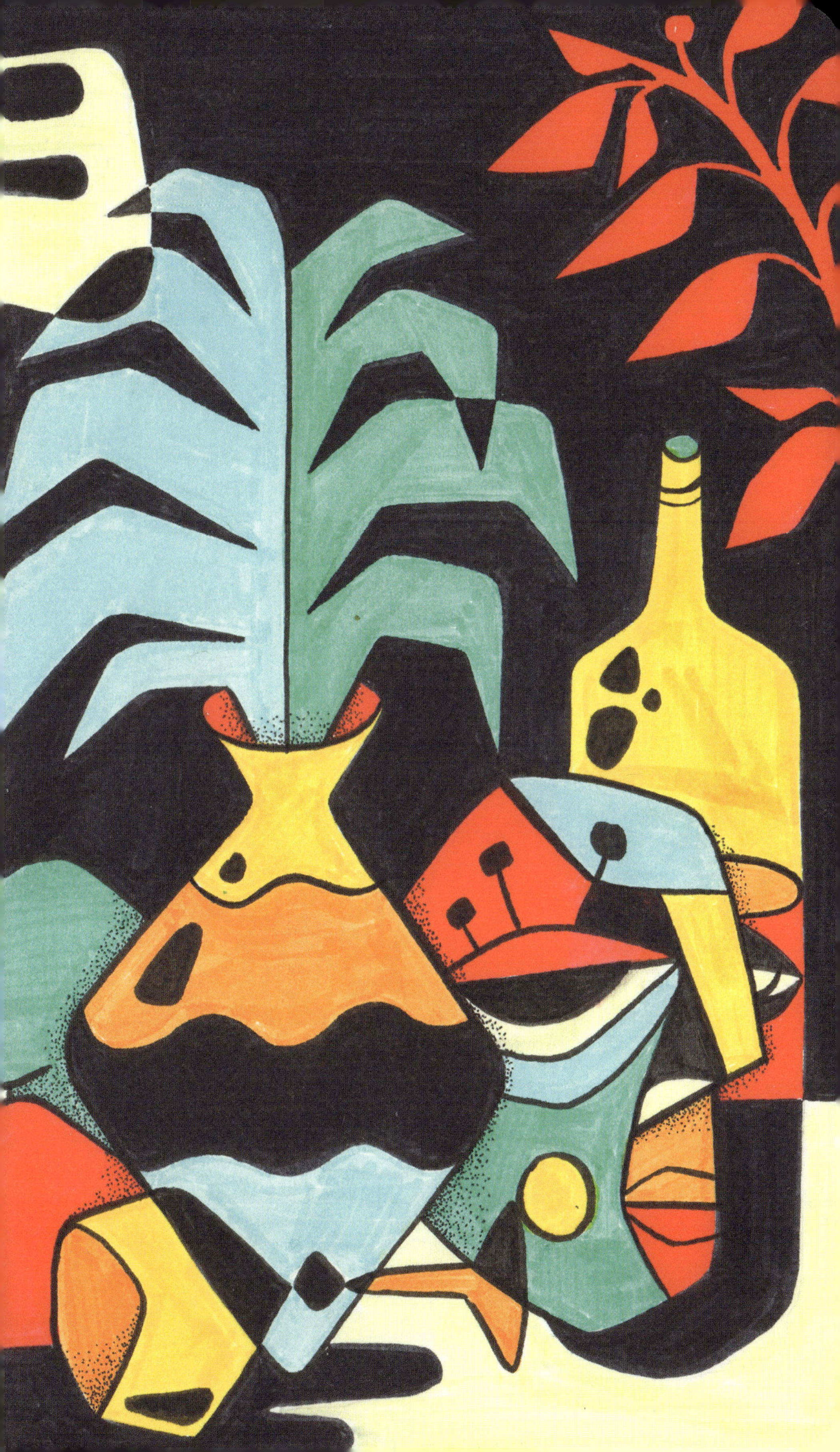

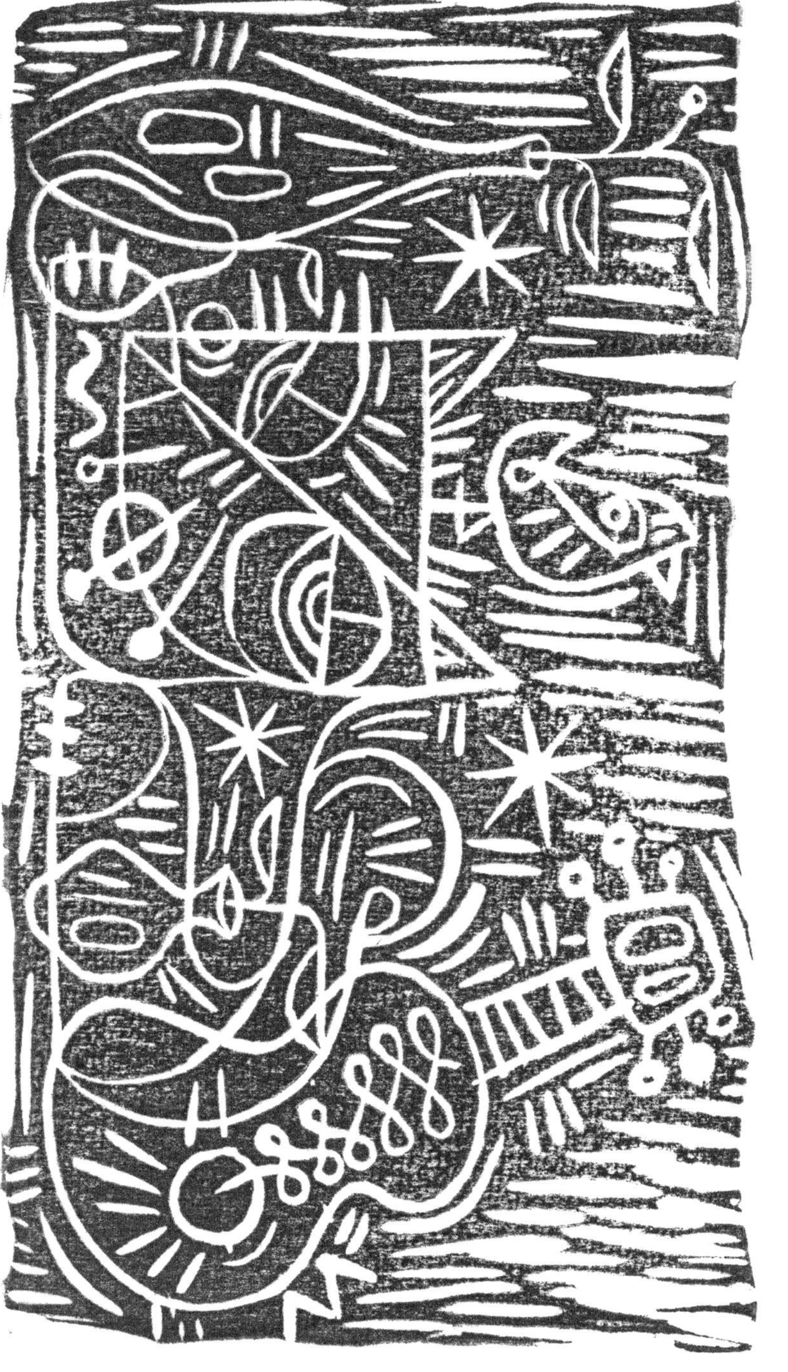

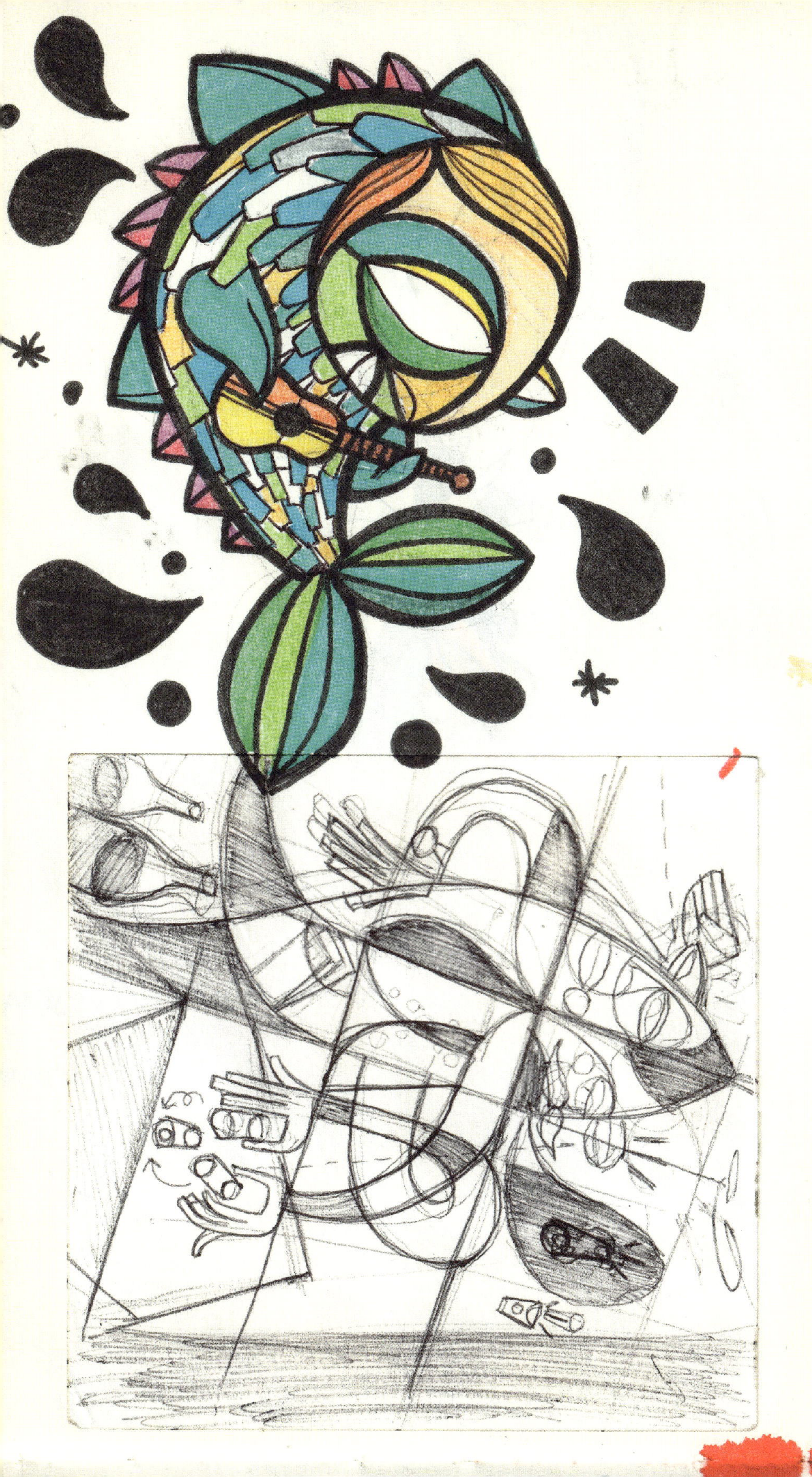

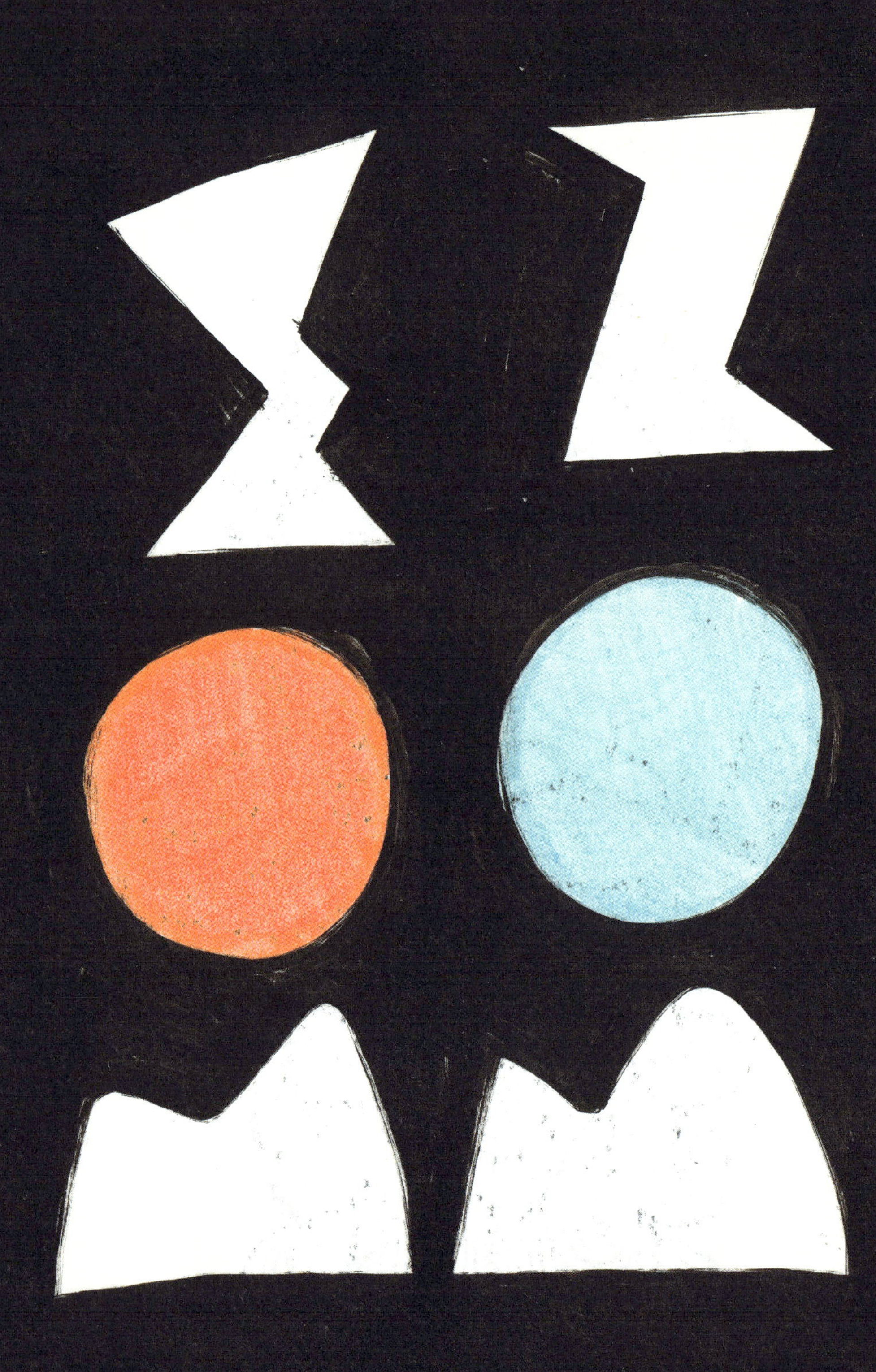

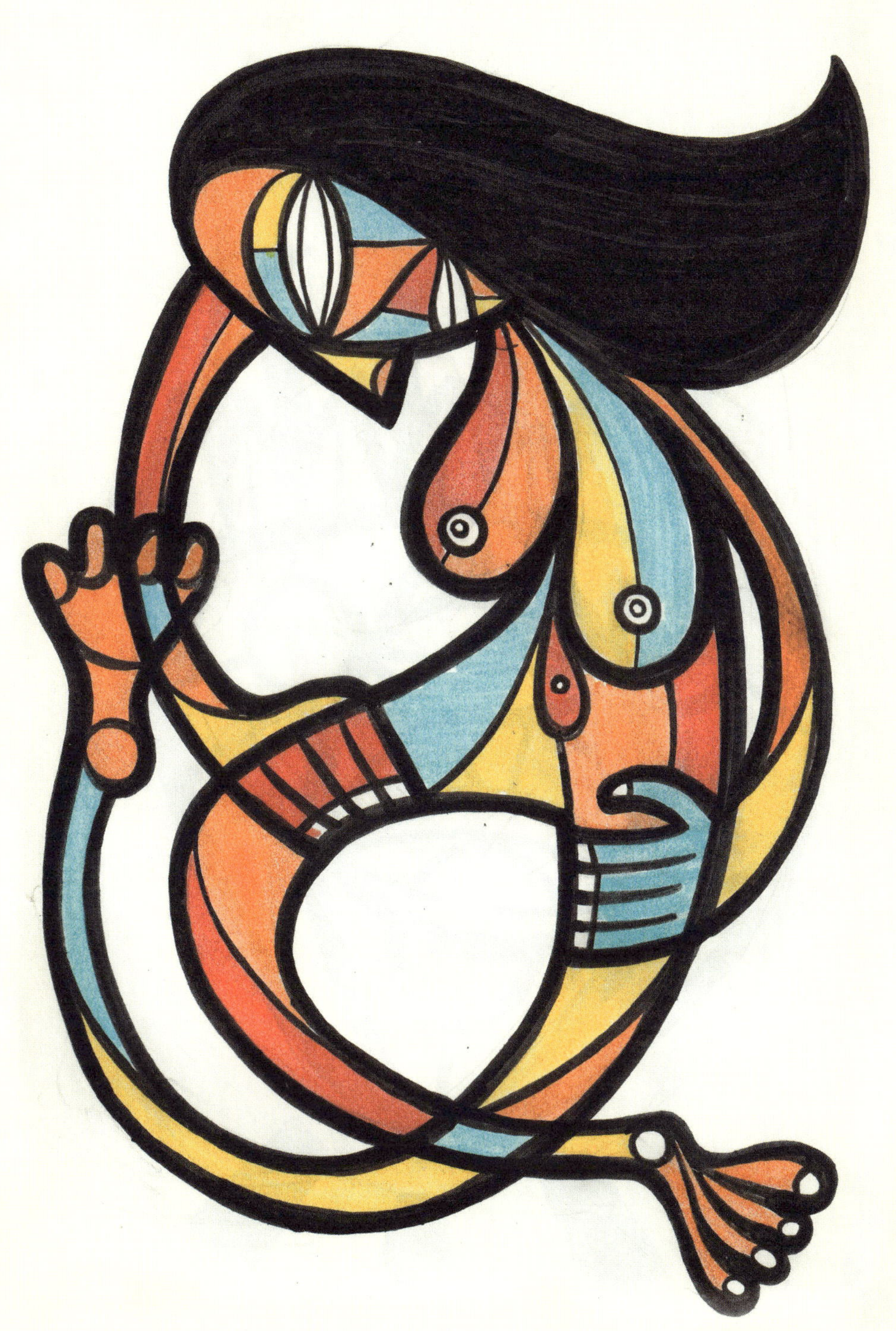

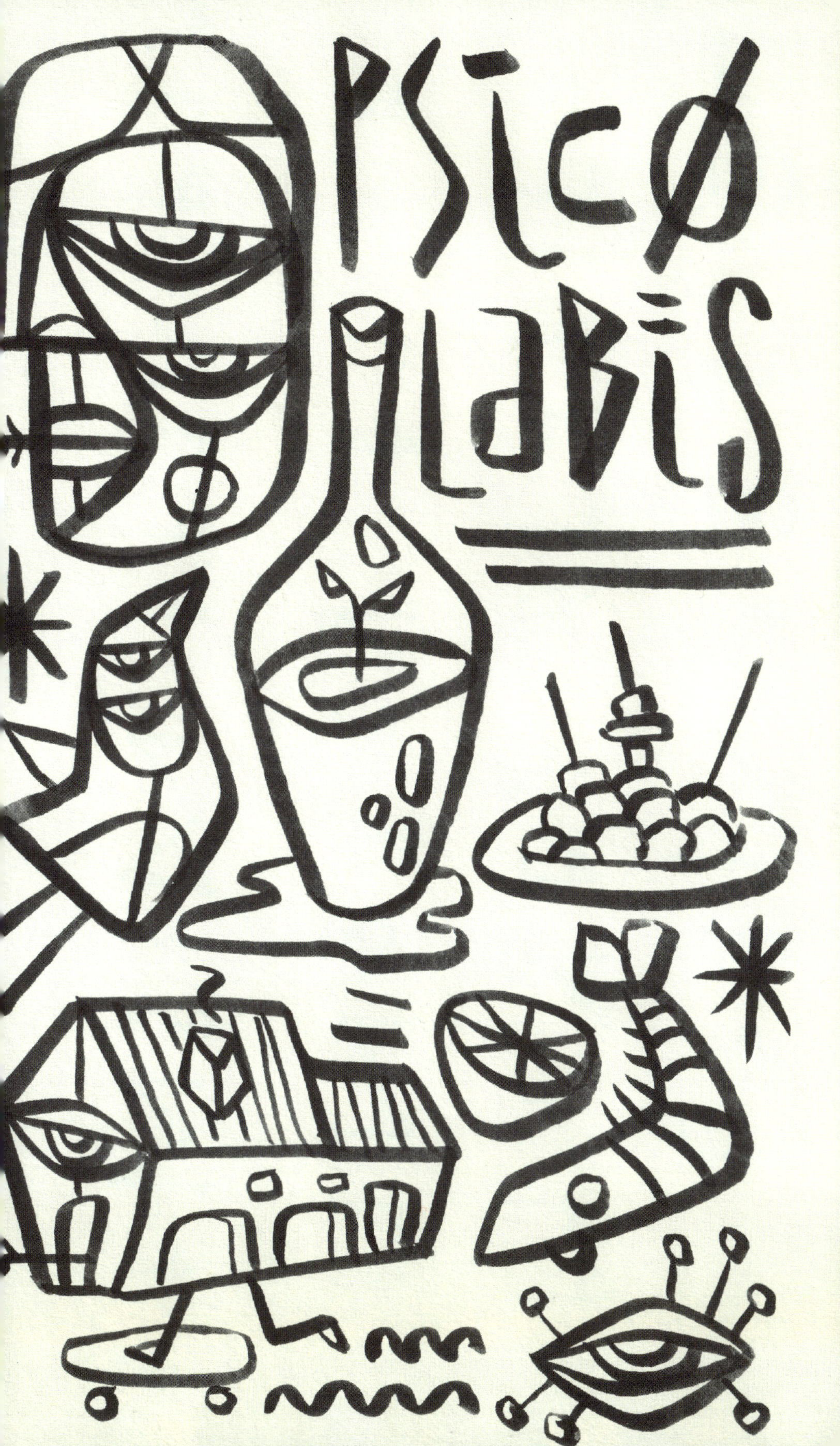
PSICO
SILABIS

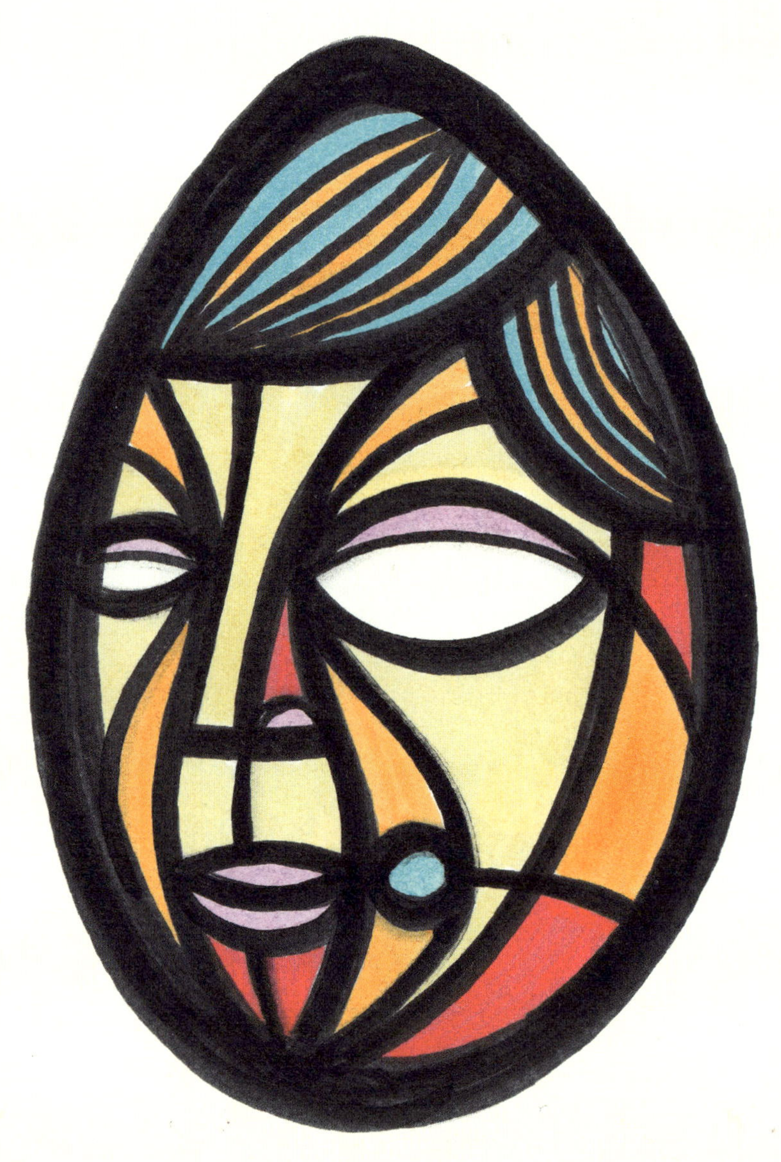

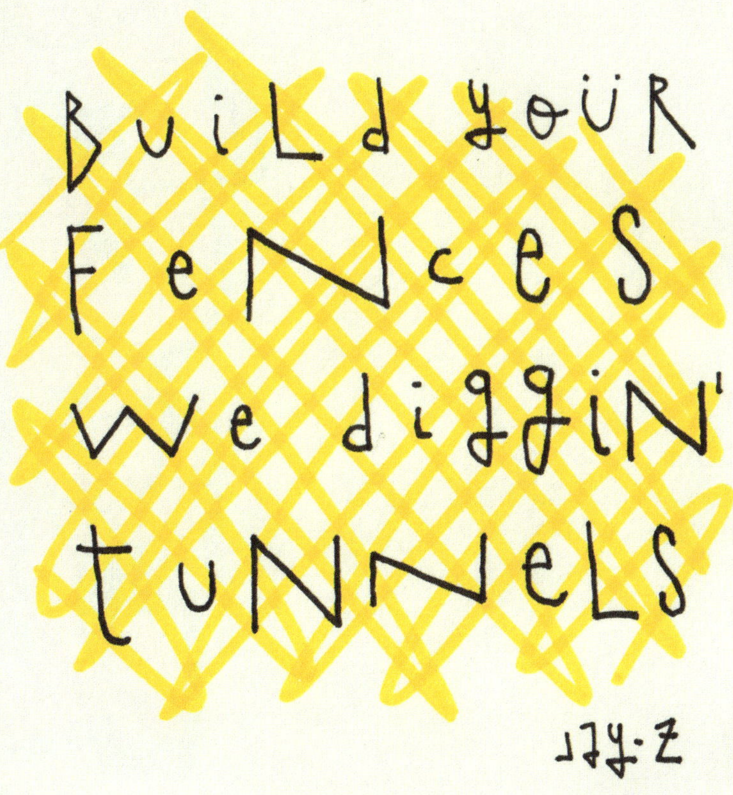
BUILD YOUR
FENCES
WE DIGGIN'
TUNNELS

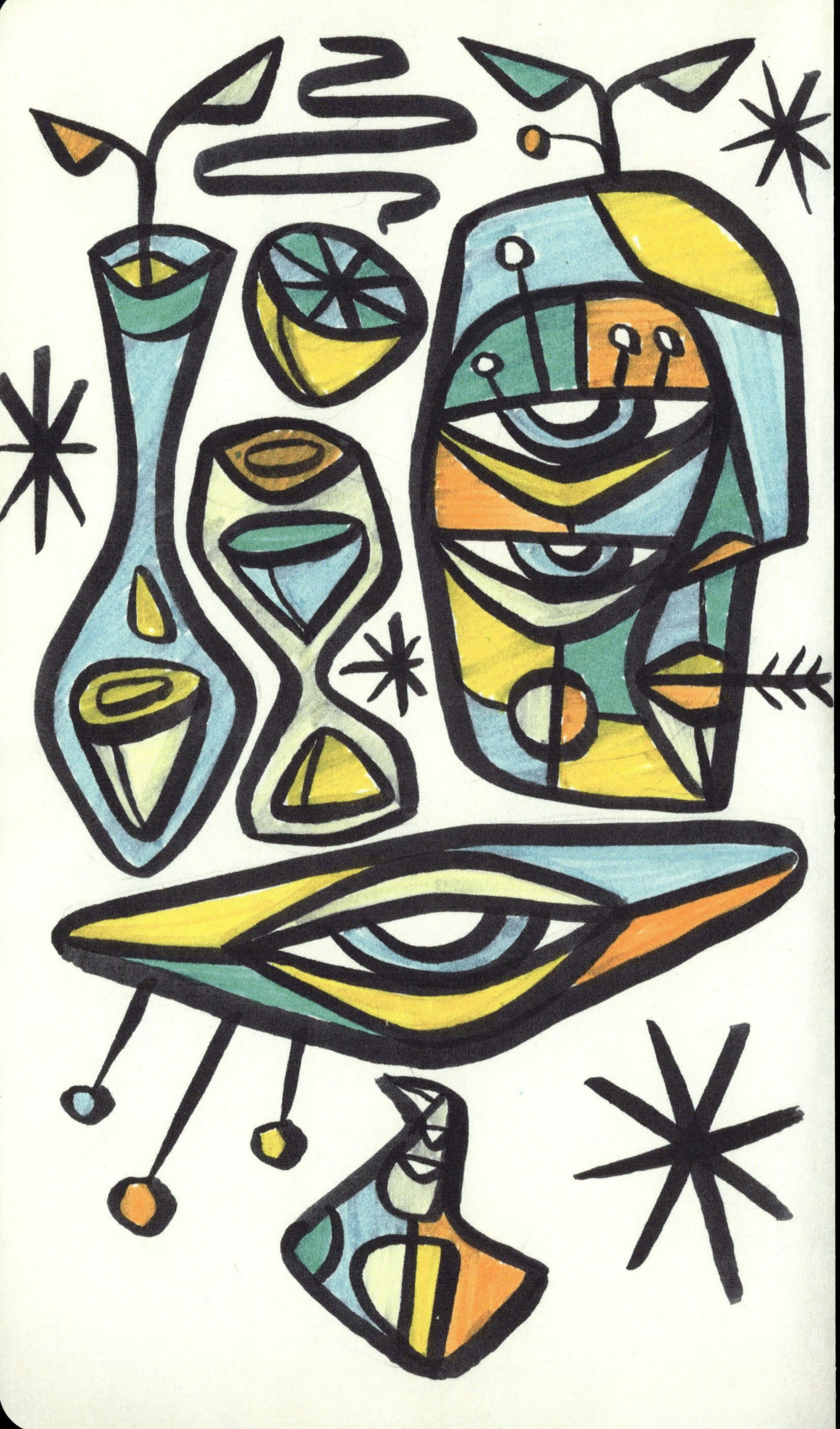

2017

KOMPL
eted·H
eRew go
WE

2018

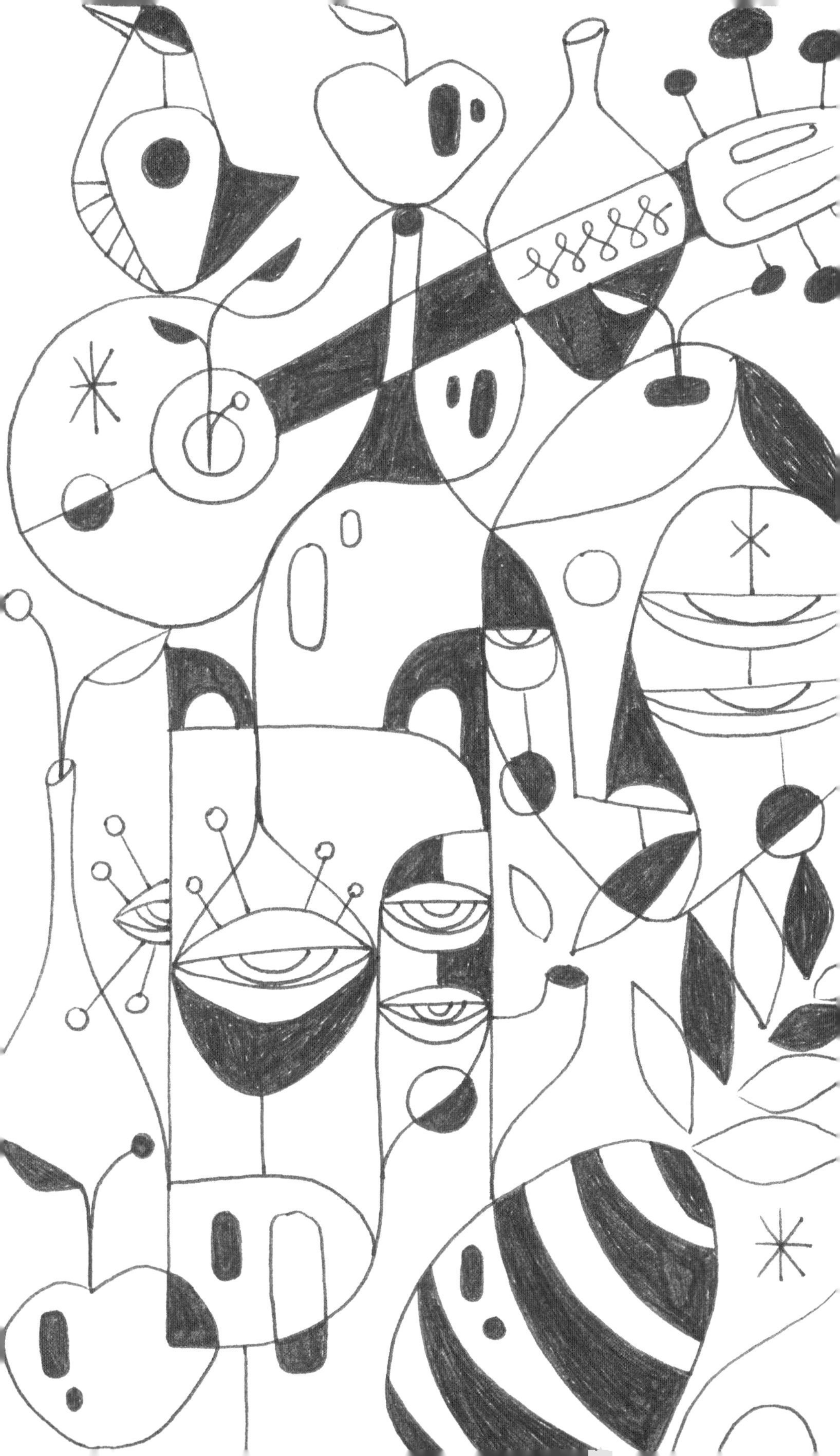

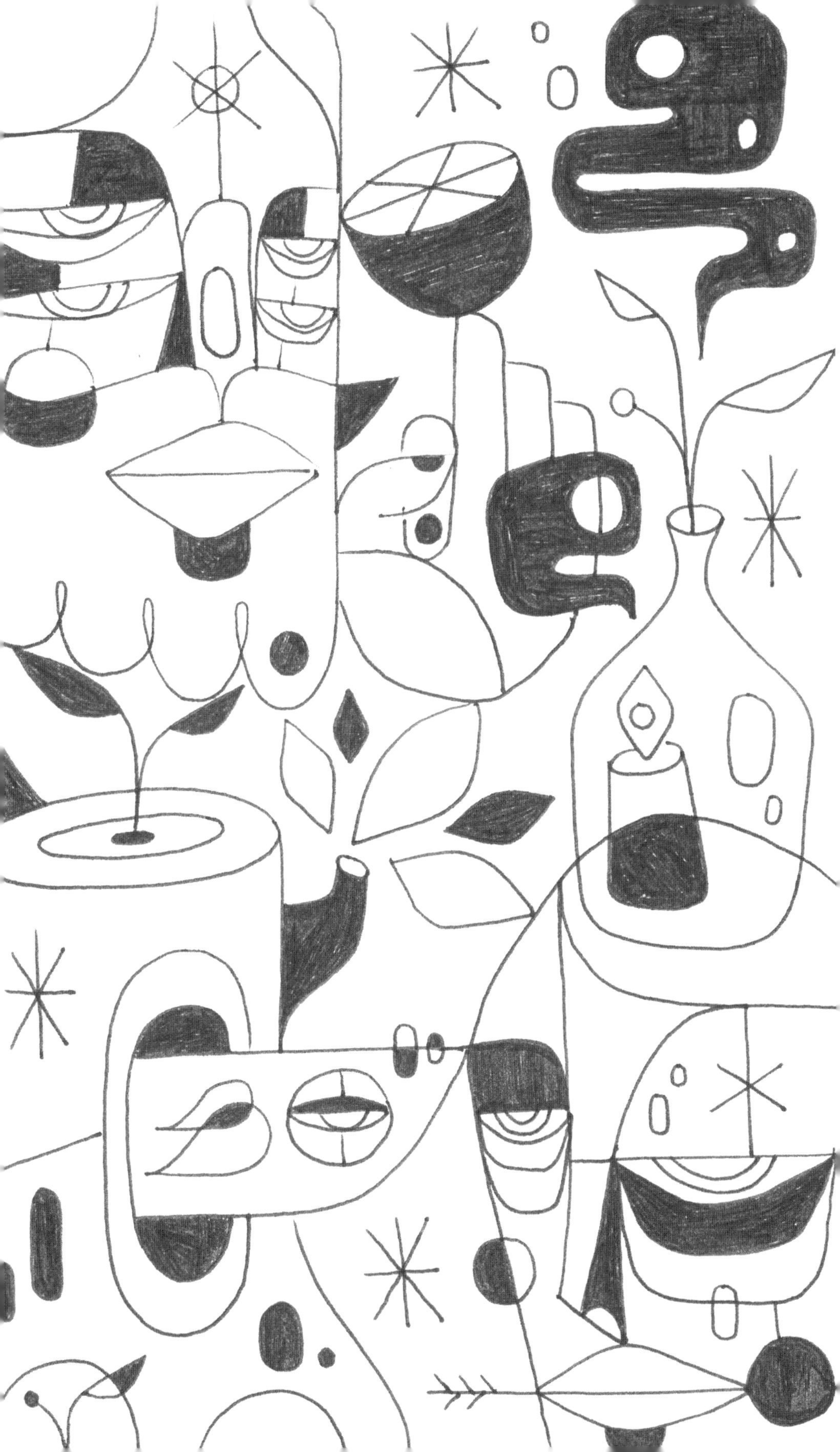

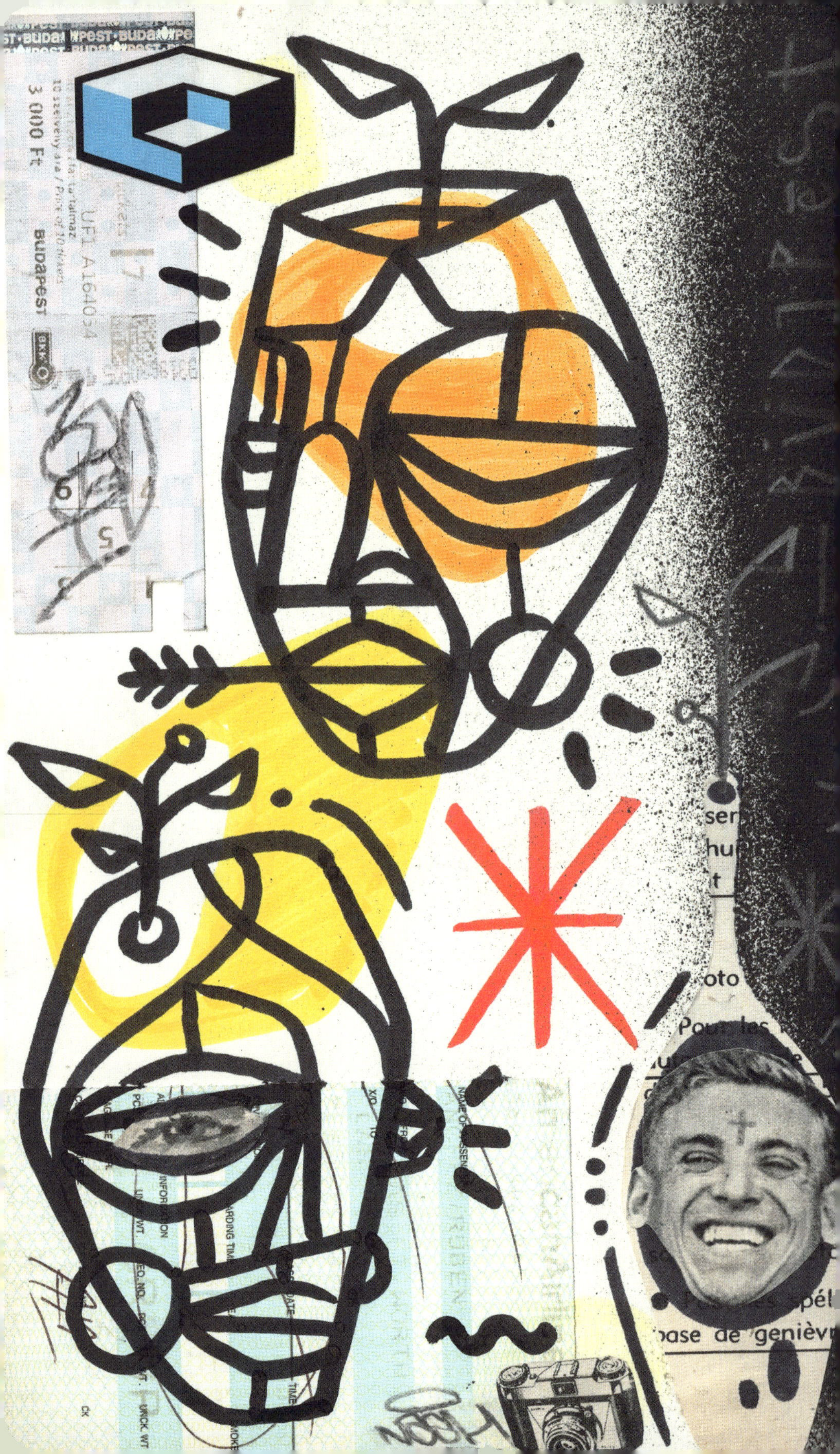

3 000 Ft
BUDAPEST
UF1 A164034
BKK
BUDAPEST

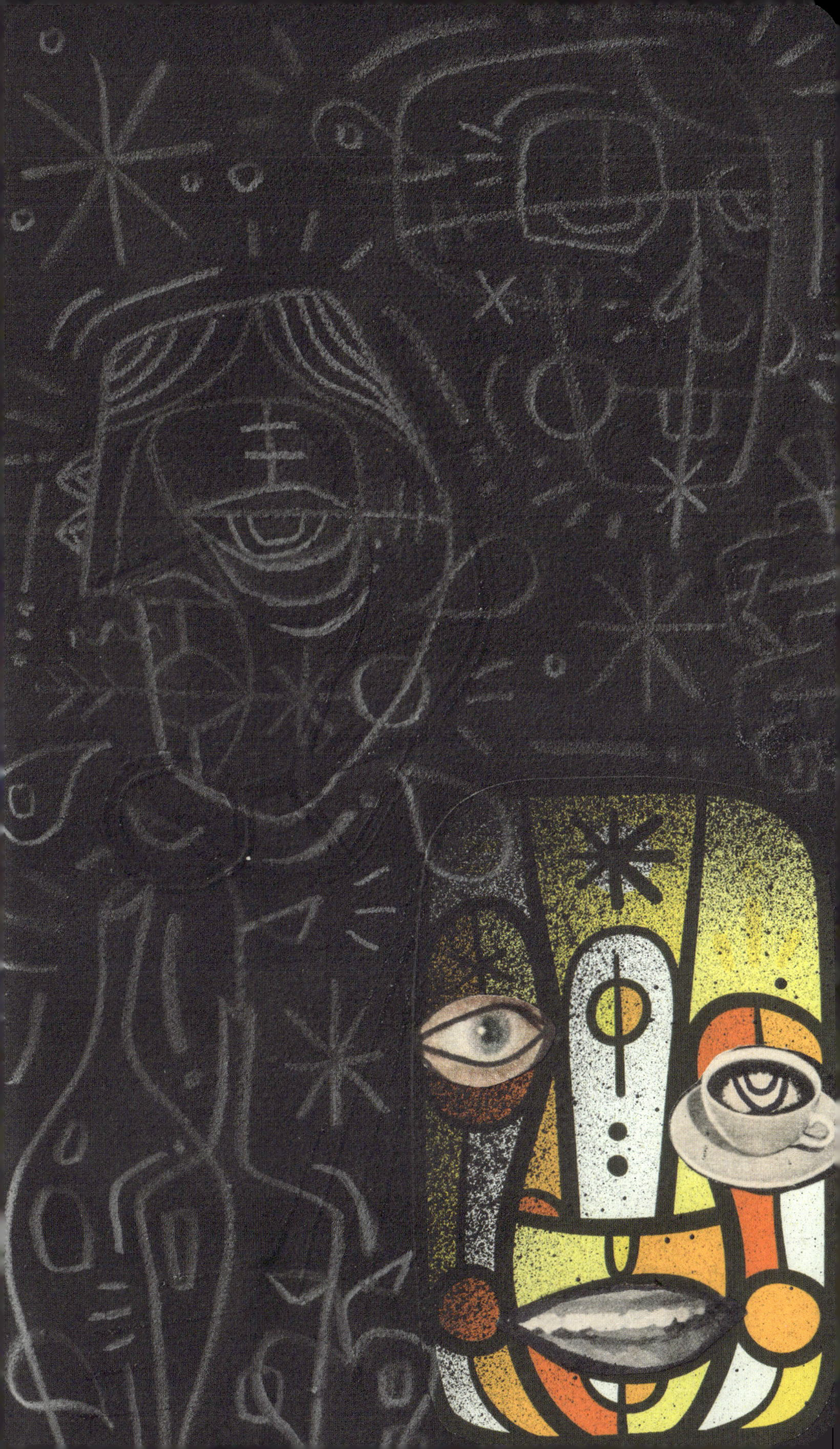

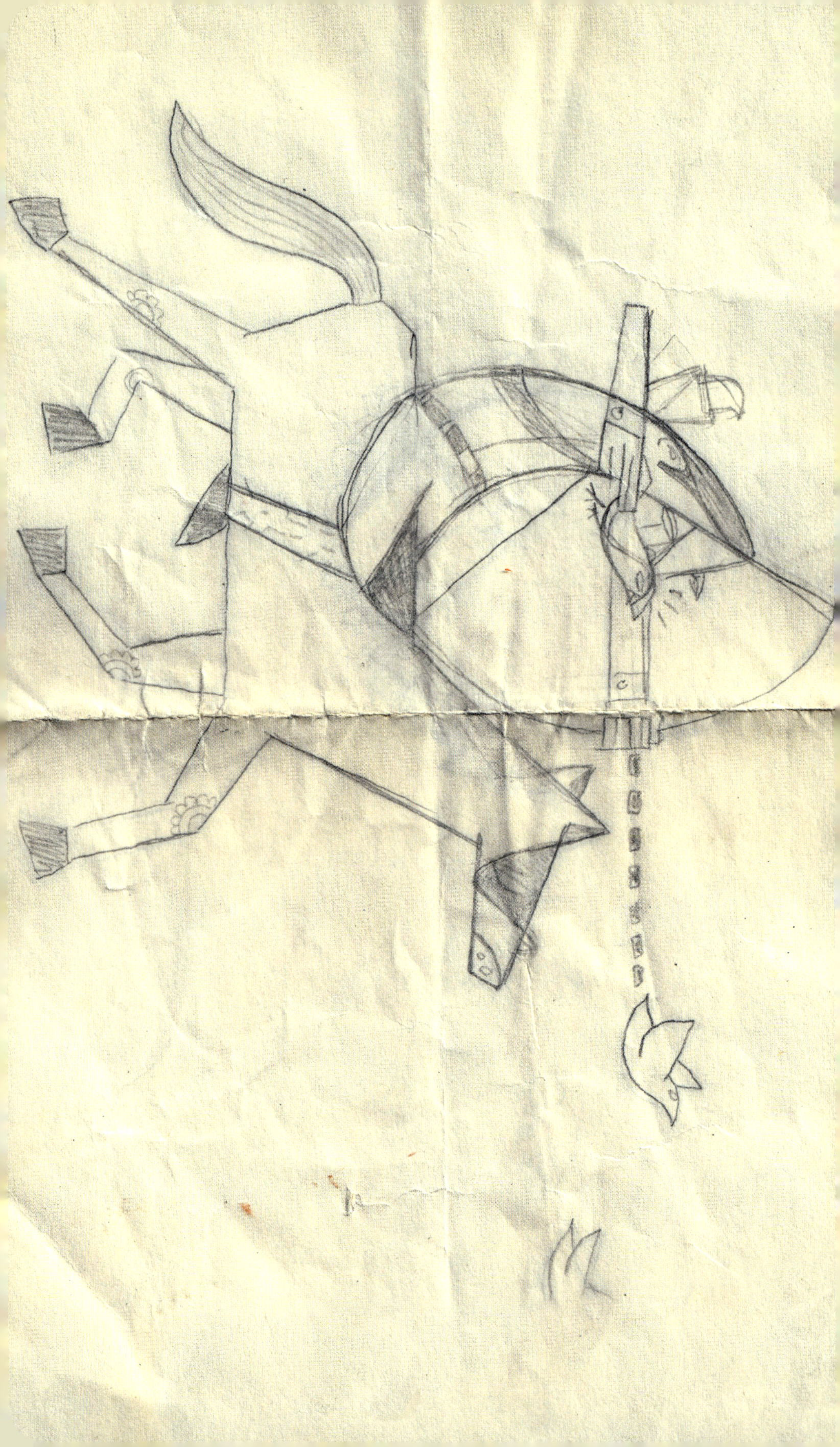

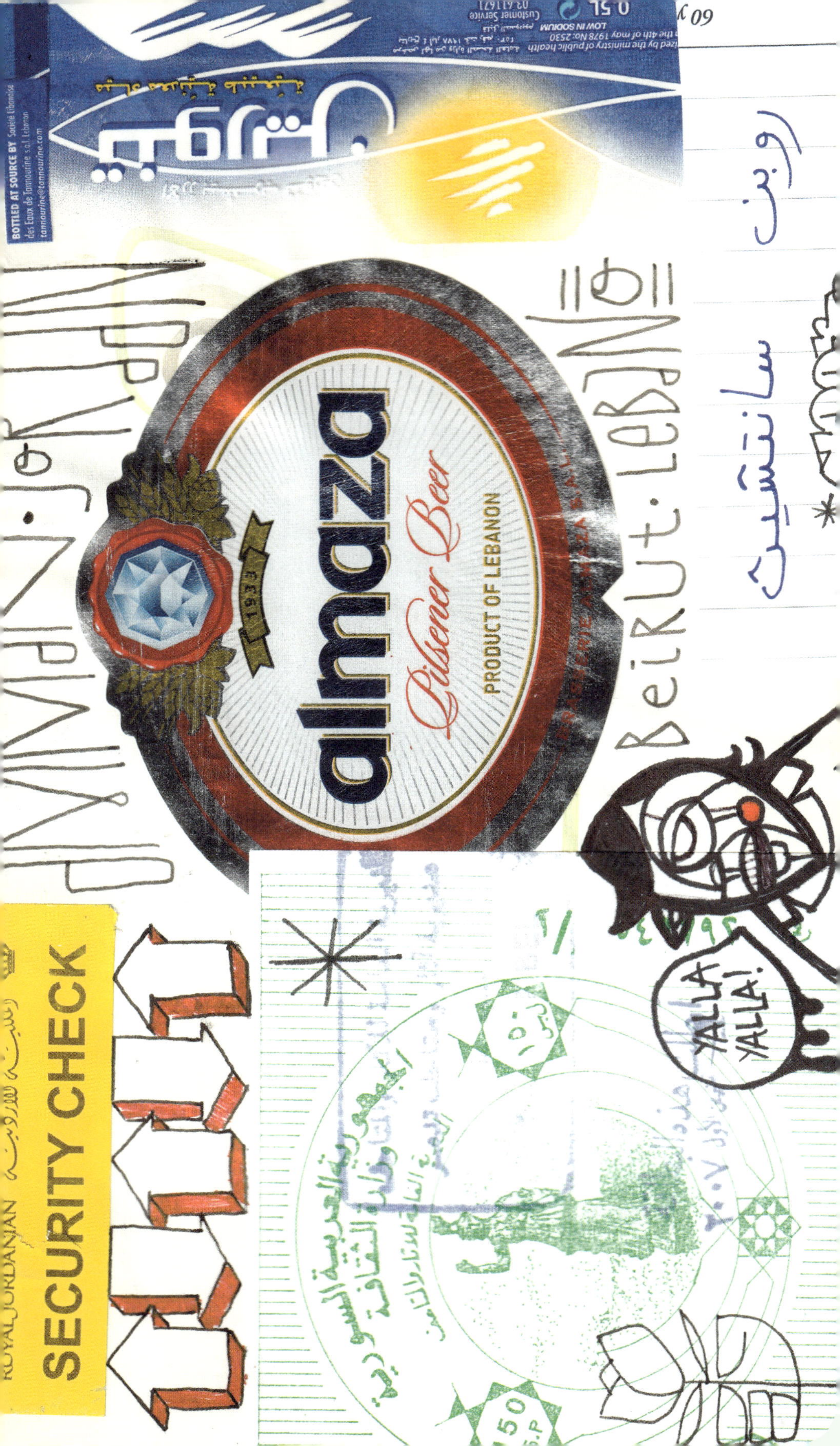

تنّورين
BOTTLED AT SOURCE BY Société libanaise
des Eaux de Tannourine s.a.l Lebanon
tannourine@tannourine.com
LOW IN SODIUM
Customer Service
03 411471
0.5L
zed by the ministry of public health
on the 4th of may 1978 No: 2530
60 y
almaza
Pilsener Beer
1933
PRODUCT OF LEBANON
BeiRut · LeBANoN
YALLA YALLA!
ROYAL JORDANIAN
SECURITY CHECK
150
S.P.

emoción
↓
curiosidad
↓
investigación
↓
reflexión
↓
concepto
~~~~~~~~~~~
~~~~~~~~~~~

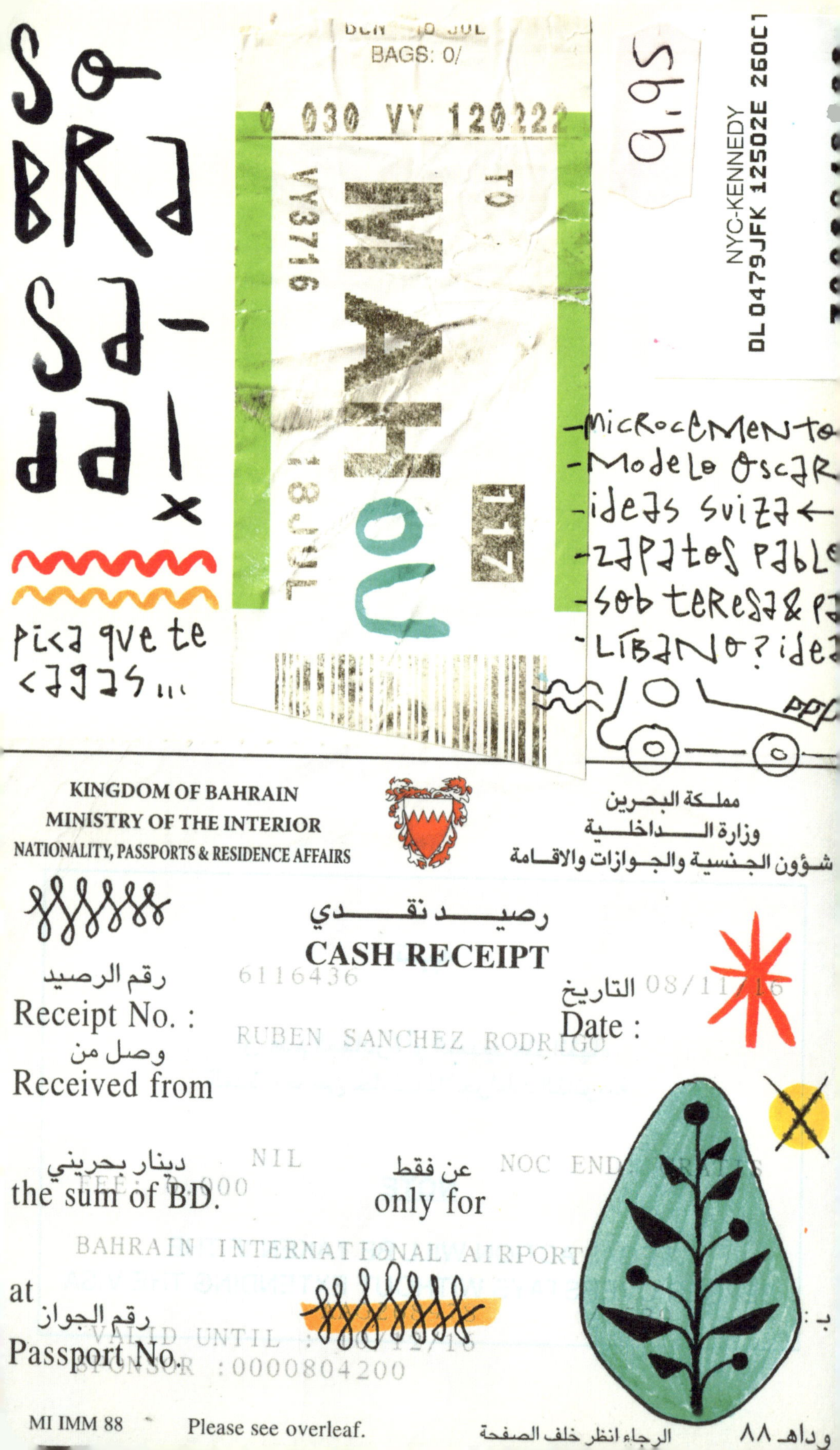
SOBRASAIX
pica que te cagas...
BAGS: 0/
0 030 VY 120222
VY3716
MAHOU
18 JUL
TO
117
NYC-KENNEDY
DL 0479JFK 12502E 260C1
9,95
- microcemento
- modelo oscar
- ideas suiza ←
- zapatos pablo
- sob teresa & pa
- libano? ide
KINGDOM OF BAHRAIN
MINISTRY OF THE INTERIOR
NATIONALITY, PASSPORTS & RESIDENCE AFFAIRS
مملكة البحرين
وزارة الـداخليـة
شؤون الجنسية والجوازات والاقـامة
رصيـد نقـدي
CASH RECEIPT
6116436
RUBEN SANCHEZ RODRIGO
رقم الرصيد
Receipt No. :
وصل من
Received from
التاريخ
Date :
08/11/16
NIL
NOC END
عن فقط
دينار بحريني
the sum of BD.
only for
BAHRAIN INTERNATIONAL AIRPORT
at
رقم الجواز
Passport No.
VALID UNTIL
SPONSOR : 0000804200
MI IMM 88
Please see overleaf.
الرجاء انظر خلف الصفحة
واه ٨٨

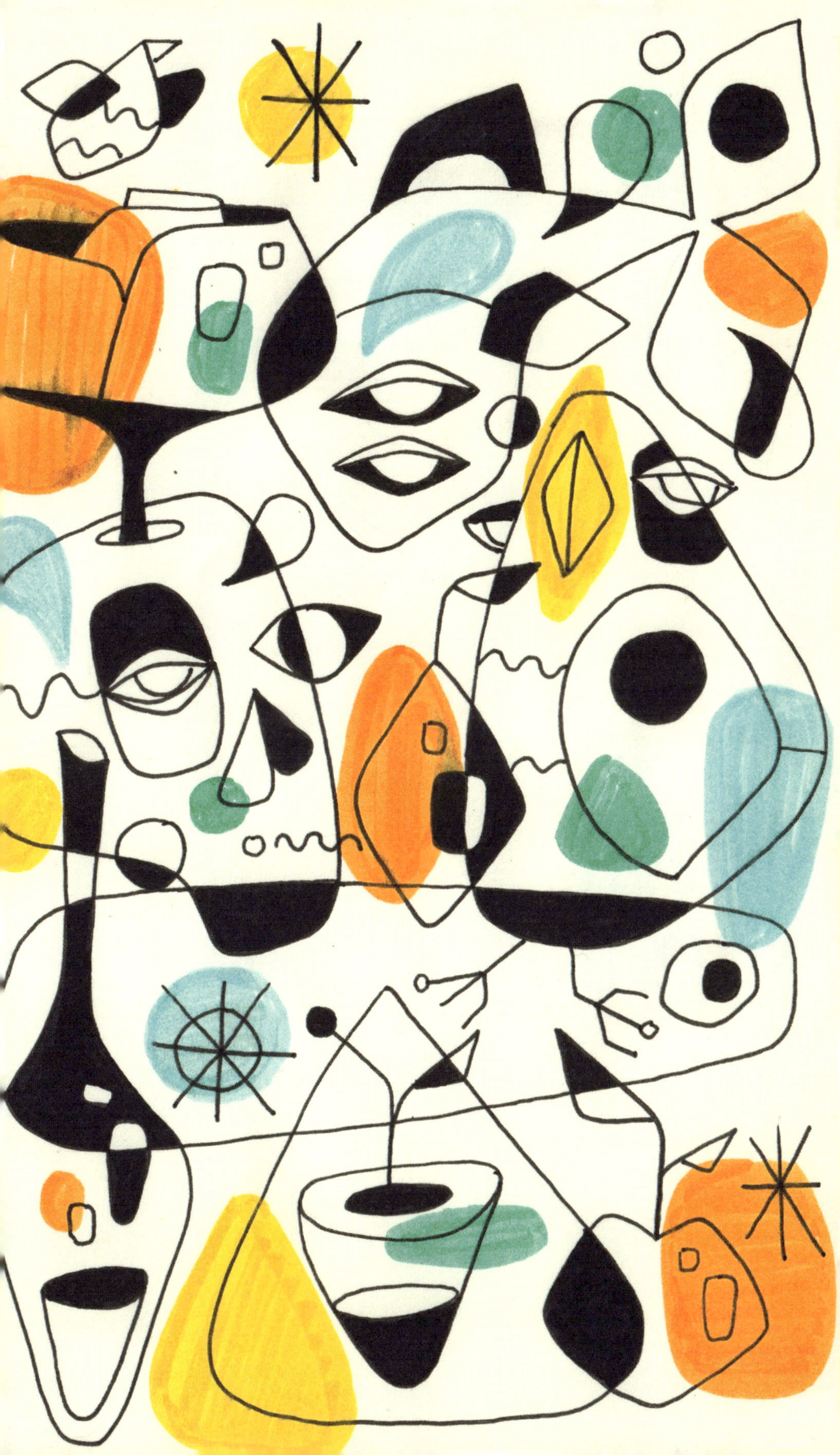

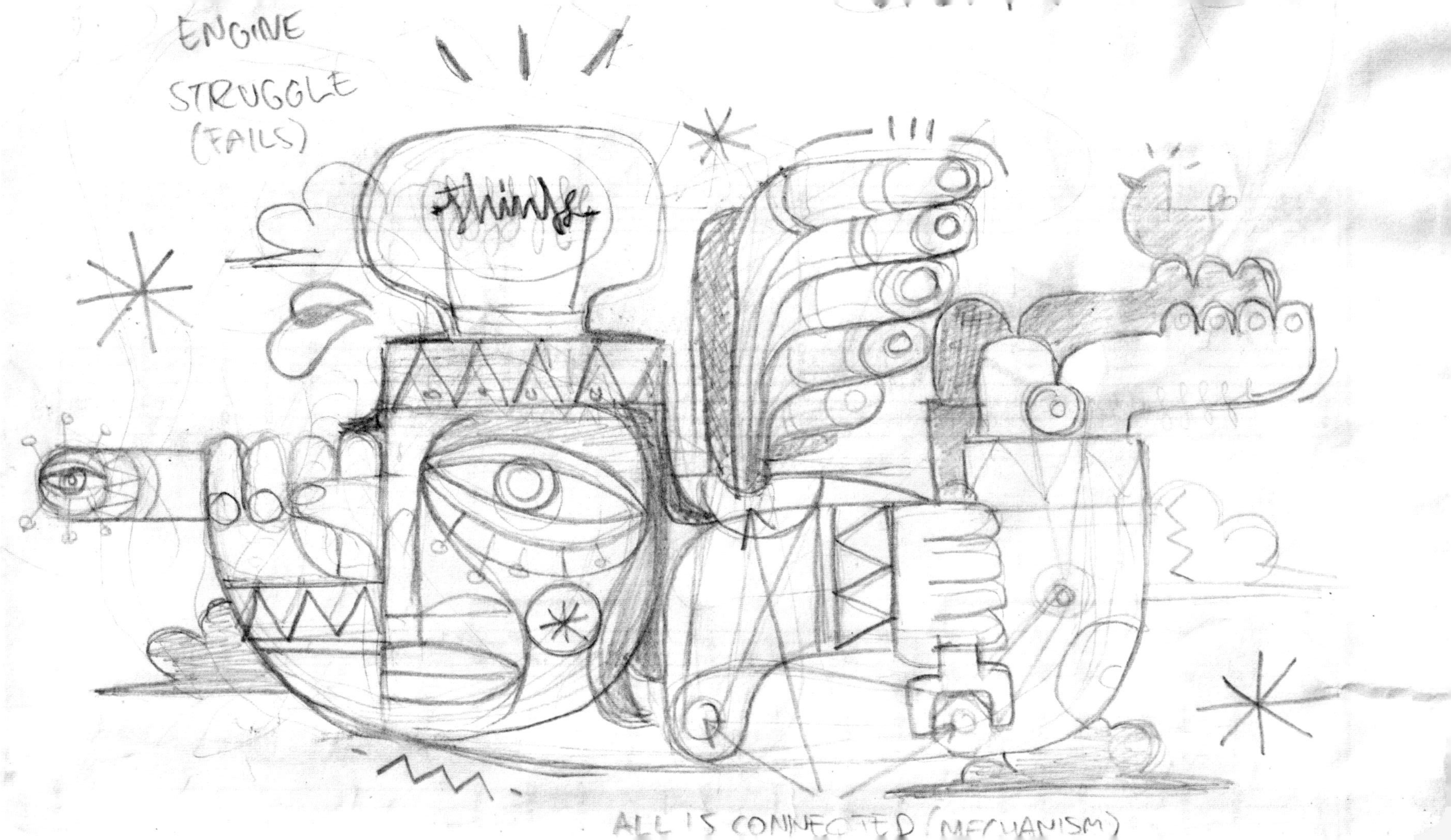

ENGINE
STRUGGLE
(FAILS)
ALL IS CONNECTED (MECHANISM)

MadRid 19

MadRid 19

MadRid 19

MadRid 19

MadRid 19

MadRid 19

MadRid 19

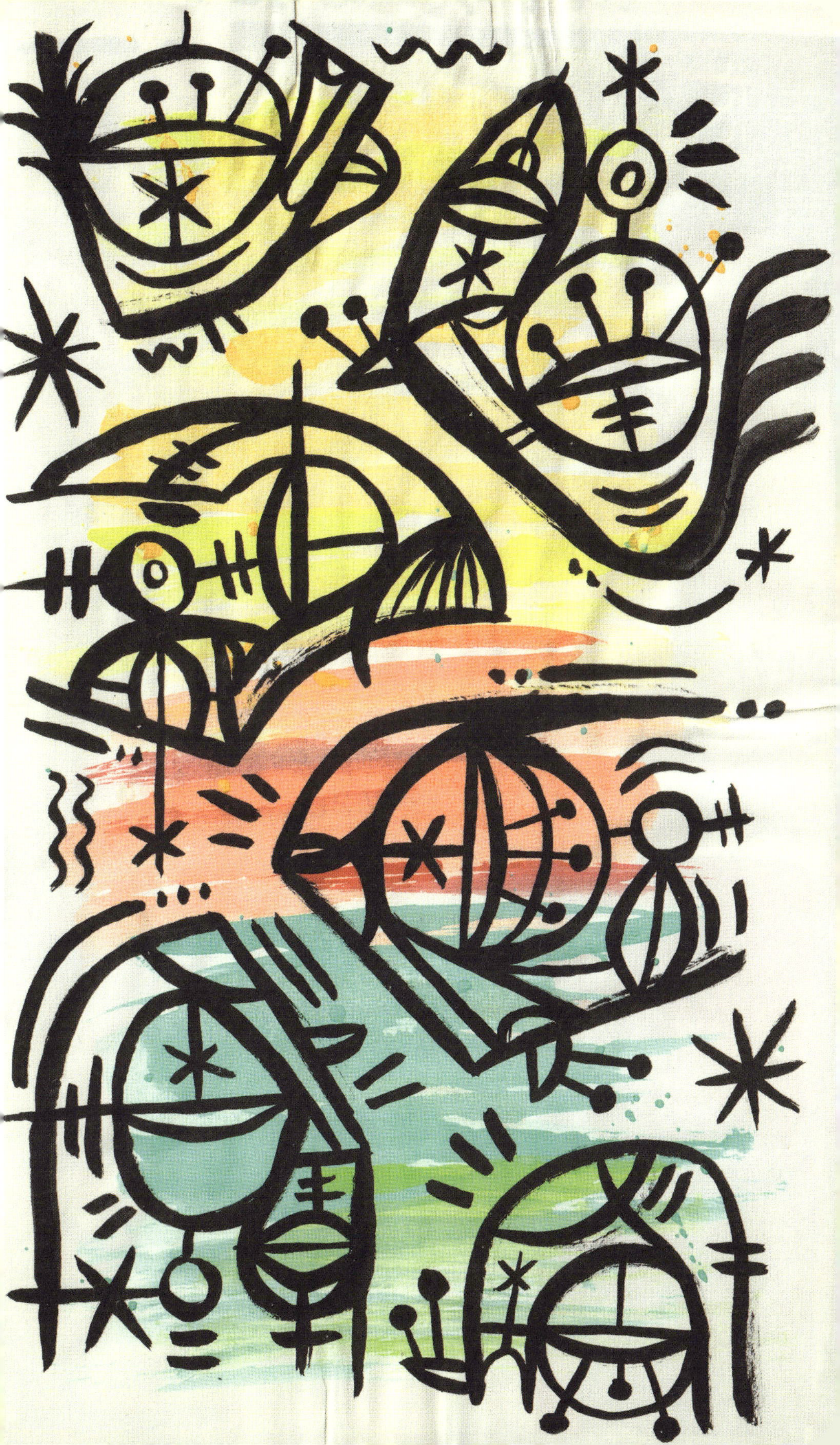

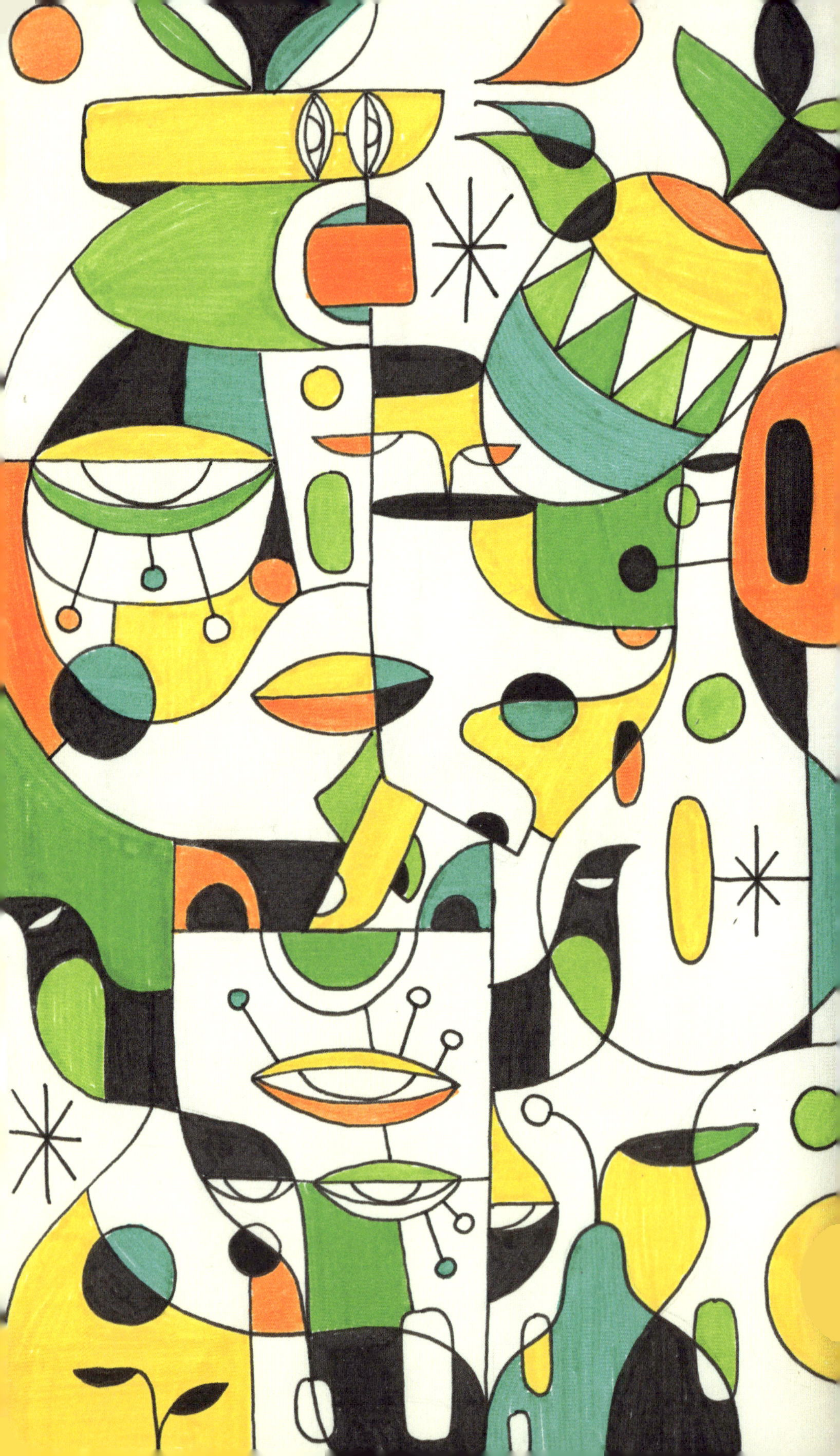

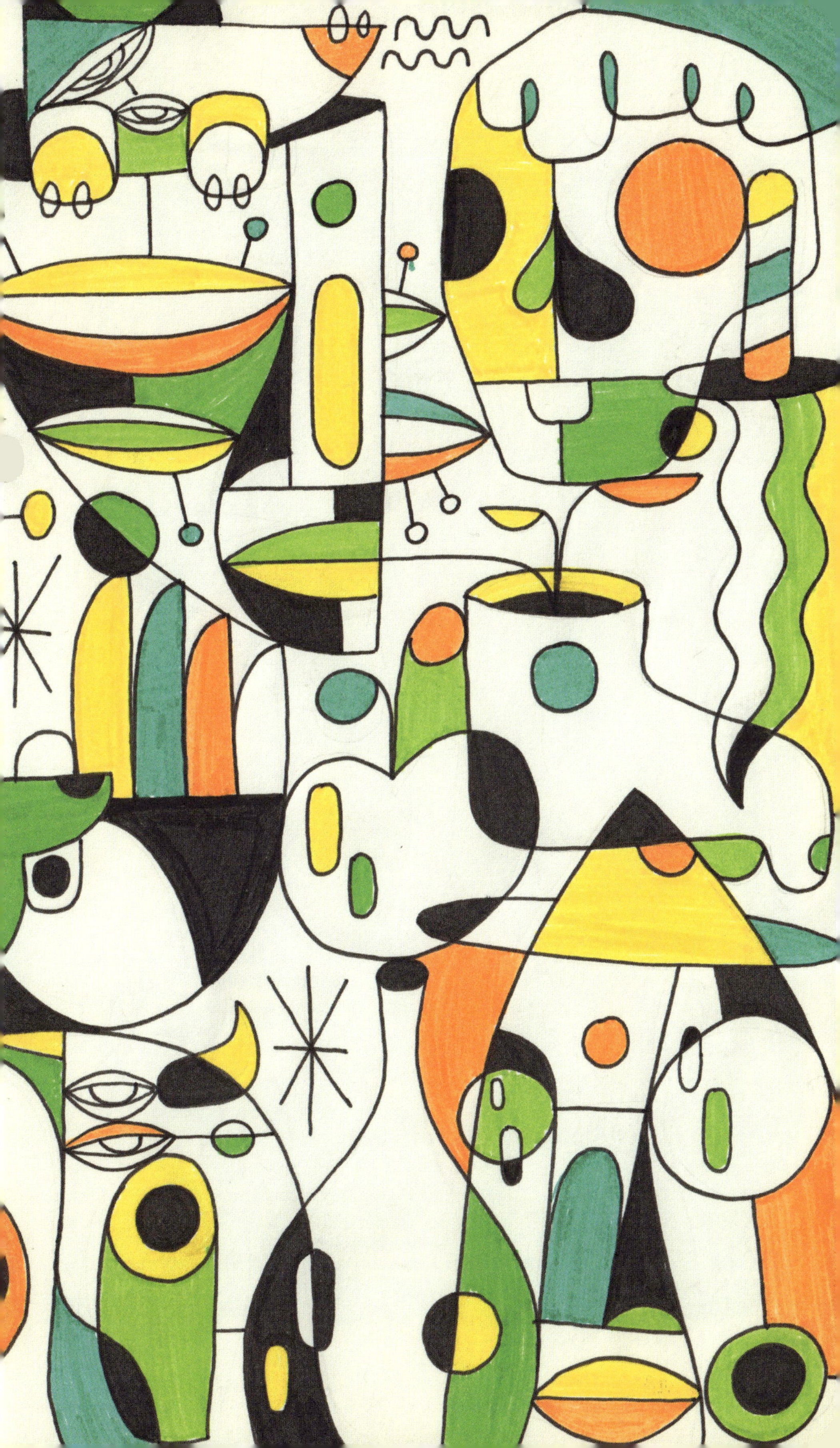

BULL
RUN

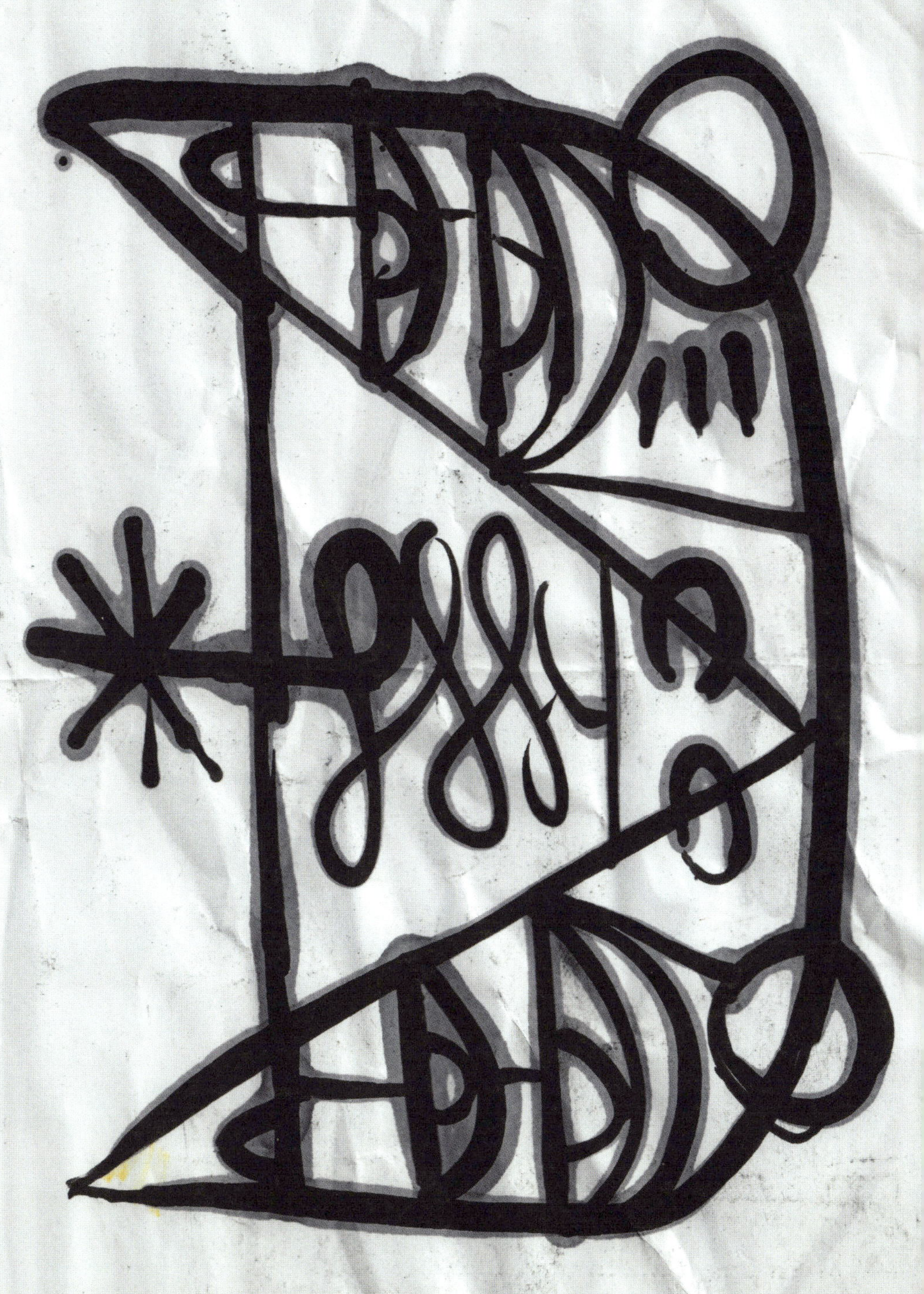

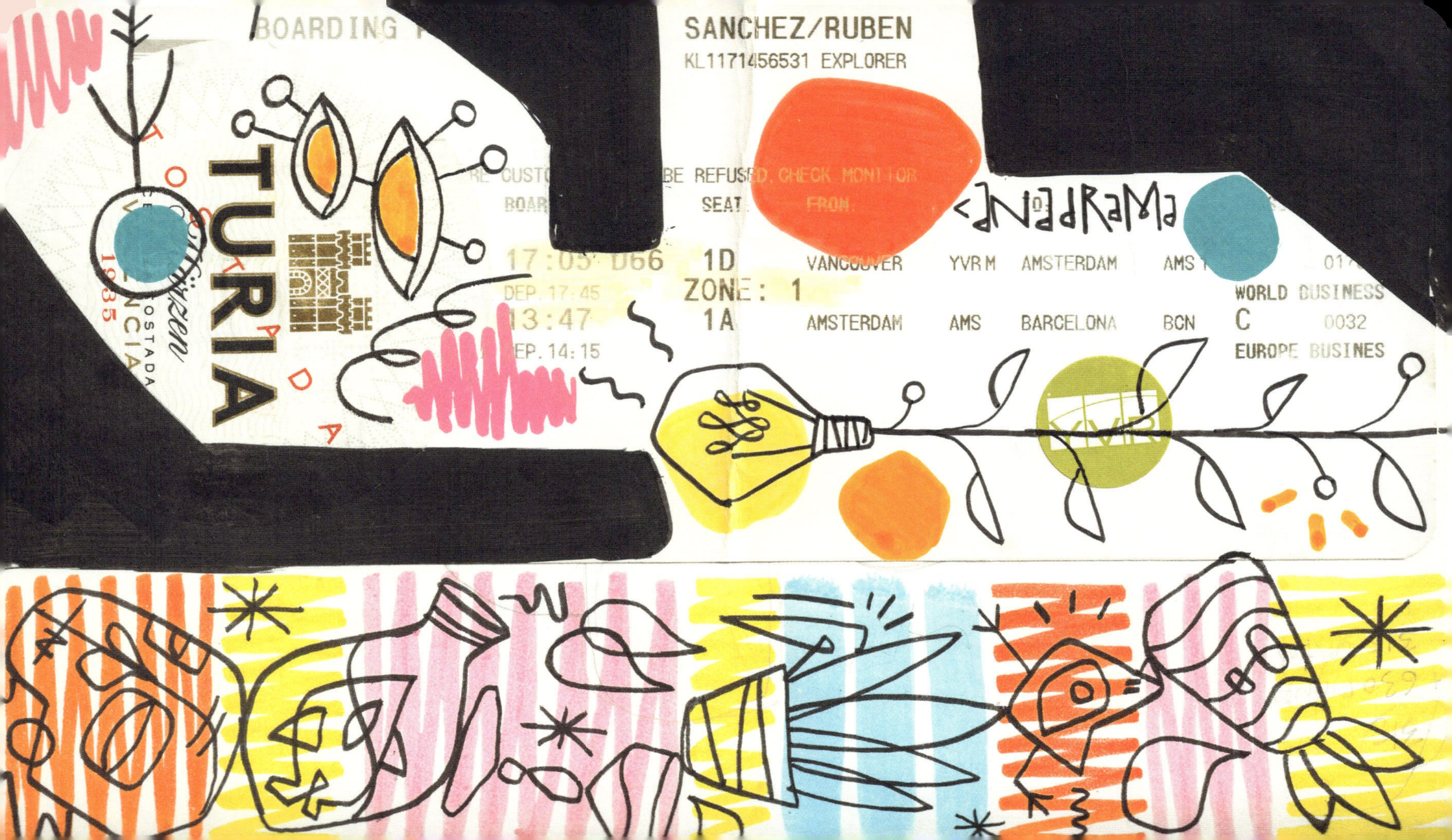
BOARDING
SANCHEZ/RUBEN
KL1171456531 EXPLORER
RE CUSTO... BE REFUSED. CHECK MONITOR
BOAR... SEAT FROM.
17:05 D66 1D VANCOUVER YVRM AMSTERDAM AMS 01
DEP. 17:45 ZONE: 1 WORLD BUSINESS
13:47 1A AMSTERDAM AMS BARCELONA BCN C 0032
DEP. 14:15 EUROPE BUSINES
TURIA
TOSTADA
VALENCIA
1935

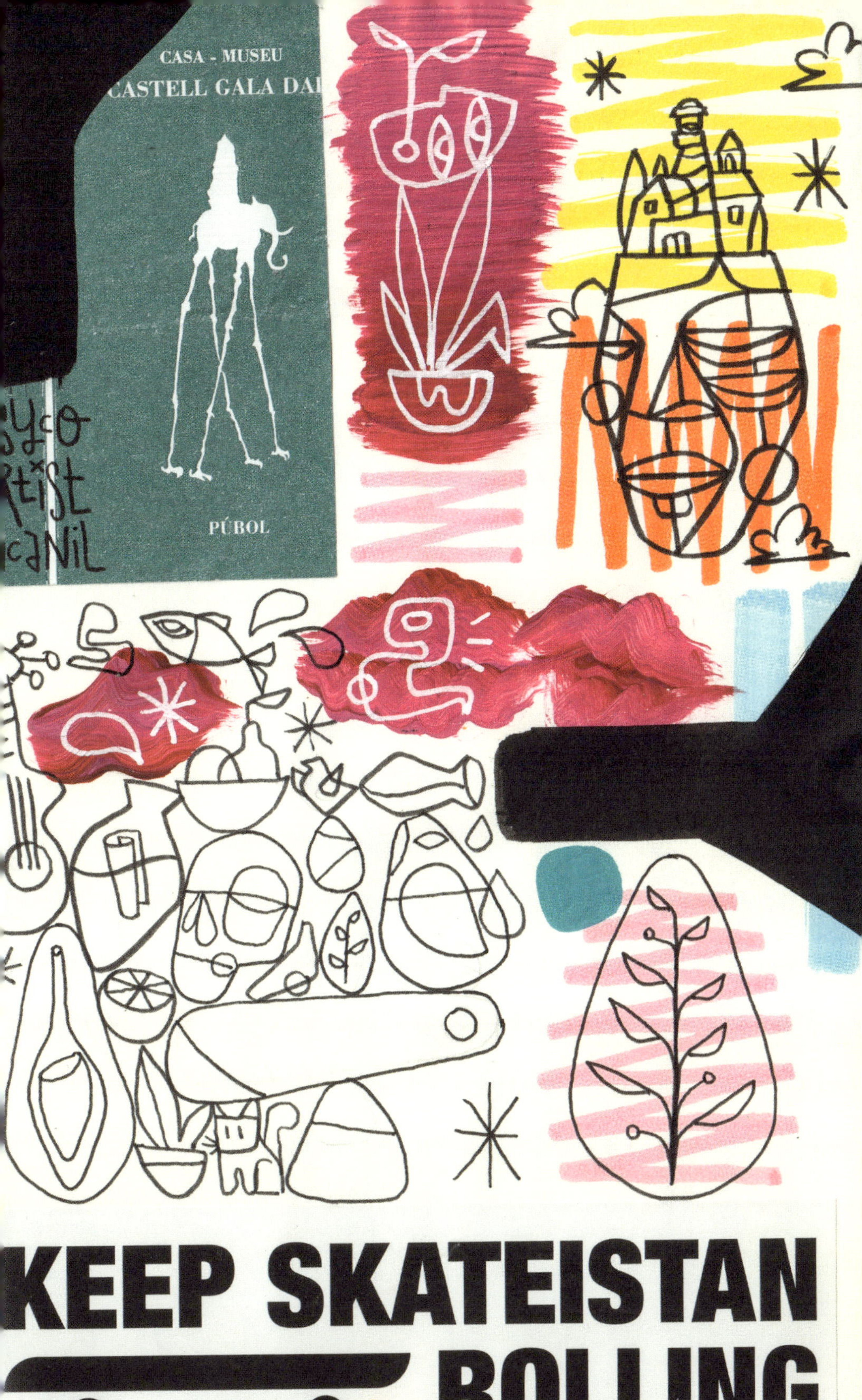

CASA - MUSEU
CASTELL GALA DALÍ
PÚBOL
KEEP SKATEISTAN ROLLING

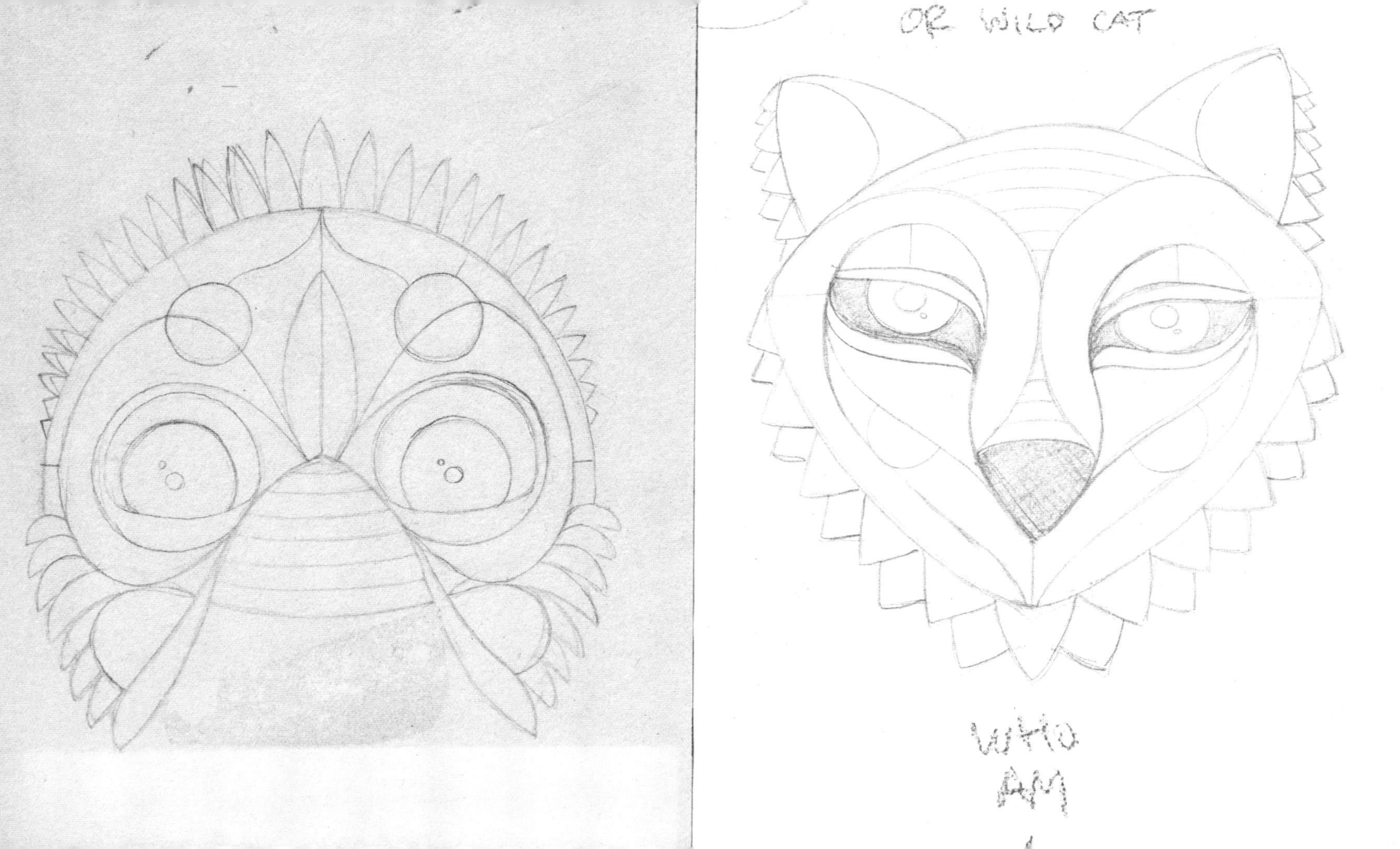
OR WILD CAT
WHO
AM

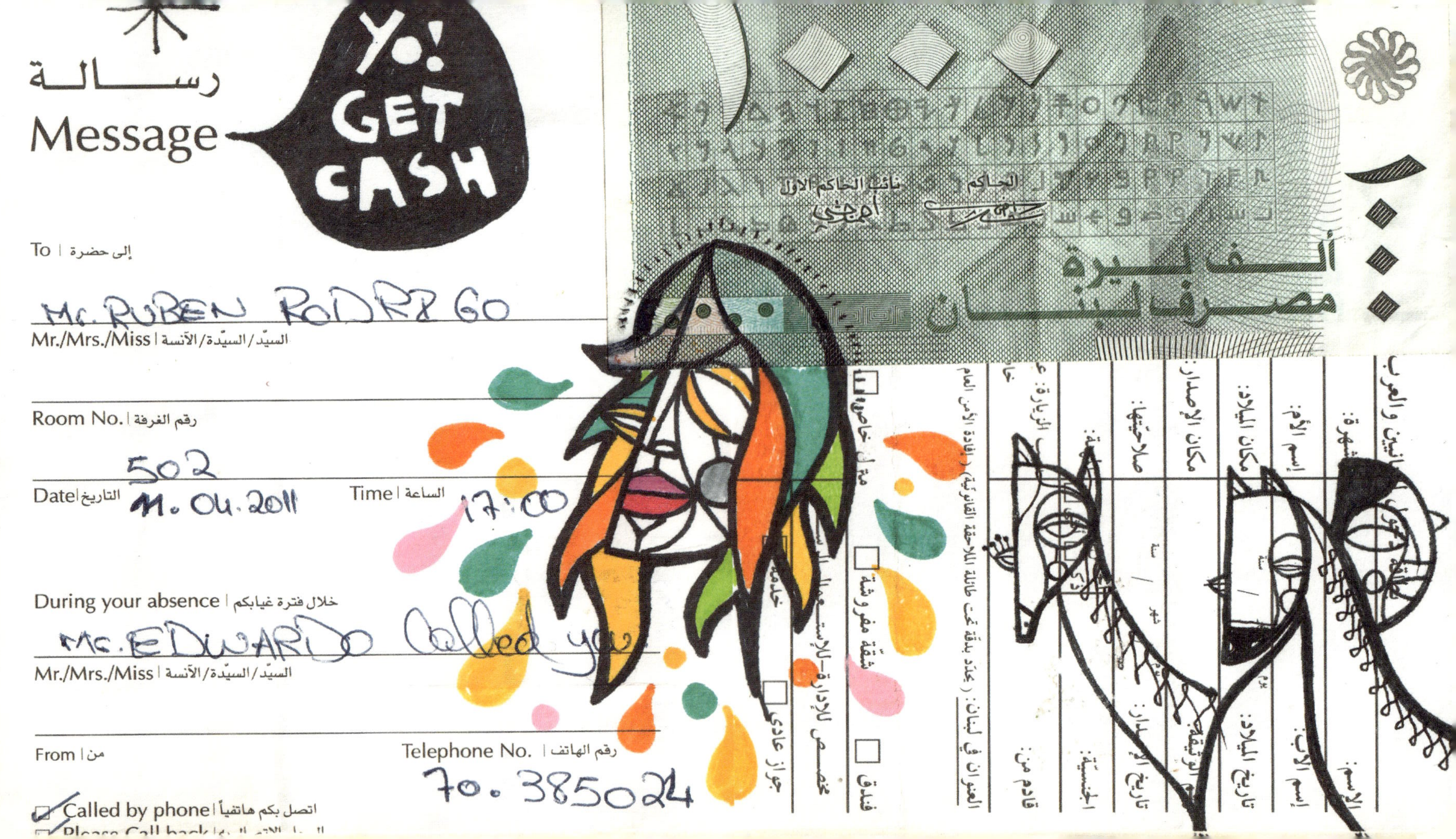
رسالة
Message
YO! GET CASH
إلى حضرة | To
Mr. RUBEN RODRIGO
السيّد/السيّدة/الآنسة | Mr./Mrs./Miss
رقم الغرفة | Room No.
502
التاريخ | Date
11. 04. 2011
الساعة | Time
17:00
خلال فترة غيابكم | During your absence
Mr. EDWARDO called you
السيّد/السيّدة/الآنسة | Mr./Mrs./Miss
من | From
رقم الهاتف | Telephone No.
70. 385024
اتصل بكم هاتفياً | Called by phone
Please Call back

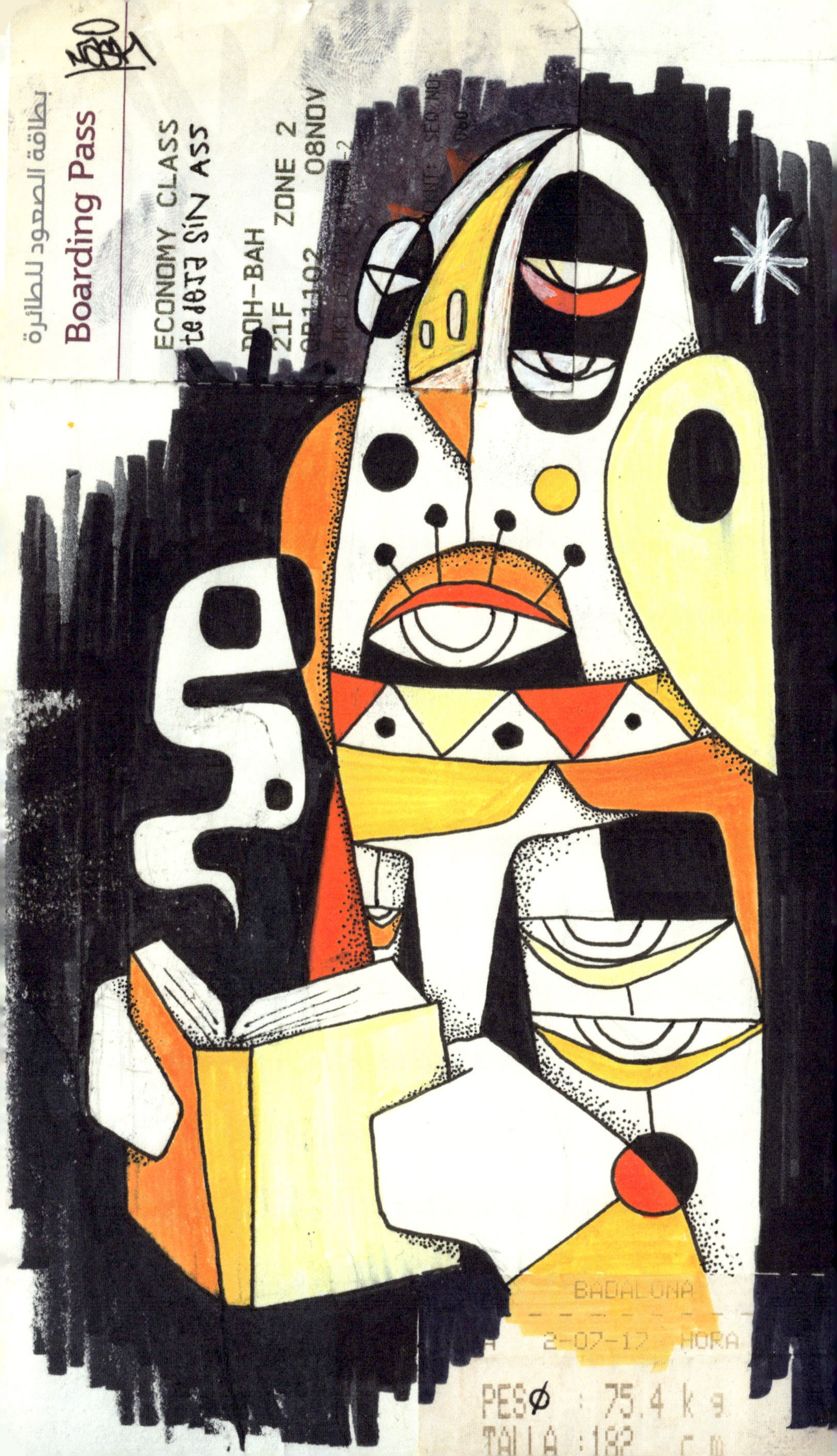
بطاقة الصعود إلى الطائرة
Boarding Pass
ECONOMY CLASS
te dera sin ass
DOH-BAH
21F ZONE 2
QR1102 08NOV
BADALONA
2-07-17 HORA
PESØ : 75.4 kg.
TALLA : 182

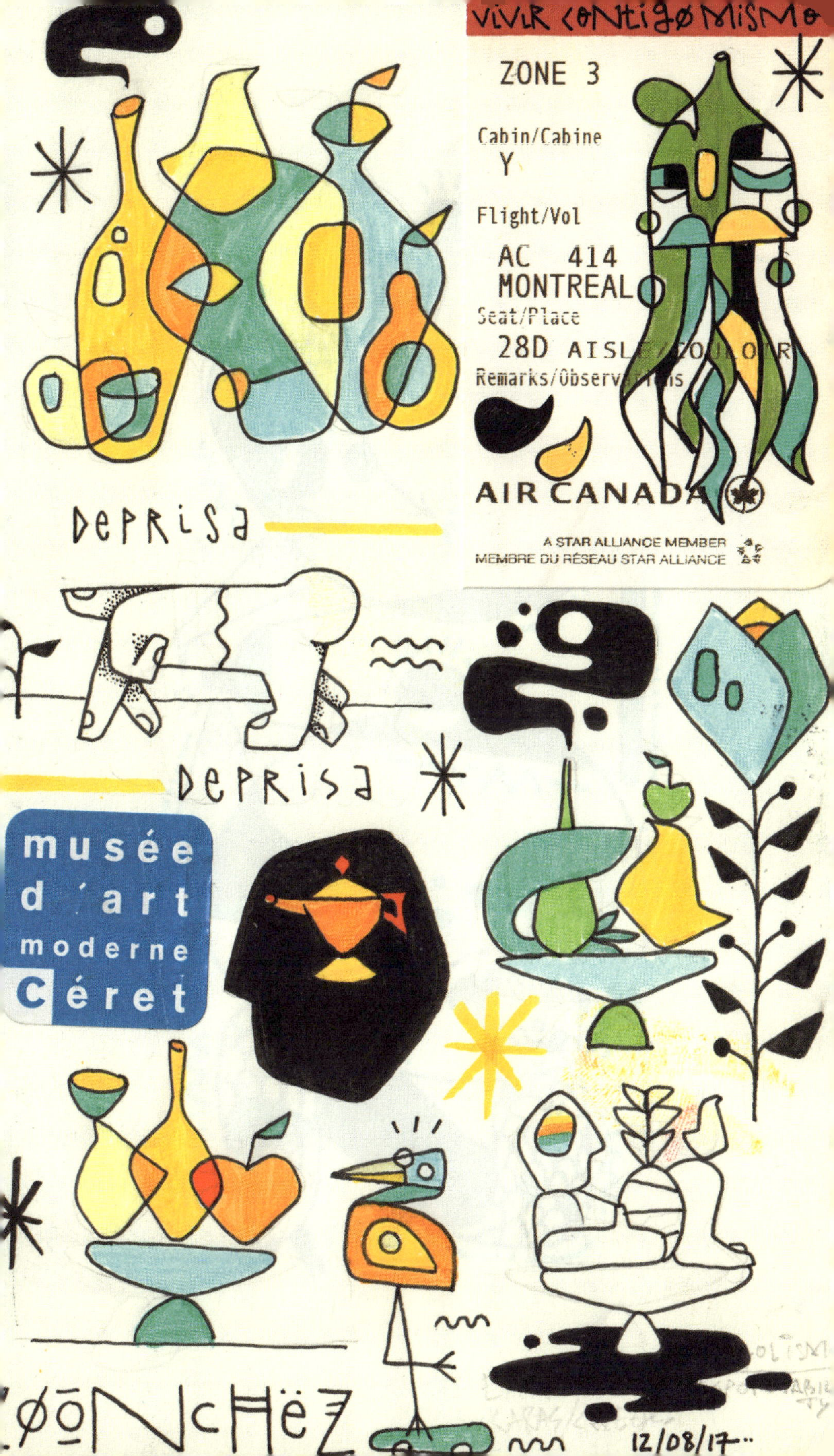

ViVıR CoNTigo MiSMo
ZONE 3
Cabin/Cabine
Y
Flight/Vol
AC   414
MONTREAL
Seat/Place
28D AISLE/COULOIR
Remarks/Observations
AIR CANADA
A STAR ALLIANCE MEMBER
MEMBRE DU RÉSEAU STAR ALLIANCE
deprisa
deprisa
musée
d'art
moderne
Céret
SàNcHëz
12/08/17

Muy seguro de
mis insegur-
idades ~~~~~~~

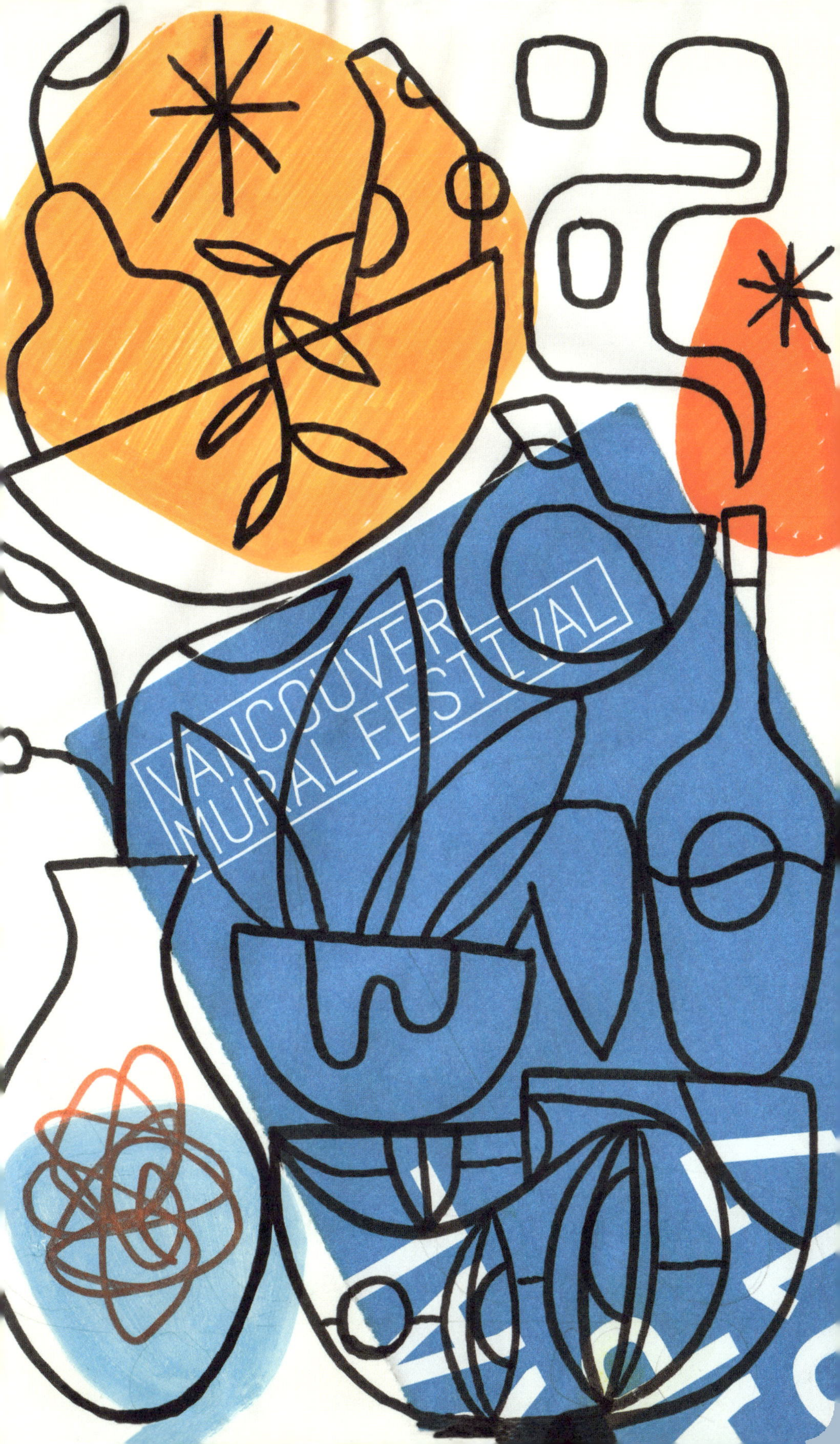

VANCOUVER
MURAL FESTIVAL

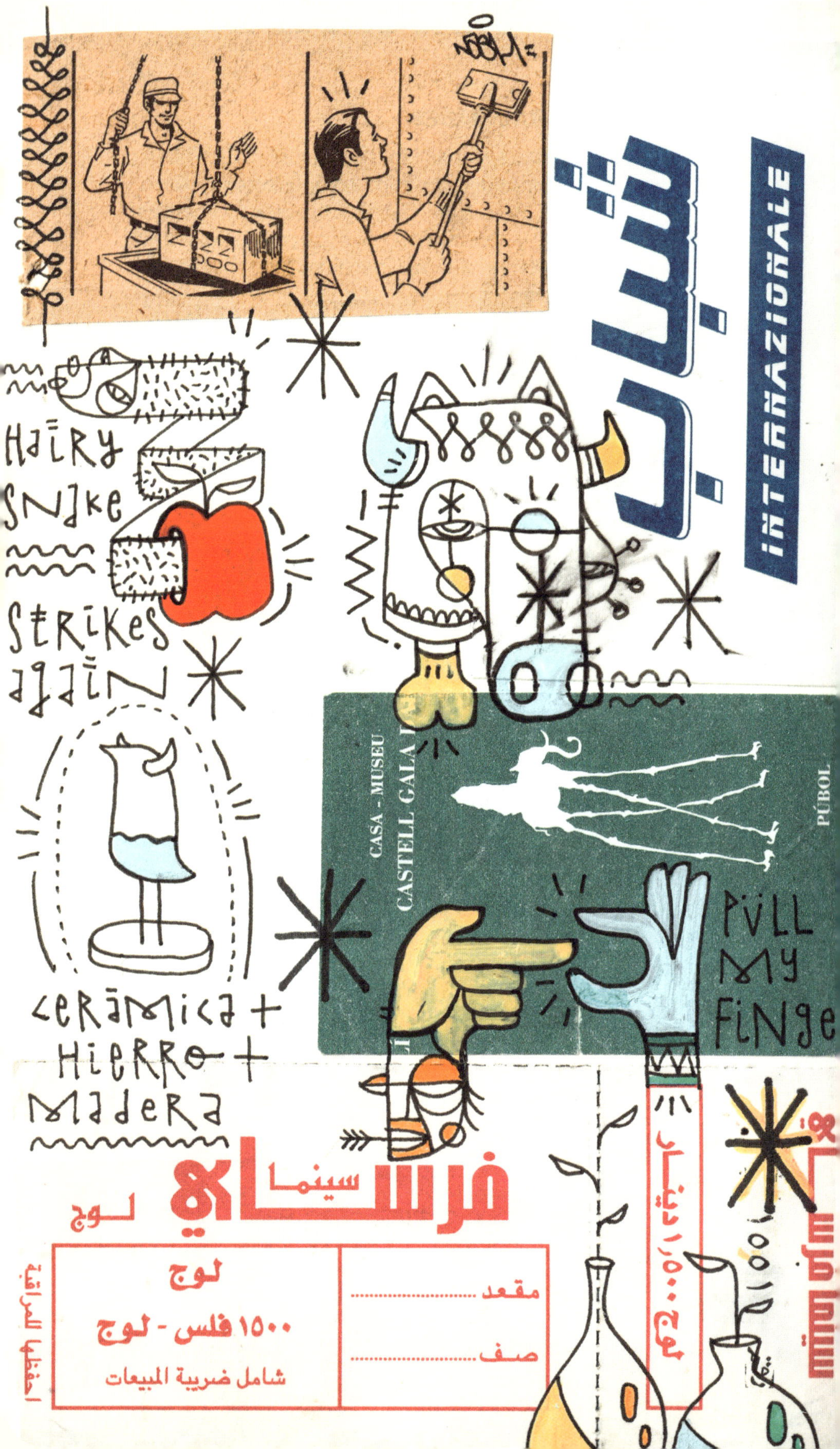
HAIRY
SNAKE
STRIKES
AGAIN
CERAMICA +
HIERRO +
MADERA
CASA - MUSEU
CASTELL GALA
PÚBOL
PULL
MY
FINGE
INTERNAZIONALE
سينما فرسان
لوج
لوج
مقعد
١٥٠٠ فلس - لوج
صف
شامل ضريبة المبيعات

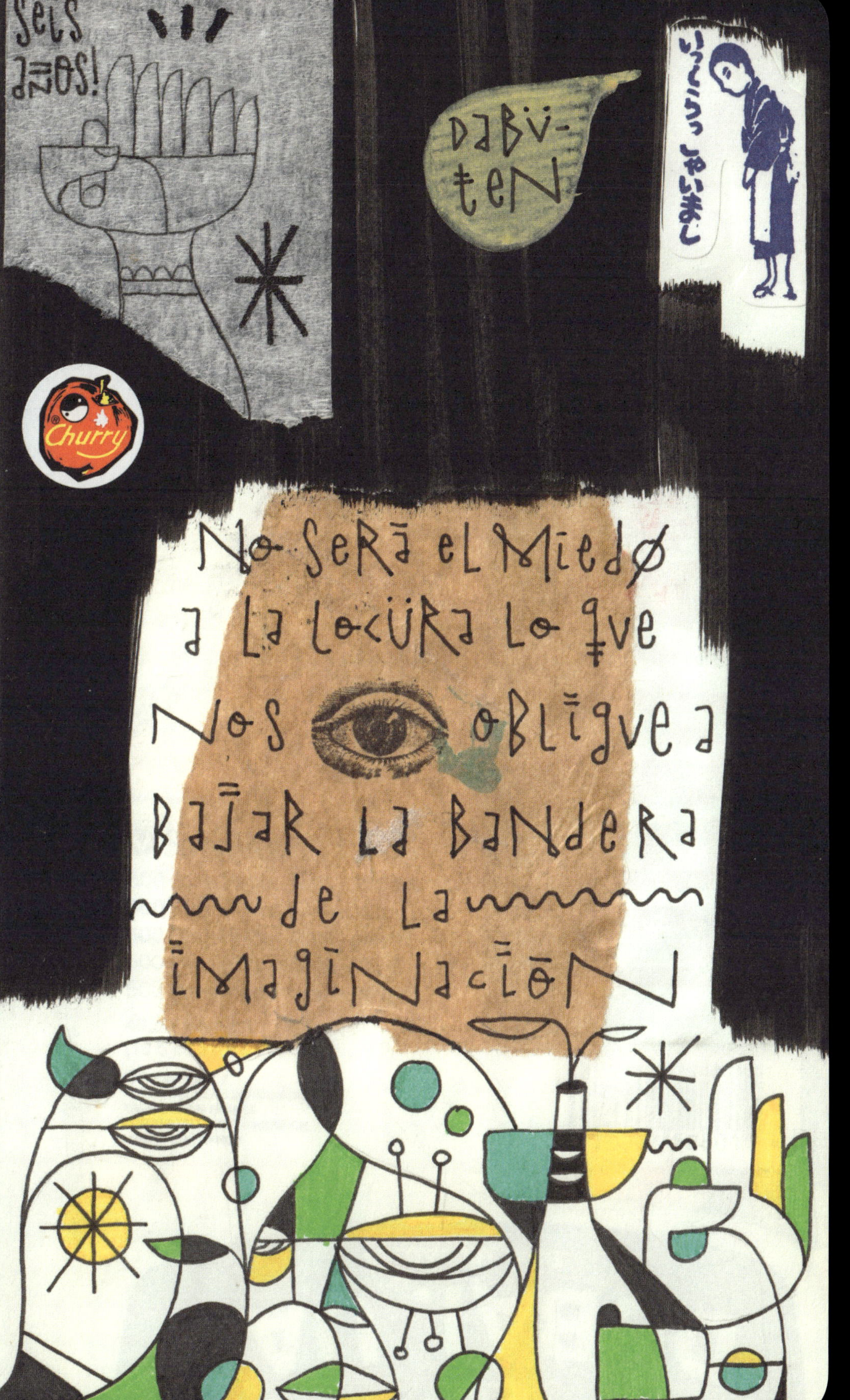

SEiS AÑOS!
DABÜ-TeN
Churry
No seRā el Miedø
a La LoCÜRa Lo que
Nos oBLīgue a
Bāāar La BaNdera
de La
iMagiNacīōN

LA SUERTE Y
LA INTELIGE
NCIA SE PELE
ARON 1 DÍA

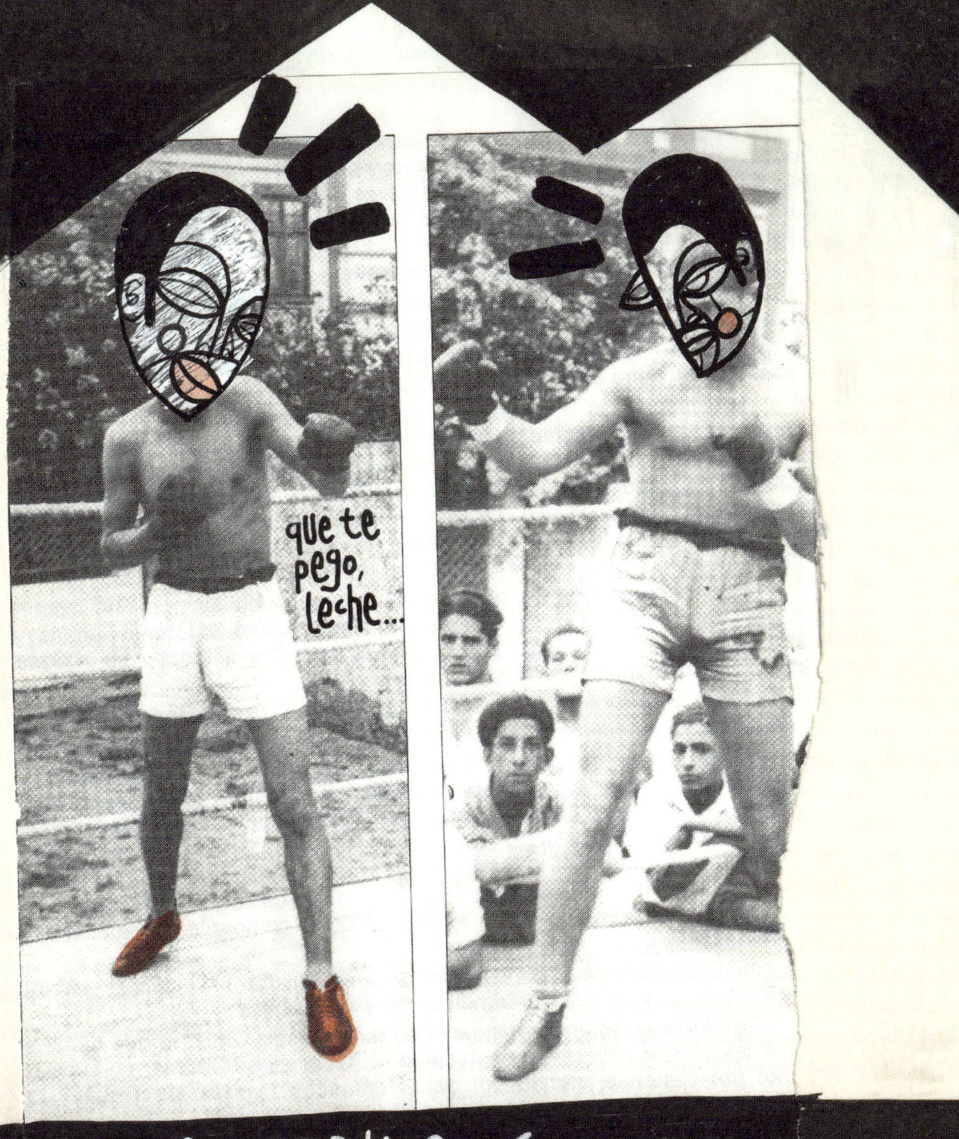

que te
pego,
leche...
6 asaltos 6 *

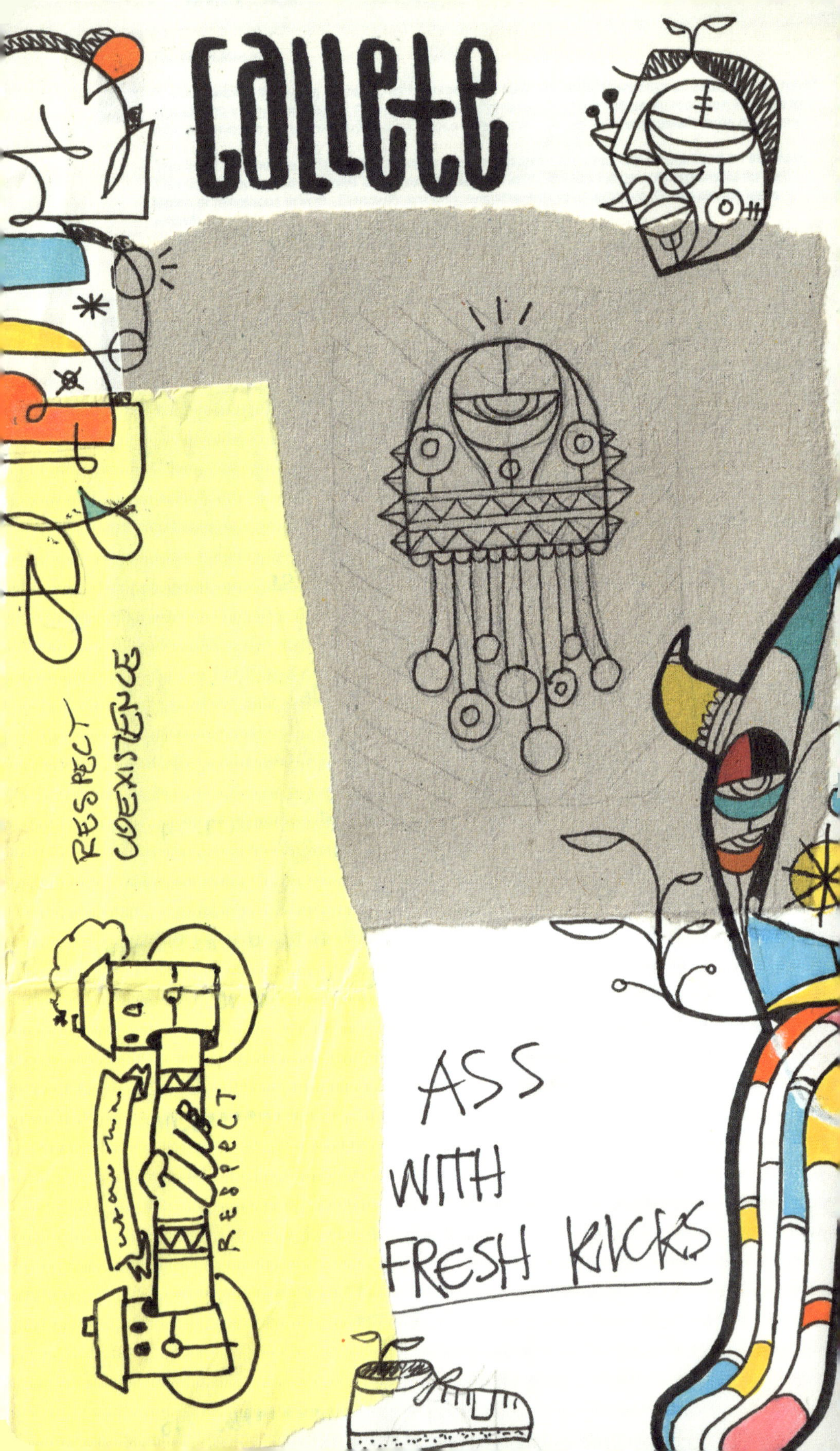

collete
RESPECT COEXISTENCE
RESPECT
ASS
WITH
FRESH KICKS

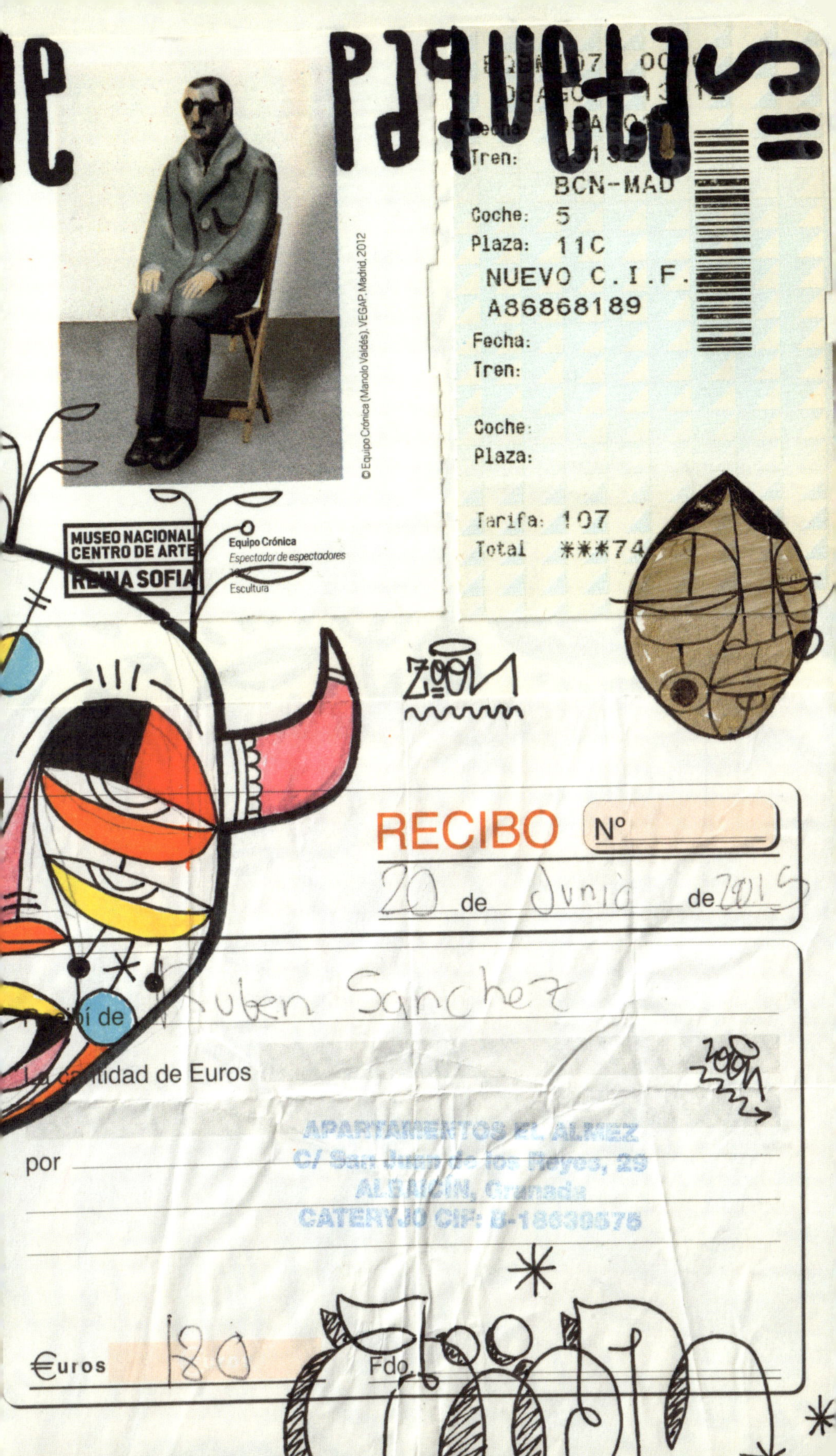
© Equipo Crónica (Manolo Valdés). VEGAP. Madrid. 2012
MUSEO NACIONAL CENTRO DE ARTE REINA SOFIA
Equipo Crónica
Espectador de espectadores
Escultura
Tren: 03132
BCN-MAD
Coche: 5
Plaza: 11C
NUEVO C.I.F.
A86868189
Fecha:
Tren:
Coche:
Plaza:
Tarifa: 107
Total ***74
RECIBO Nº
20 de Junio de 2015
Ruben Sanchez
de Euros
por
APARTAMENTOS EL ALMEZ
C/ San Juan de los Reyes, 29
ALBAICIN, Granada
CIF: G-18038575
€uros 180
Fdo.

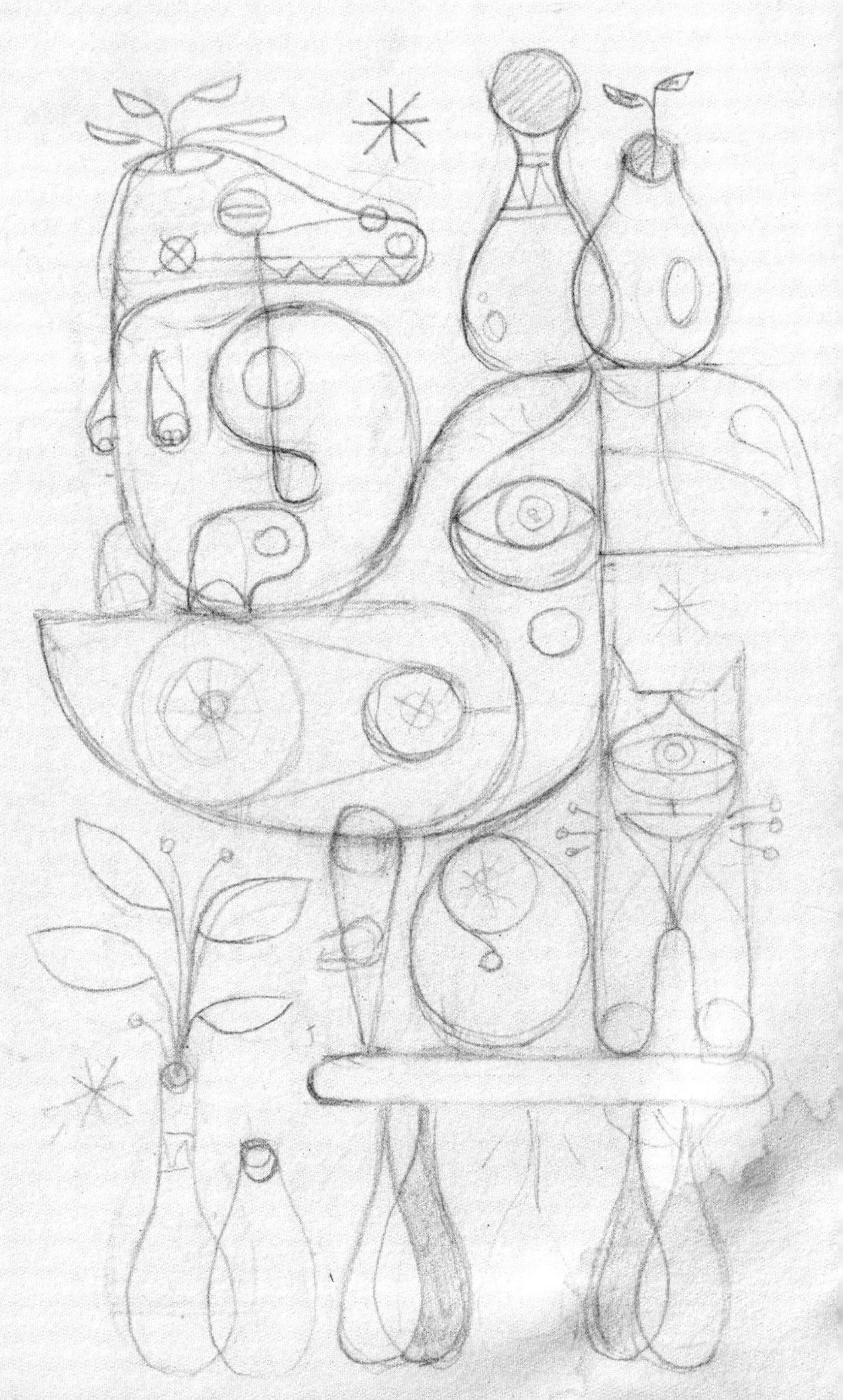

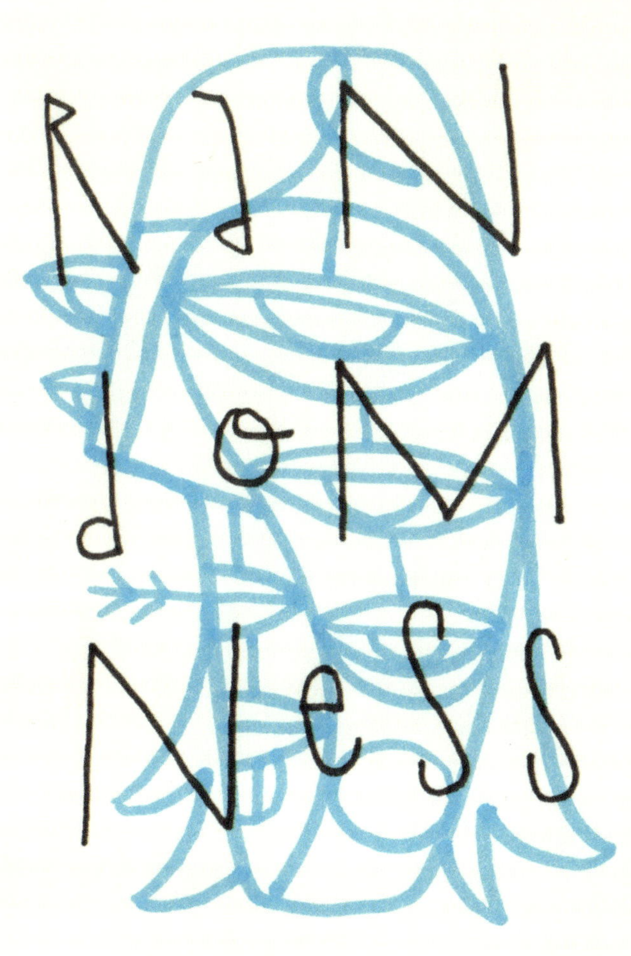
RANDOMNESS

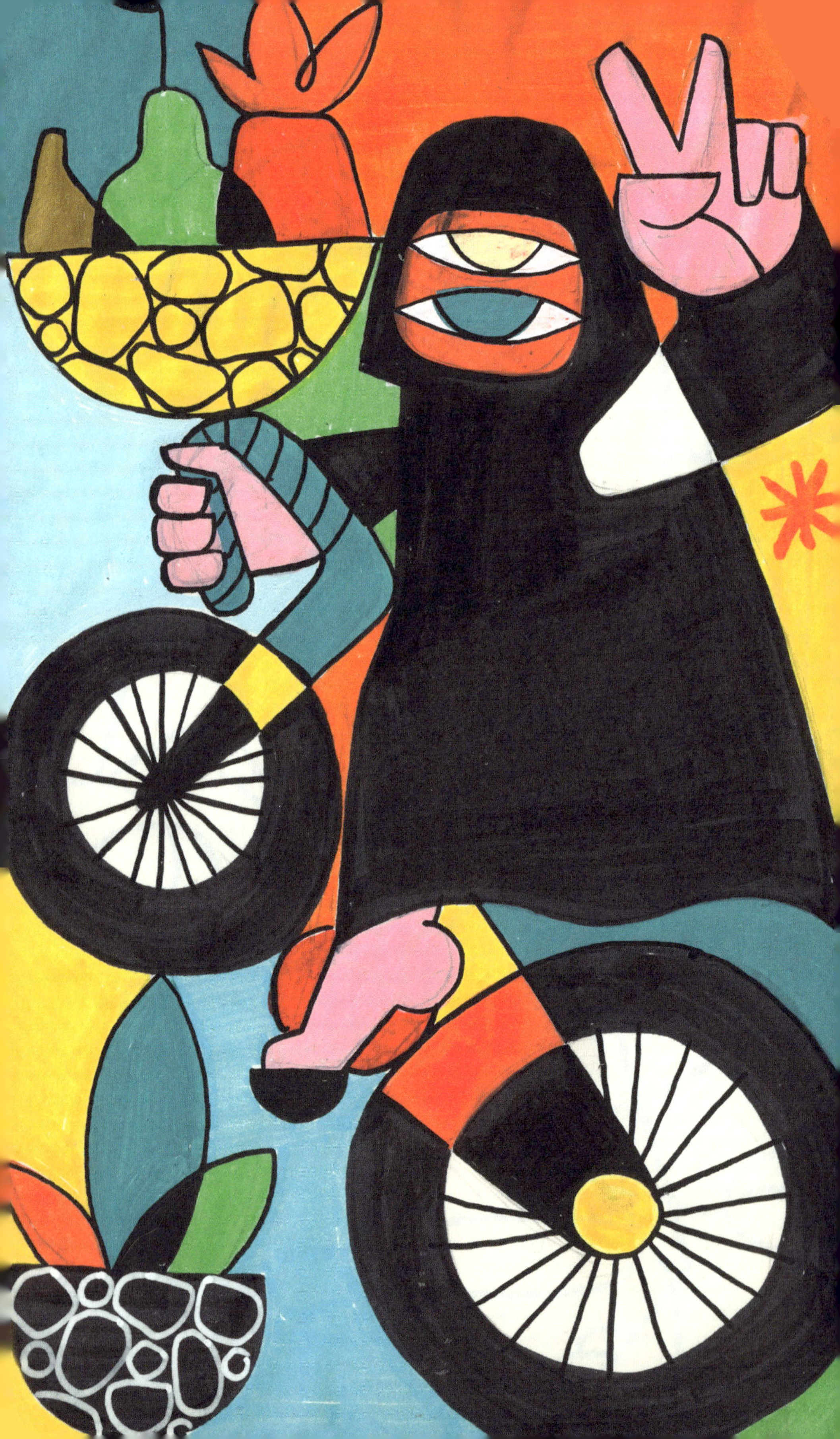

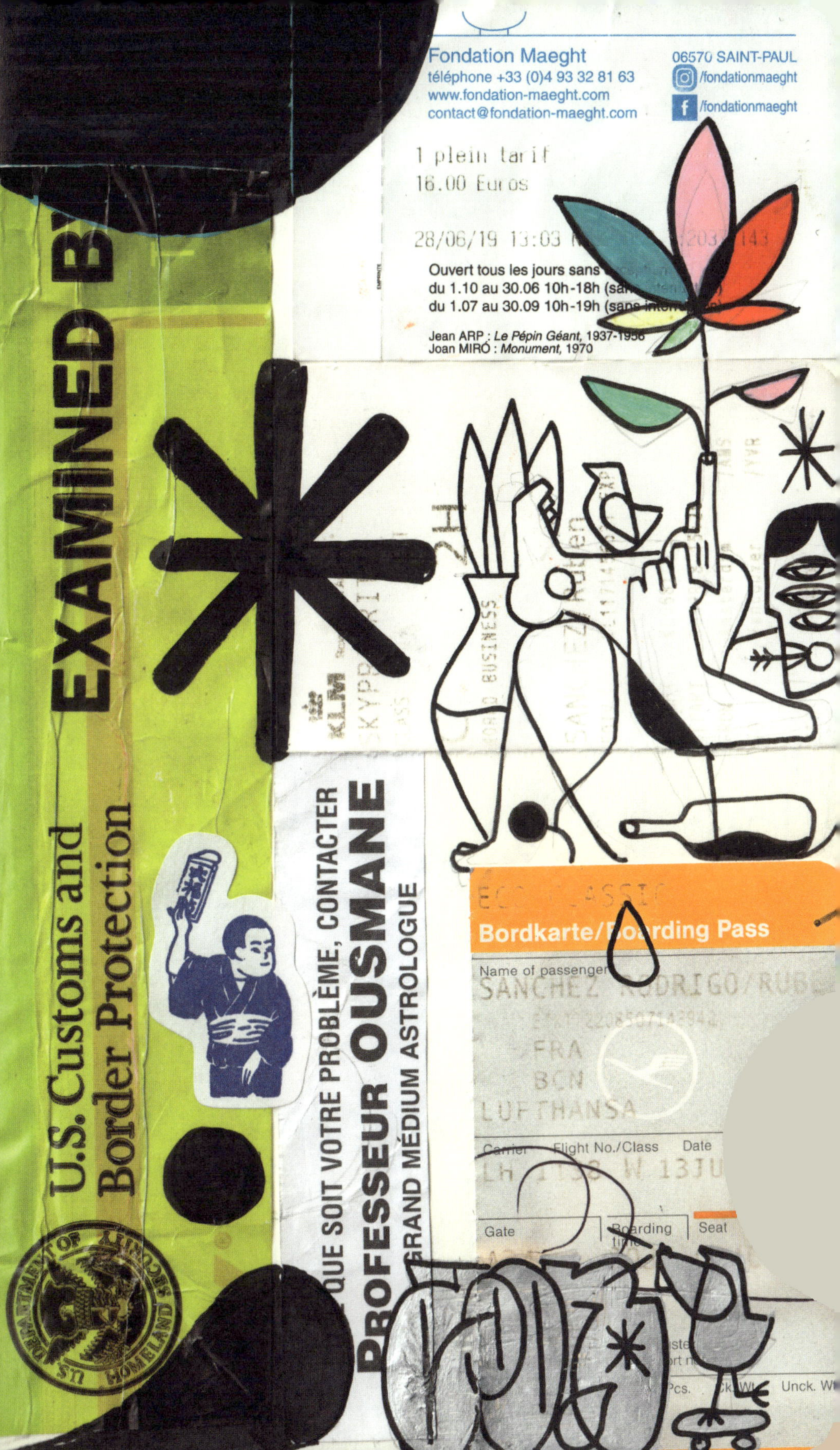
EXAMINED BY
U.S. Customs and Border Protection
Fondation Maeght
téléphone +33 (0)4 93 32 81 63
www.fondation-maeght.com
contact@fondation-maeght.com
/fondationmaeght
/fondationmaeght
06570 SAINT-PAUL
1 plein tarif
16.00 Euros
28/06/19 13:03
Ouvert tous les jours sans
du 1.10 au 30.06 10h-18h (san
du 1.07 au 30.09 10h-19h (sans inter
Jean ARP : Le Pépin Géant, 1937-1958
Joan MIRÓ : Monument, 1970
KLM
SKYPRIORITY
PASS
QUE SOIT VOTRE PROBLÈME, CONTACTER
PROFESSEUR OUSMANE
GRAND MÉDIUM ASTROLOGUE
Bordkarte/Boarding Pass
Name of passenger
SANCHEZ RODRIGO/RUBE
FRA
BCN
LUFTHANSA
Carrier   Flight No./Class   Date
LH 1158 W 13JU
Gate   Boarding   Seat
time

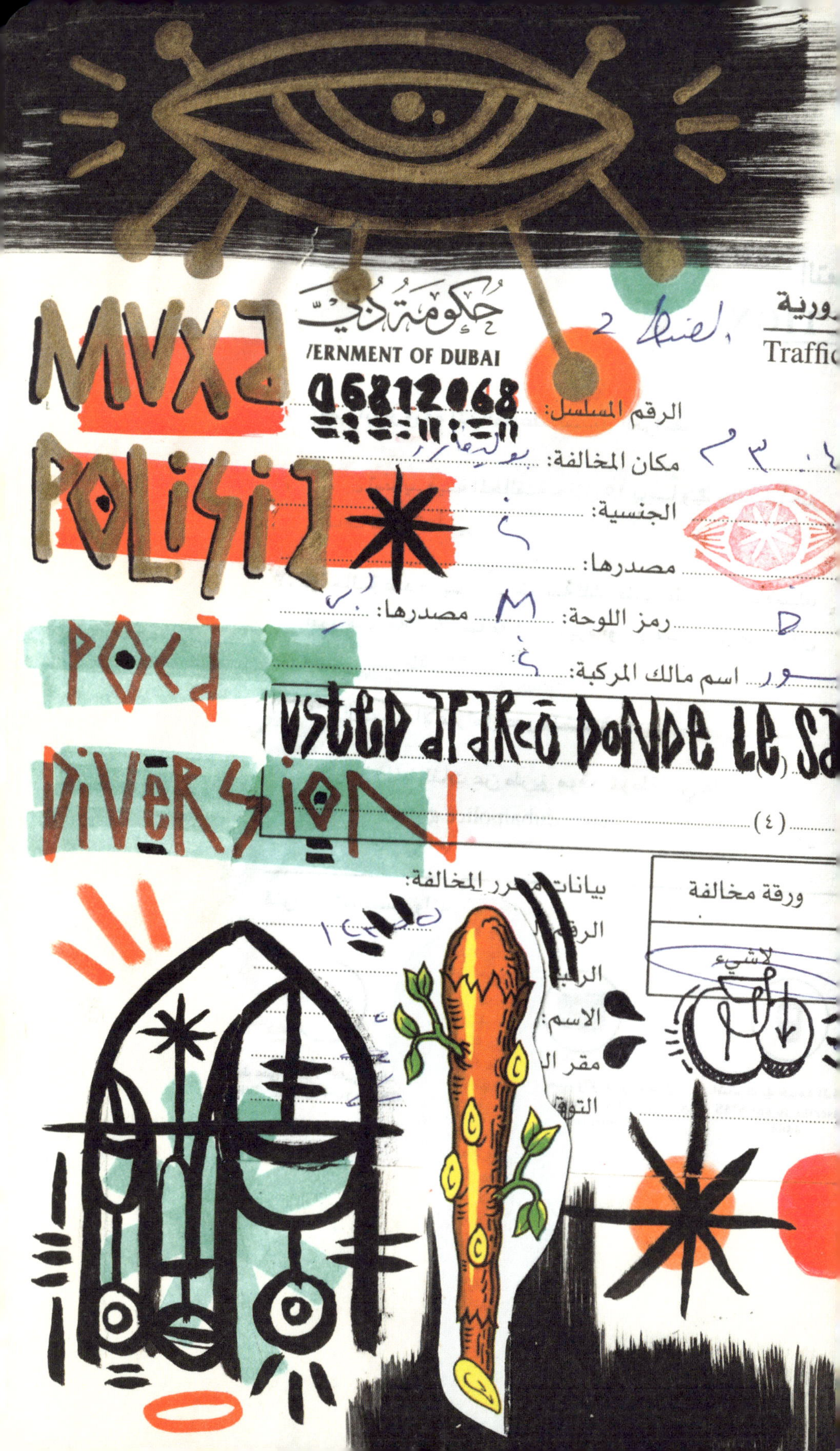

MVX
POLISIZ
POCL
DIVERSION
حكومة دبي
/ERNMENT OF DUBAI
06812068
الرقم المسلسل:
مكان المخالفة:
الجنسية:
مصدرها:
رمز اللوحة: مصدرها:
اسم مالك المركبة:
VSTED ATARCO DONDE LE S
(٤)
ورقة مخالفة
بيانات محرر المخالفة:
الرقم
الرتبة
الاسم:
مقر ال
التو
لاشيء
Traffic

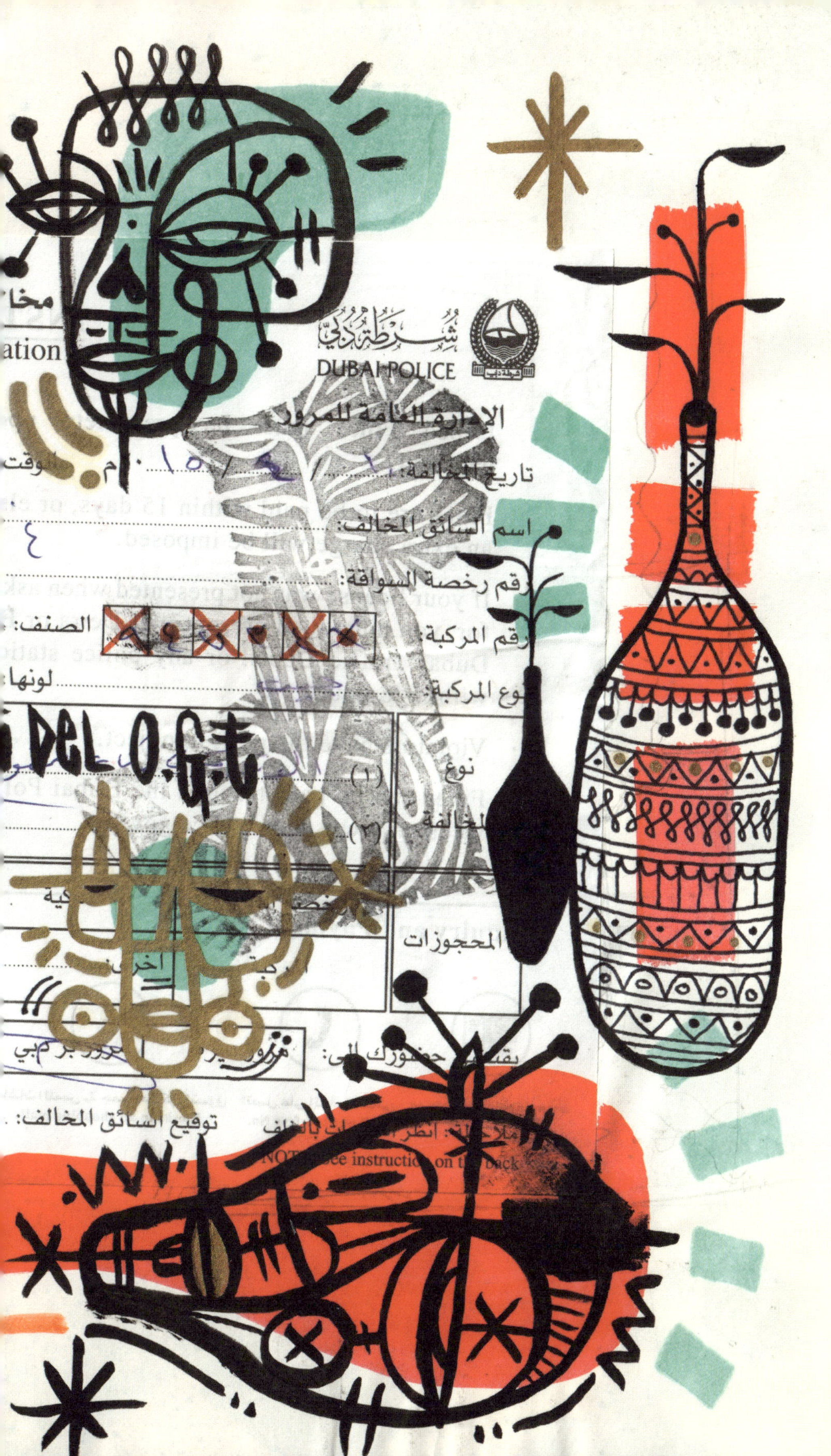
مخا
ation
مخالفة
وقت
DEL O.G.t
شرطة دبي
DUBAI POLICE
الإدارة العامة للمرور
تاريخ المخالفة:
اسم السائق المخالف:
رقم رخصة السواقة:
رقم المركبة:
الصنف:
نوع المركبة:
لونها:
نوع
المخالفة
المحجوزات
توقيع السائق المخالف:
ملاحظة: انظر
NOTE: see instructions on the back

2015

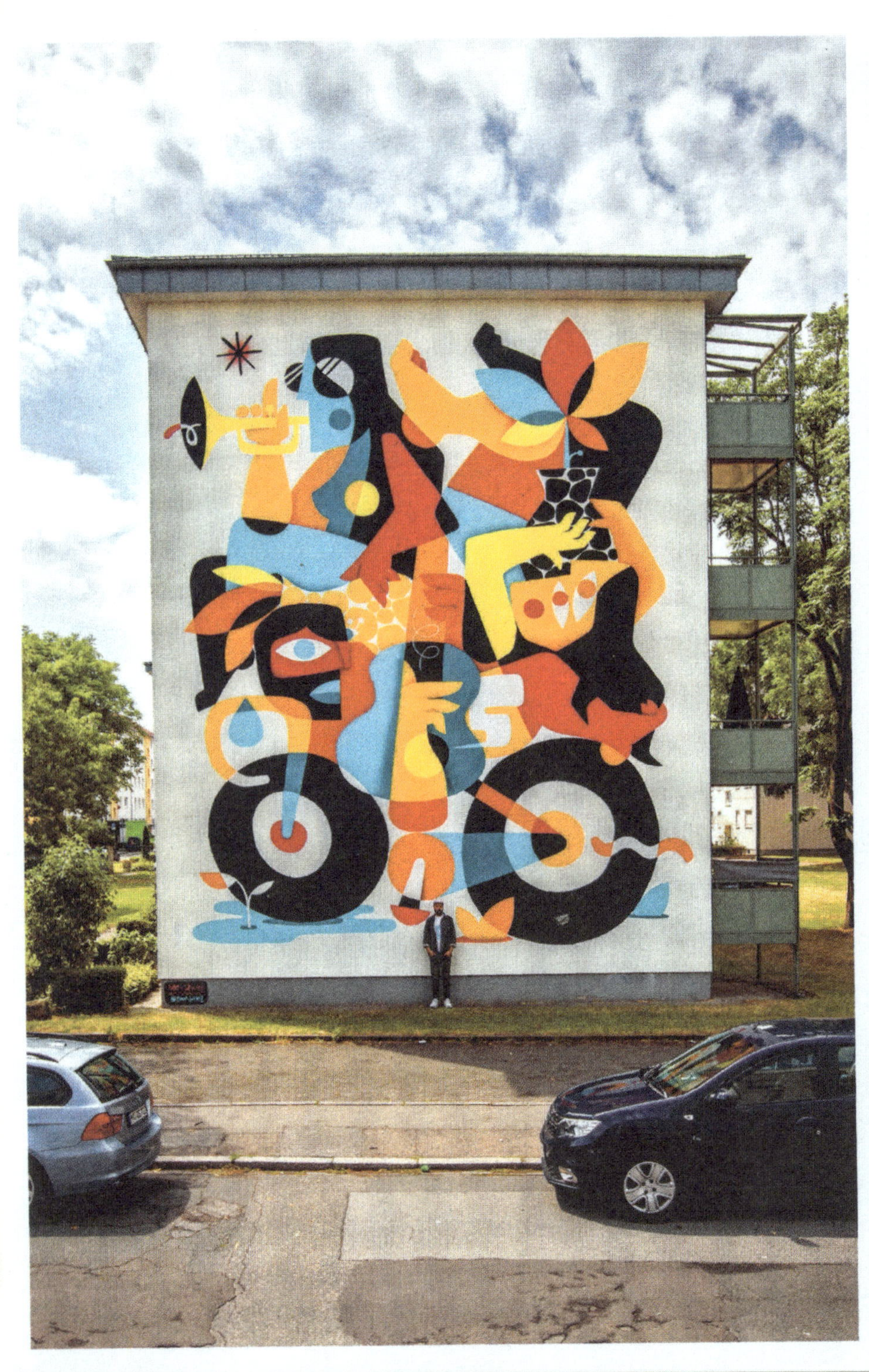

MANNHEIM, GERMANY * 2019

PERHAPS WE'RE
TRYING TO KEEP
FAR TOO MUCH
AND PERHAPS BY
DOING THAT
WE'RE NOT KEE
PING MUCH
AT ALL * HOCKNEY

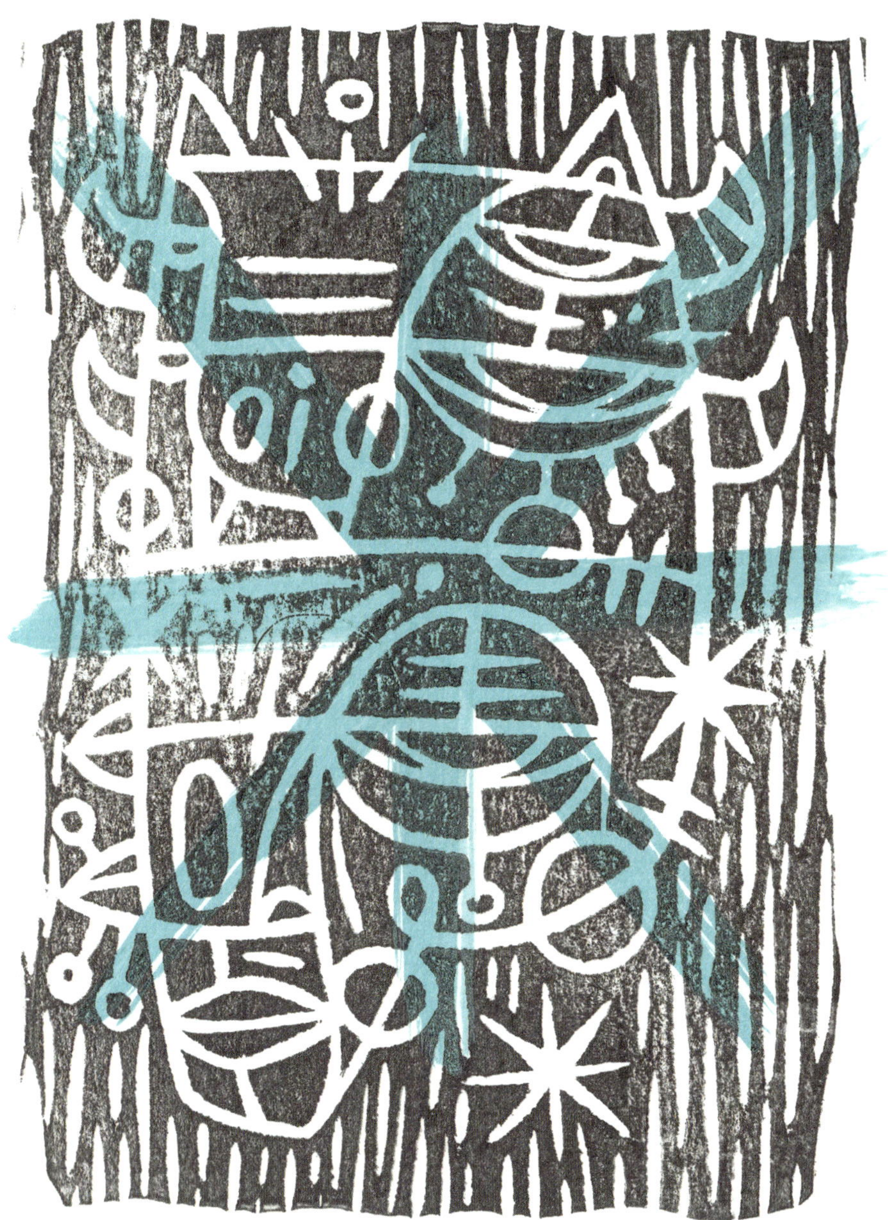

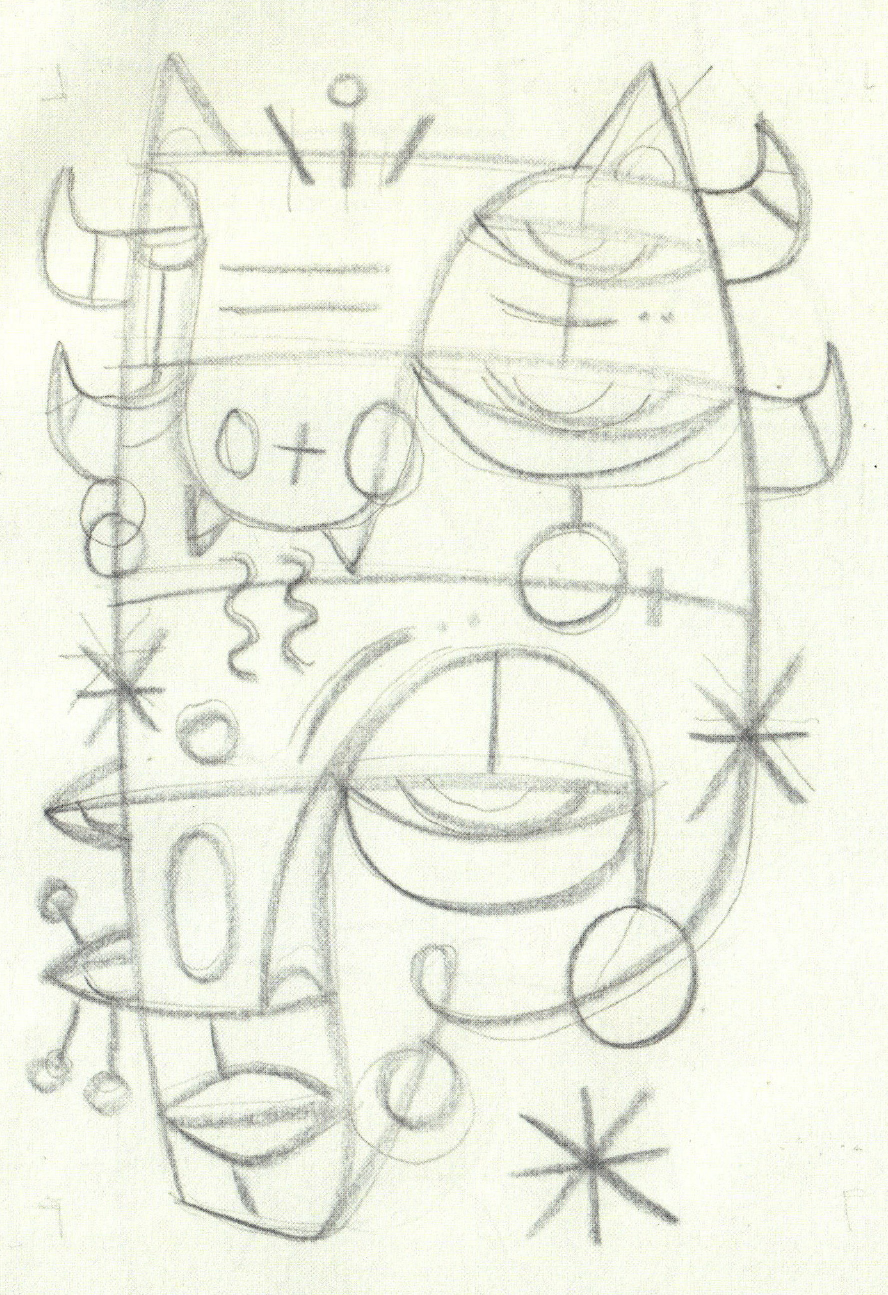

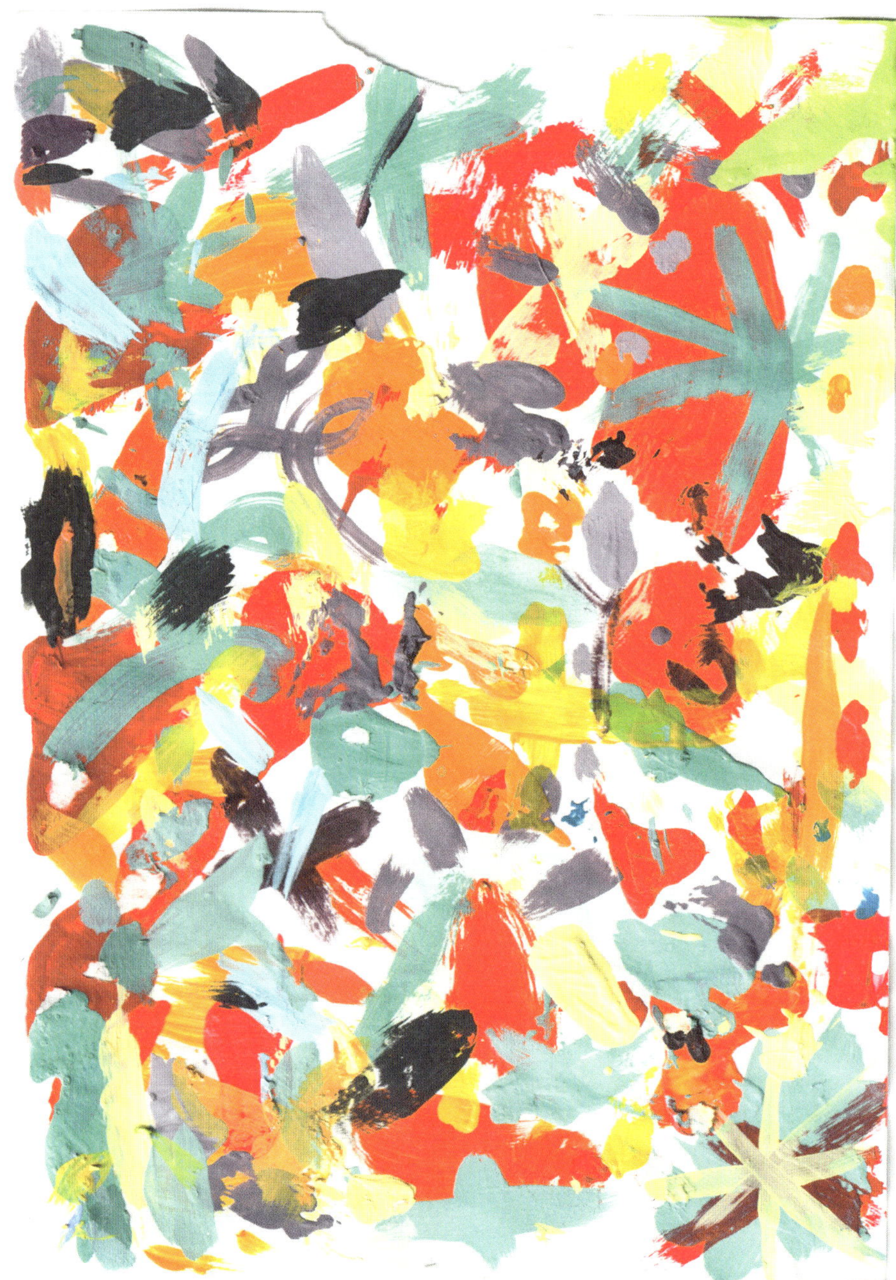

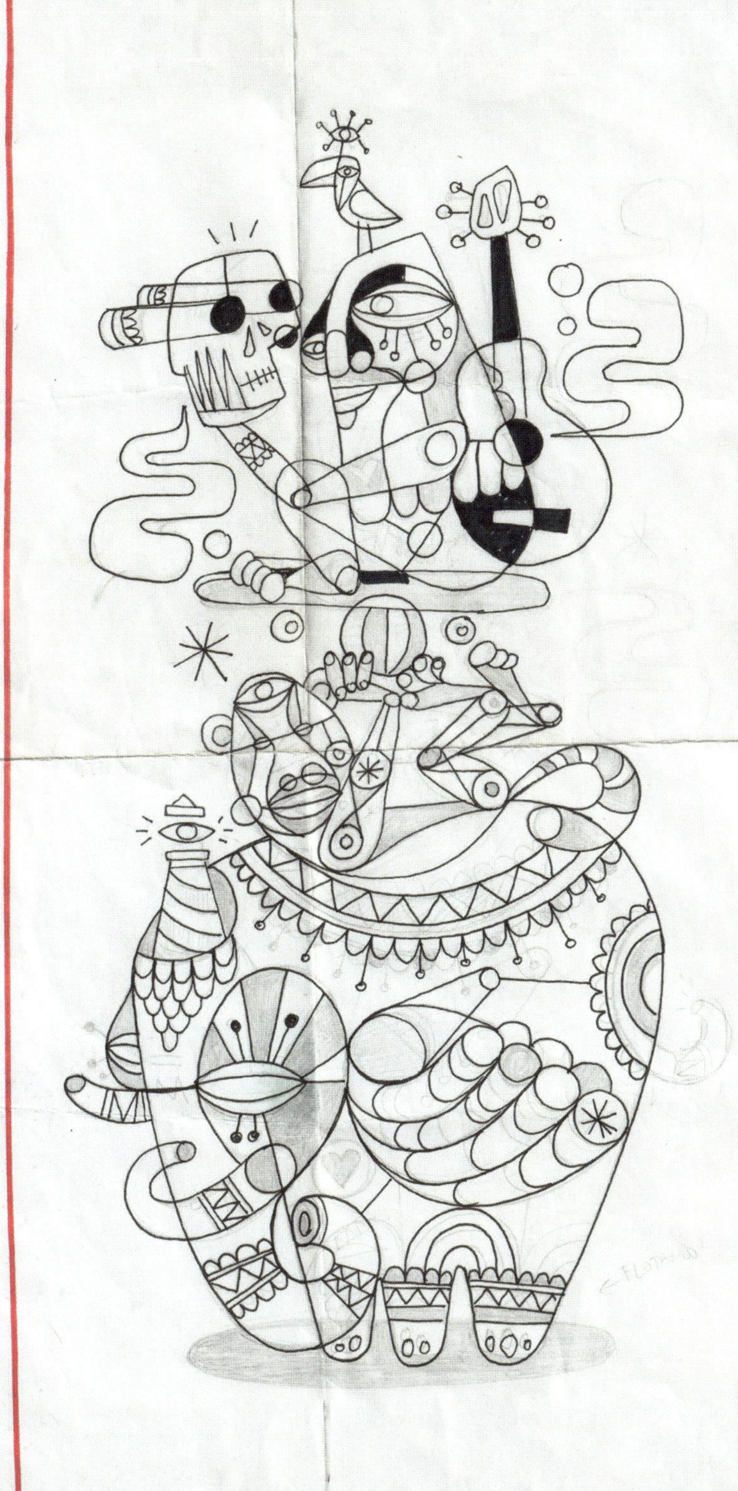

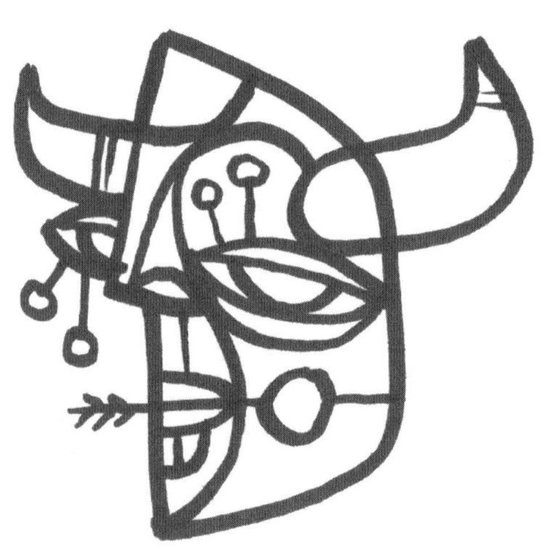

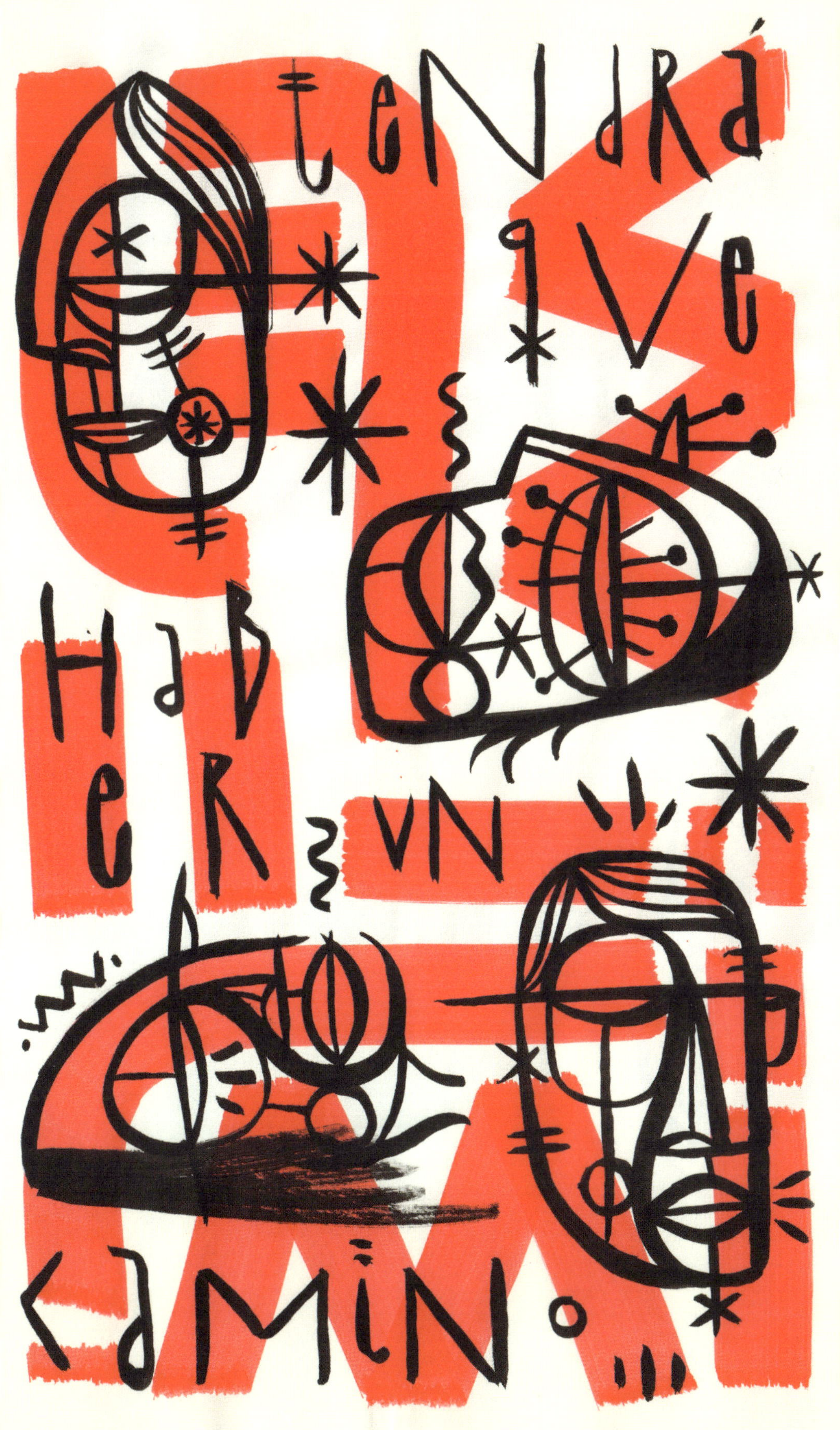
teNdrá
qVe
HaBeR
vN
caMiNo

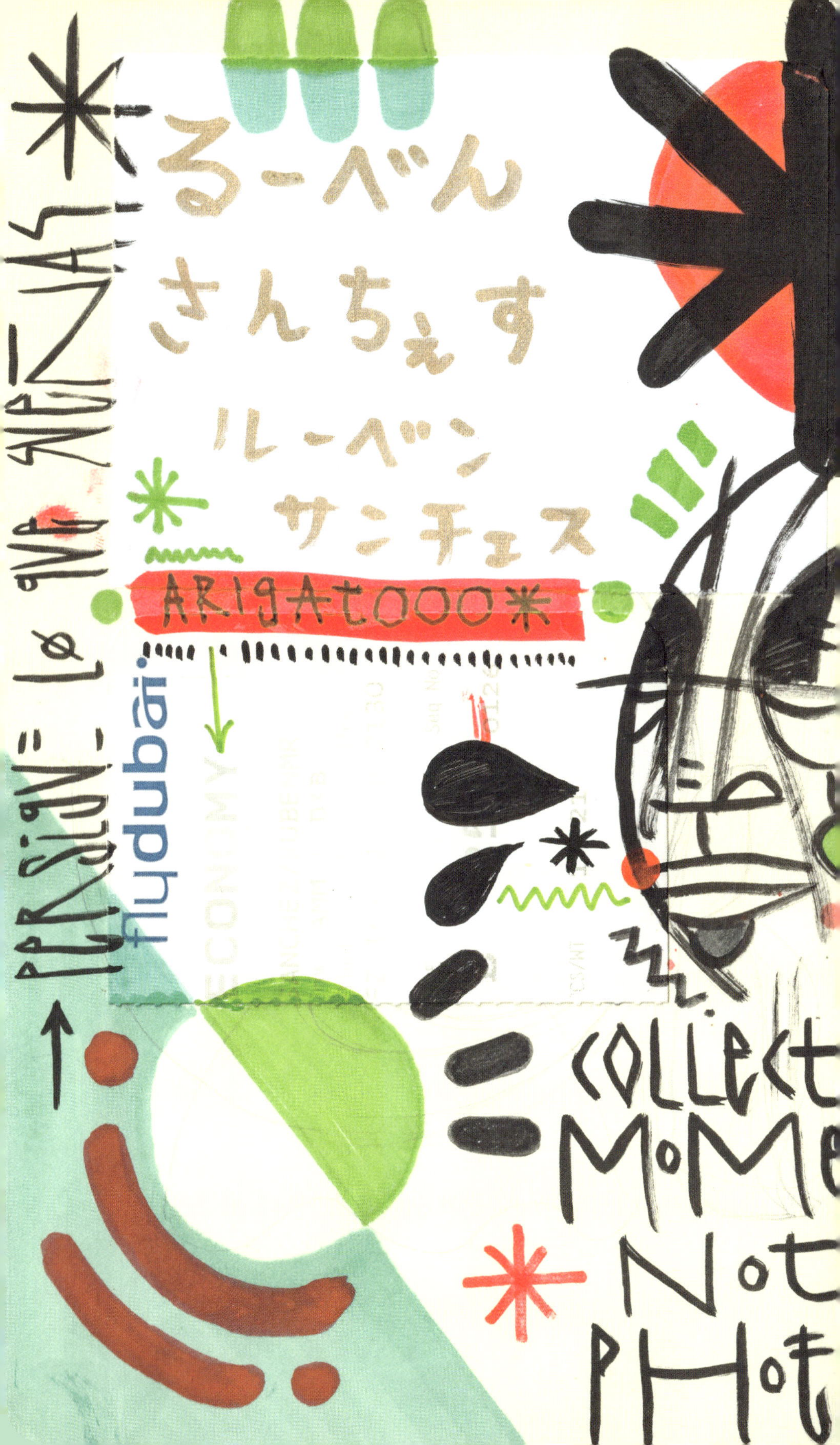
るーべん
さんちぇす
ルーベン
サンチェス
ARIGAtOOO
flydubai
ECONOMY
COLLECt
MoMe
Not
PHot

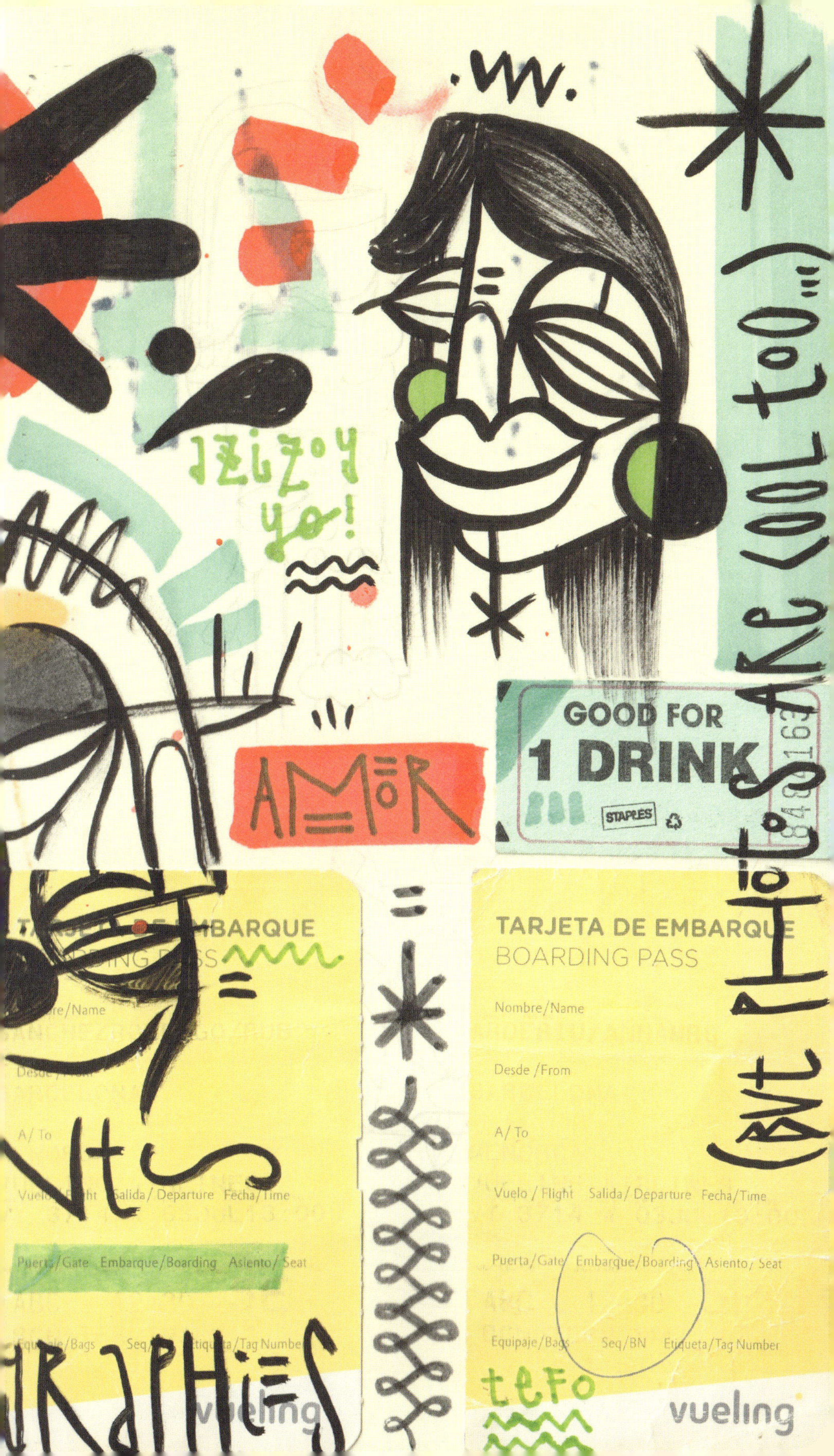
JEFGZOY
YO!
AMOR
GOOD FOR
1 DRINK
STAPLES
848163
ARE COOL TOO...)
(BVT PHotS
TARJETA DE EMBARQUE
BOARDING PASS
Nombre/Name
Desde /From
A/ To
Vuelo / Flight   Salida / Departure   Fecha/Time
Puerta/Gate   Embarque/Boarding   Asiento/ Seat
Equipaje/Bags   Seq/BN   Etiqueta/Tag Number
vueling
TARJETA DE EMBARQUE
BOARDING PASS
Nombre/Name
Desde/From
A/ To
Vuelo / Flight   Salida/ Departure   Fecha/Time
Puerta/Gate   Embarque/Boarding   Asiento/ Seat
Equipaje/Bags   Seq/BN   Etiqueta/Tag Number
vueling
RaPHiES
tefo

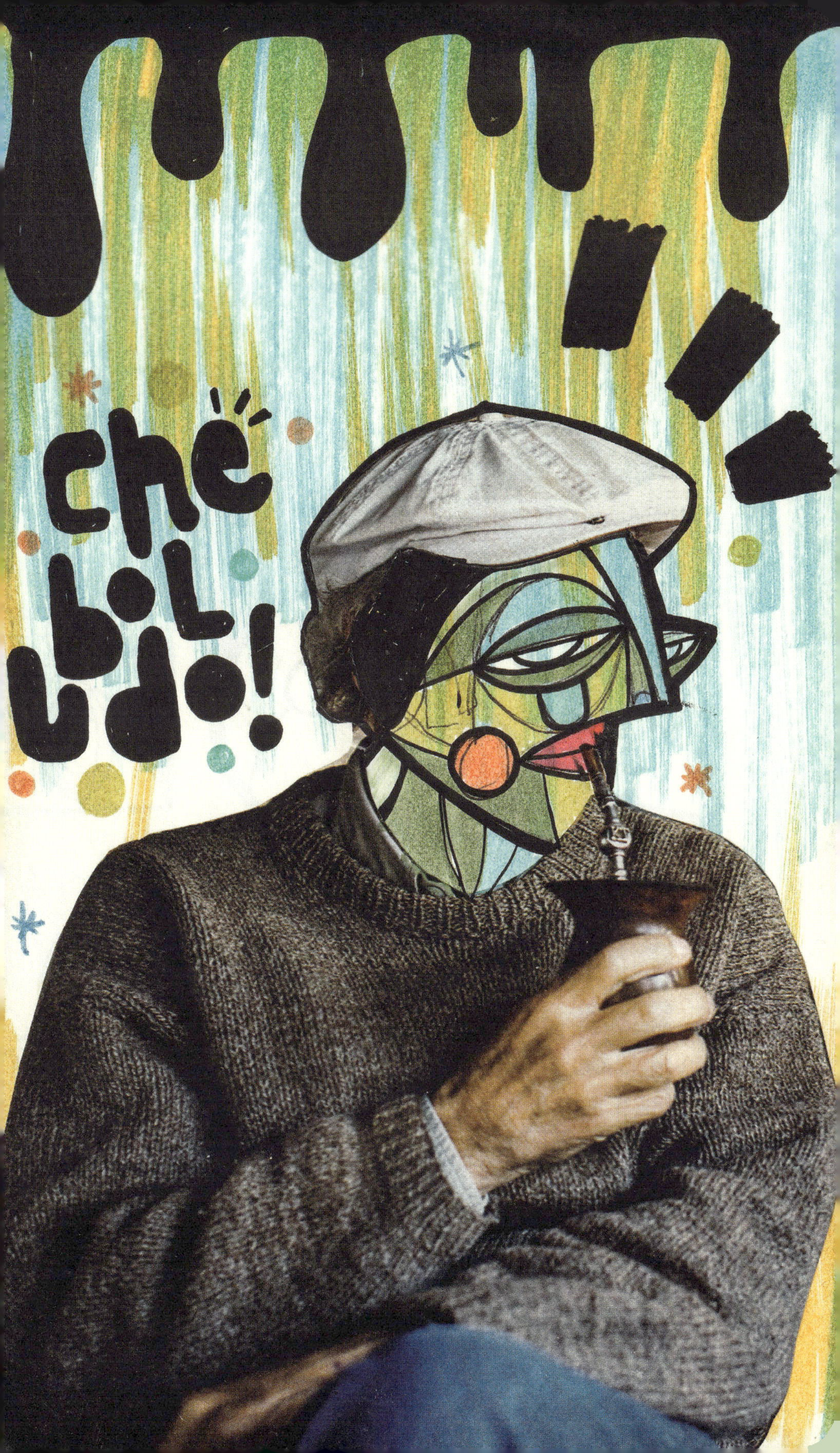

CHÉ
BO
LU
DO!

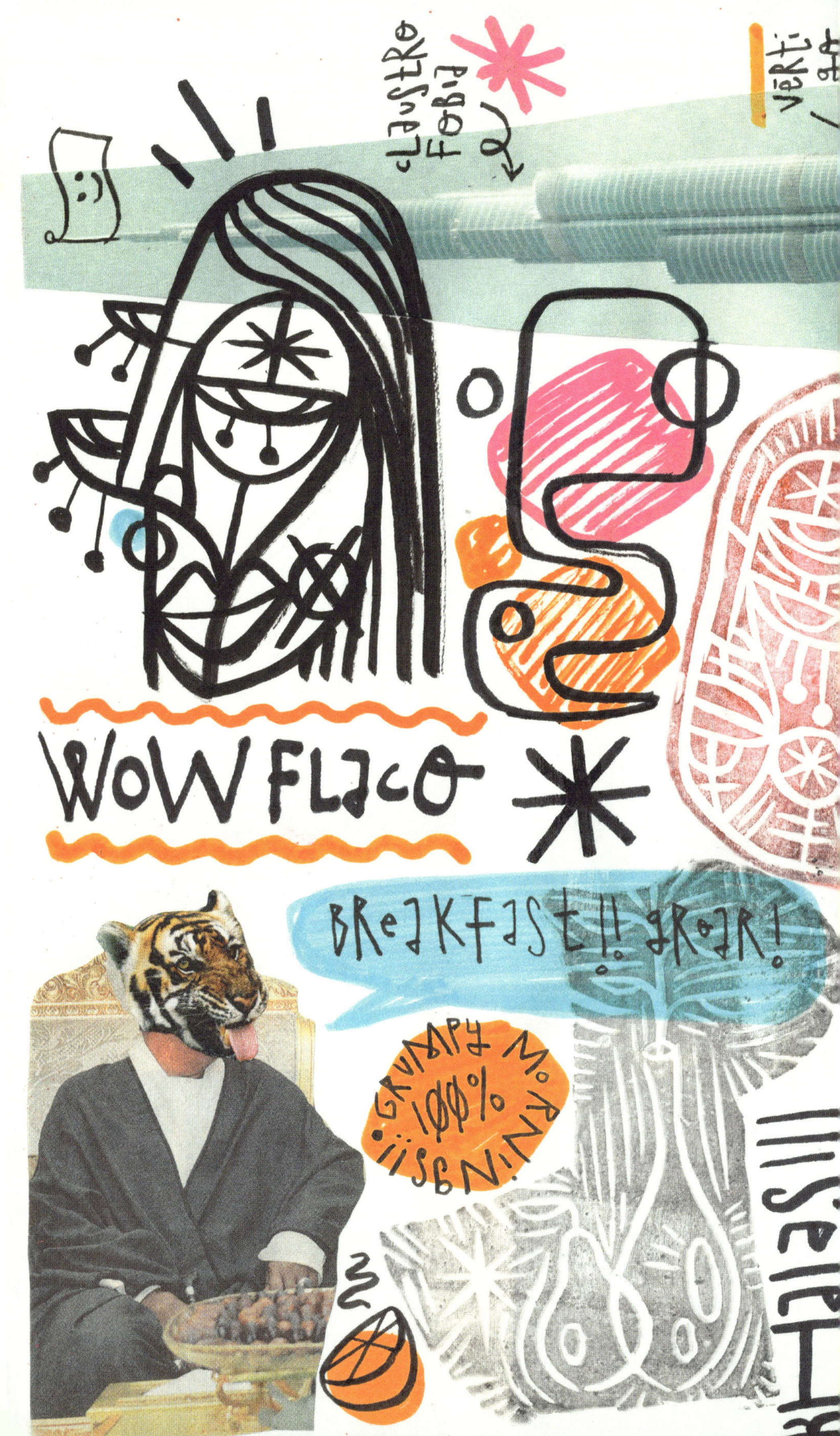

CLAUSTRO FOBIA
vertigo
WOW FLACO
BREAKFAST!! GROAR!
GRUMPY MORNING!! 100%

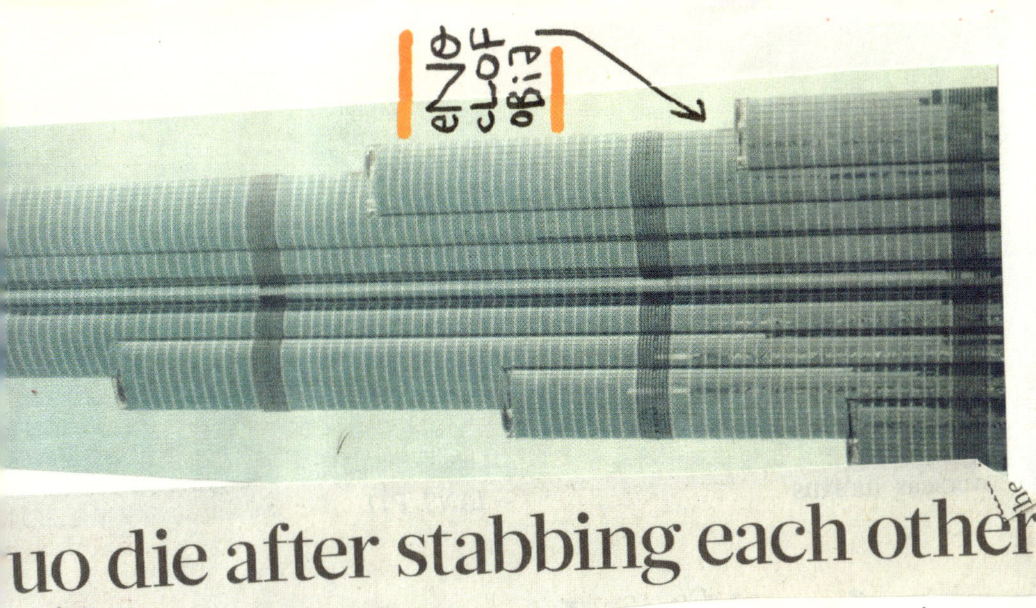

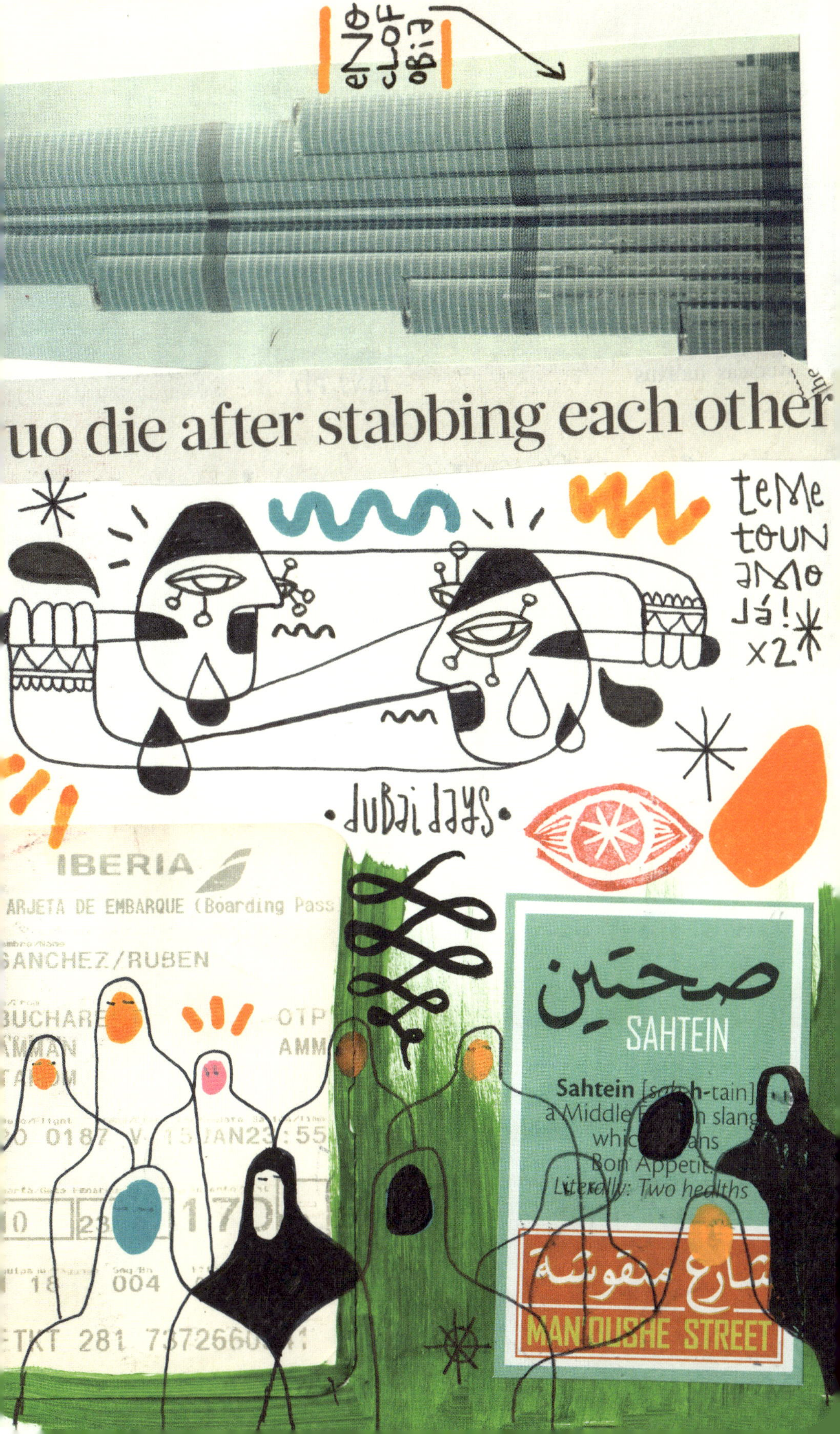

uo die after stabbing each other

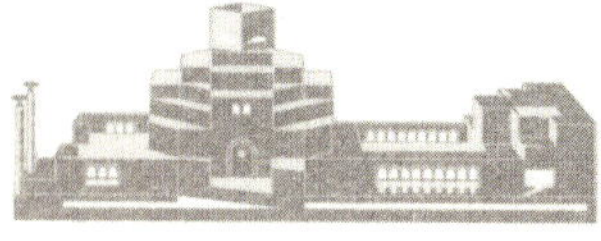

The revolution

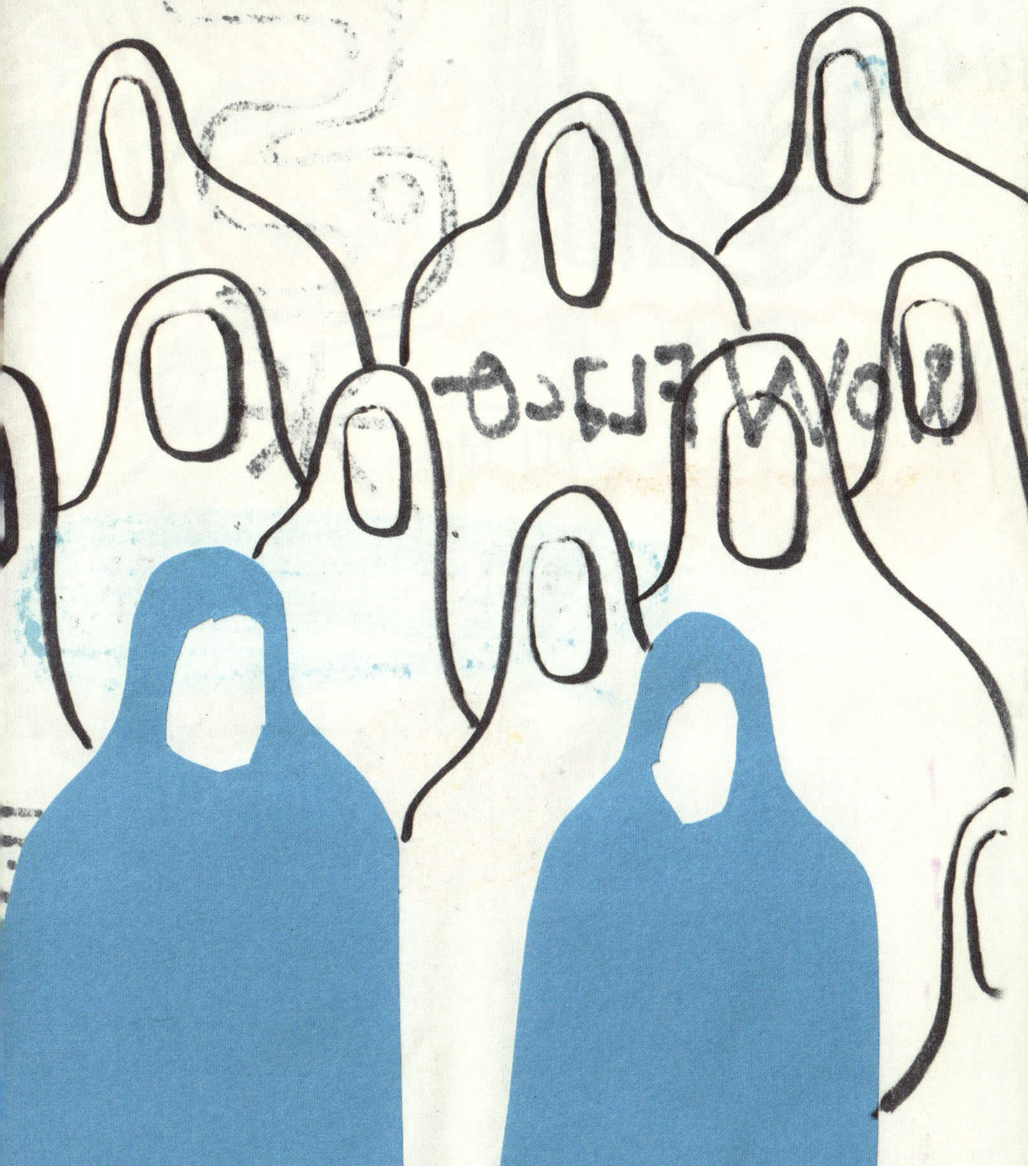

CHEUCHES

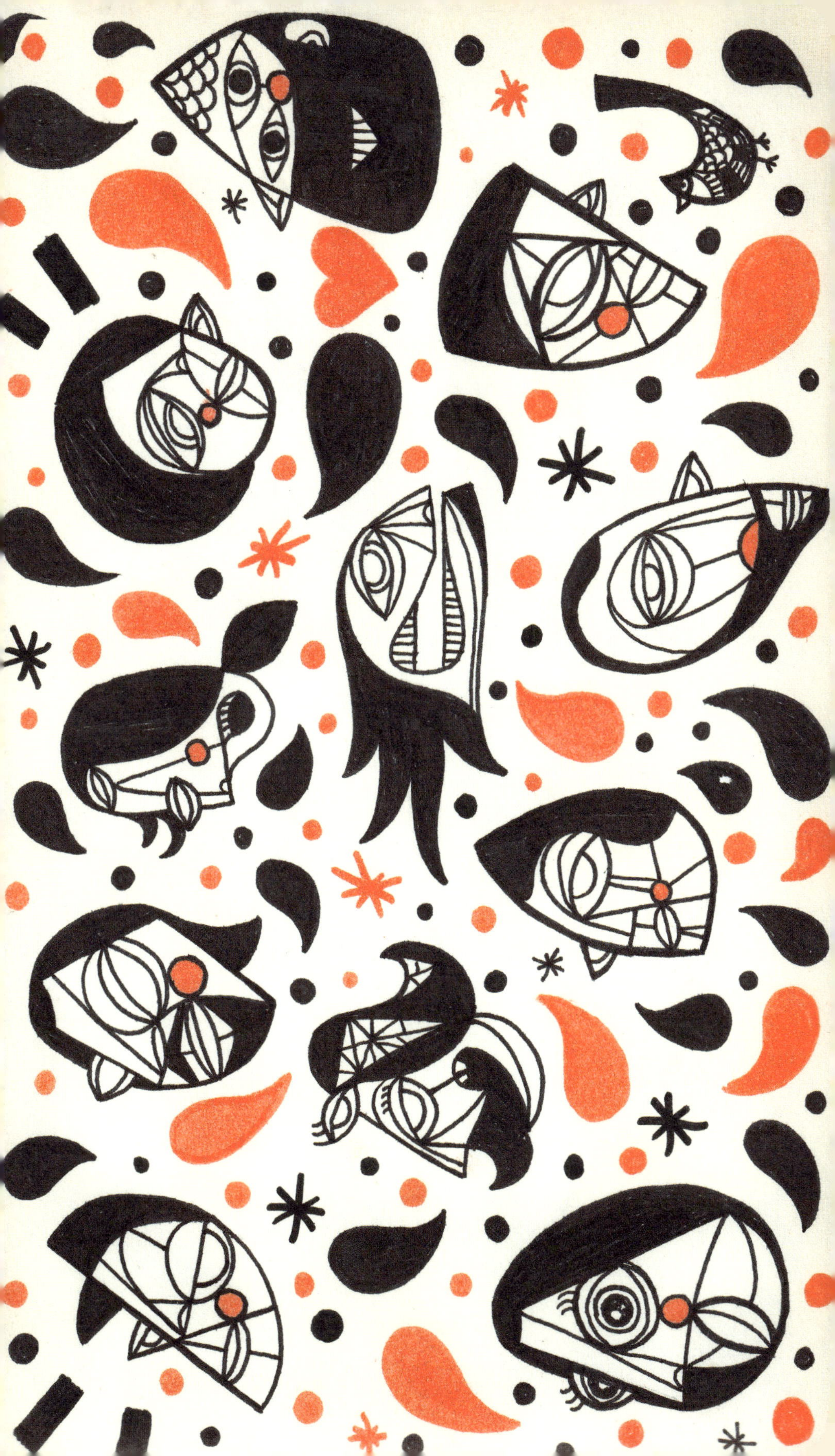

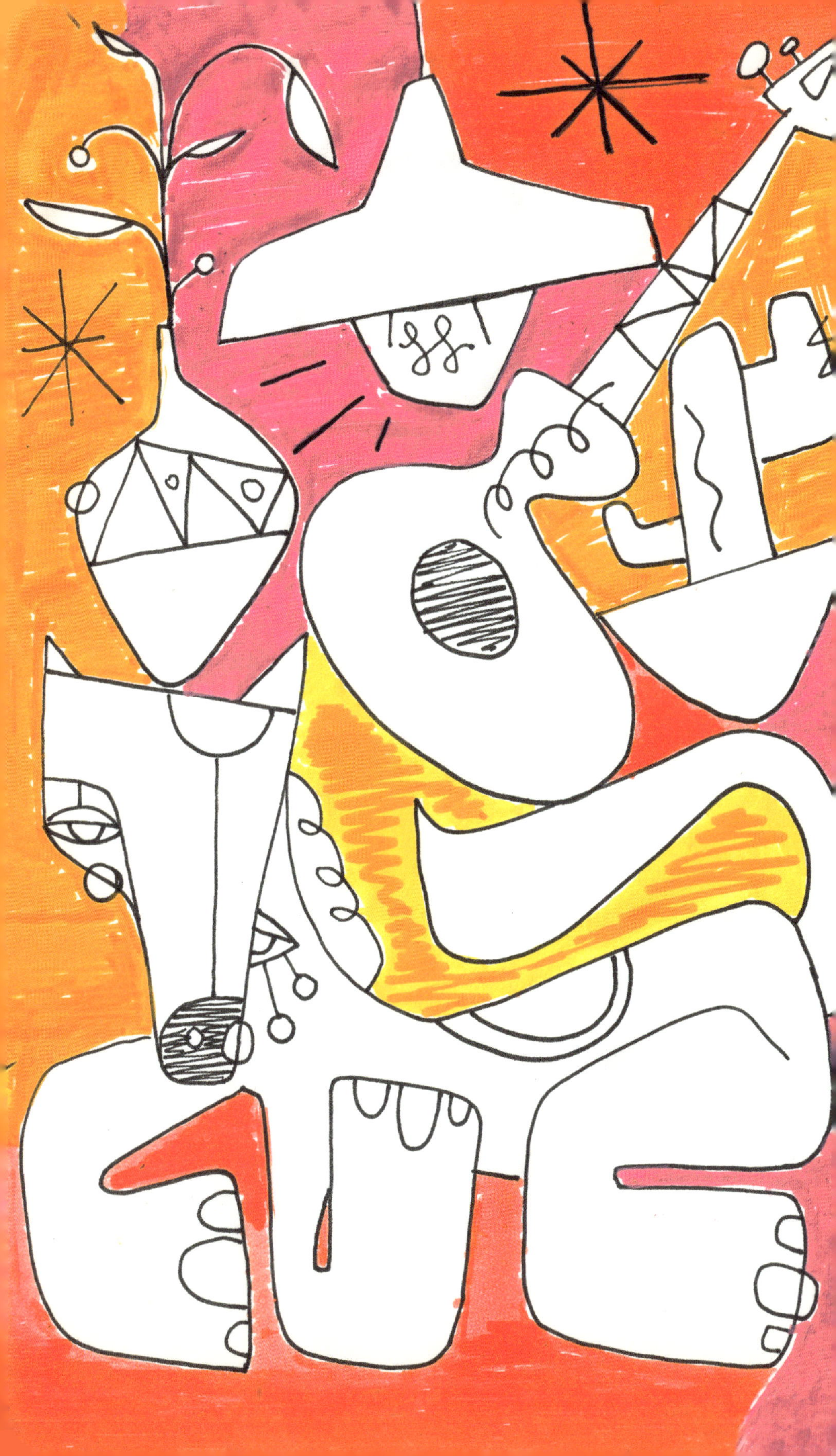

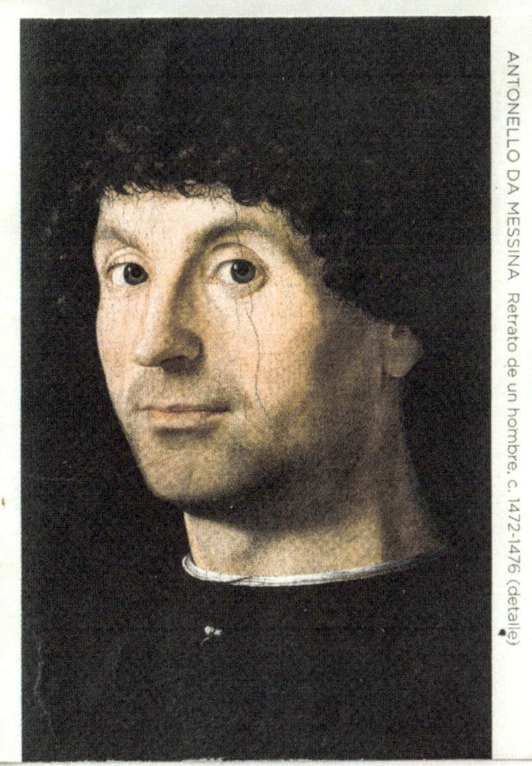

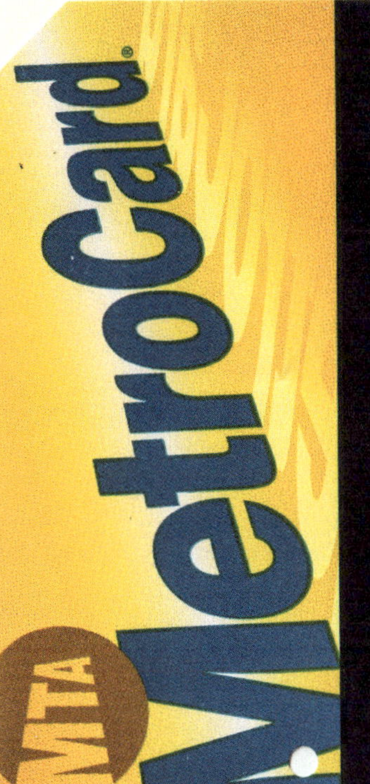

Diazepam
mg/ml

Barker Berrit

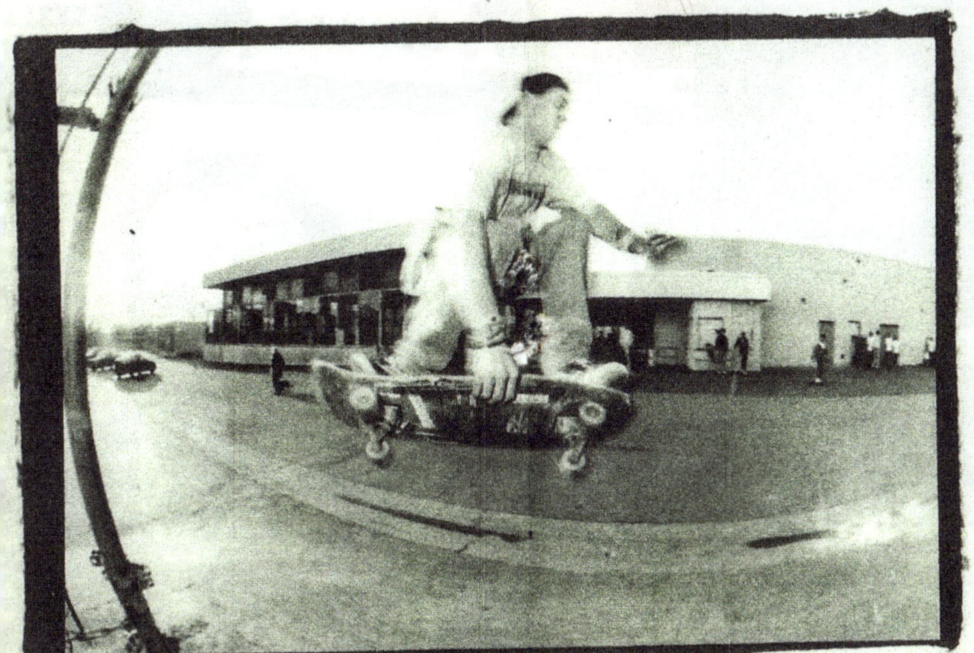

Venice High

Photo Tobin Yelland

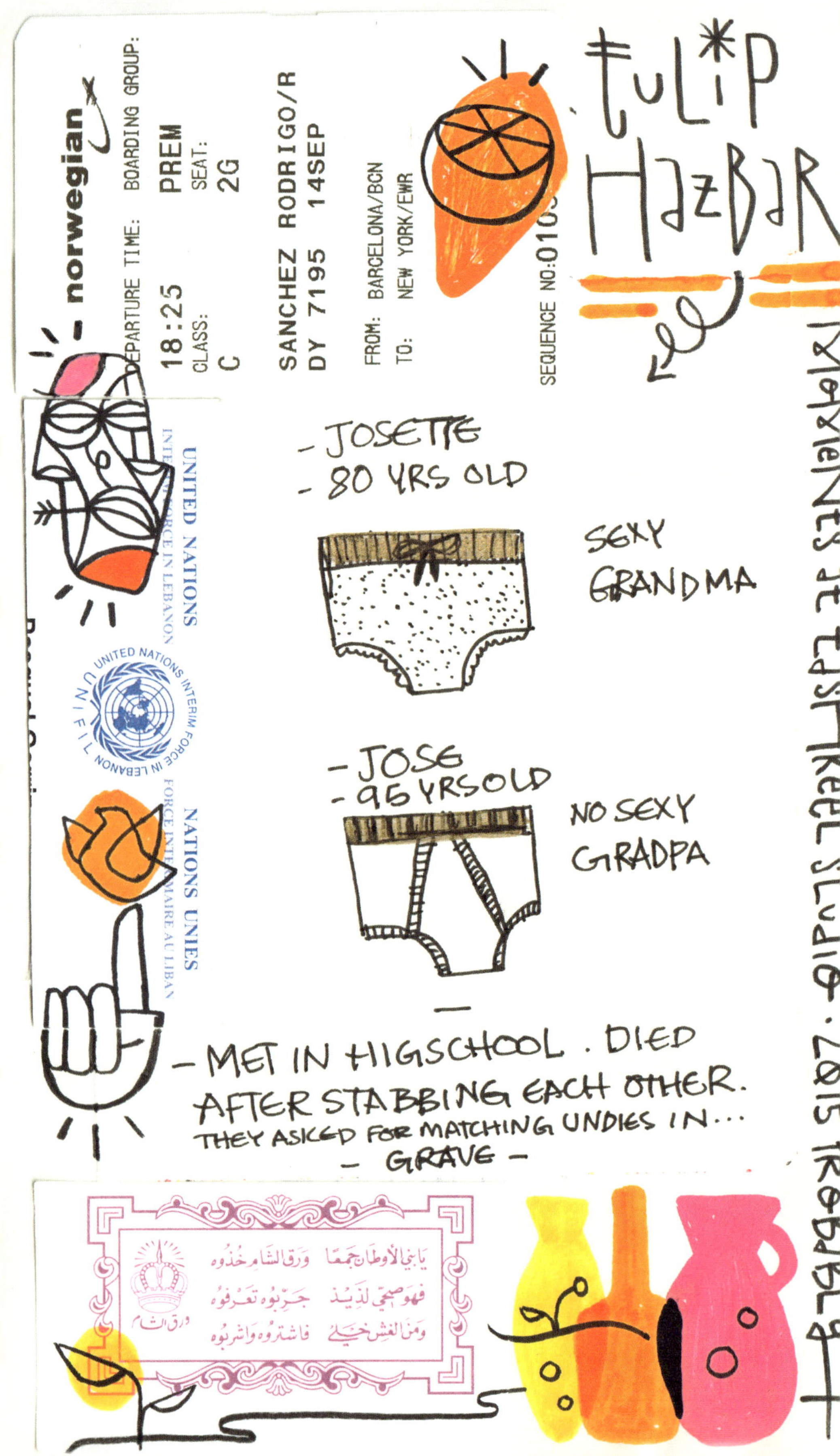

norwegian
BOARDING GROUP:
PREM
SEAT:
2G
DEPARTURE TIME:
18:25
CLASS:
C
SANCHEZ RODRIGO/R
DY 7195   14SEP
FROM: BARCELONA/BCN
TO: NEW YORK/EWR
SEQUENCE NO:010
TULIP HAZBAR
UNITED NATIONS
INTERIM FORCE IN LEBANON
UNITED NATIONS INTERIM FORCE IN LEBANON
UNIFIL
NATIONS UNIES
FORCE INTERIMAIRE AU LIBAN
- JOSETTE
- 80 YRS OLD
SEXY GRANDMA
- JOSE
- 95 YRS OLD
NO SEXY GRADPA
- MET IN HIGSCHOOL . DIED AFTER STABBING EACH OTHER. THEY ASKED FOR MATCHING UNDIES IN...
- GRAVE -
يا بني الأوطان جمعًا   ورق الشام خذوه
فهو صحي لذيذ   جربوه تعرفوه
ومن الغش خير   فاشتروه واشربوه
ورق الشام

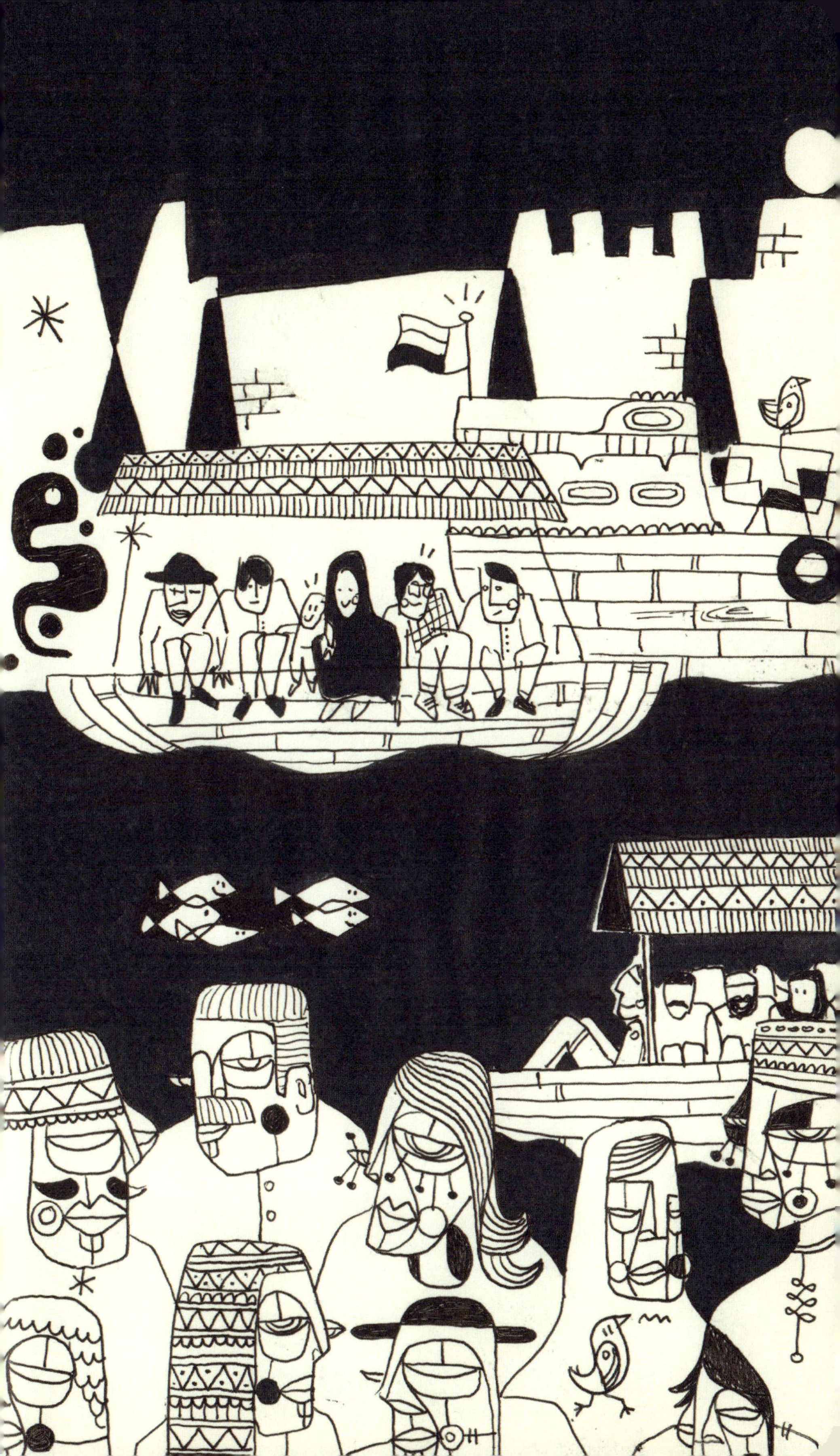

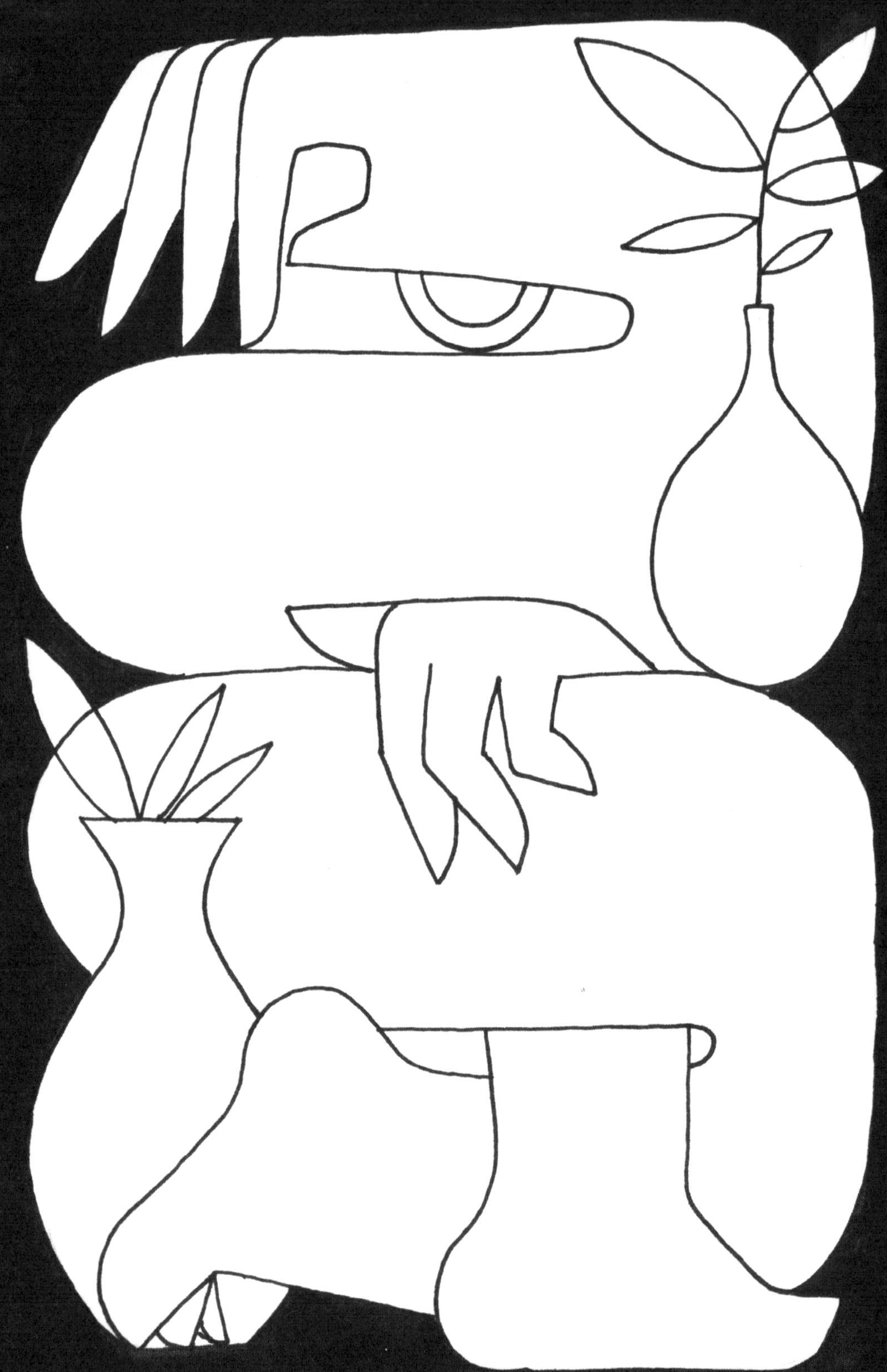

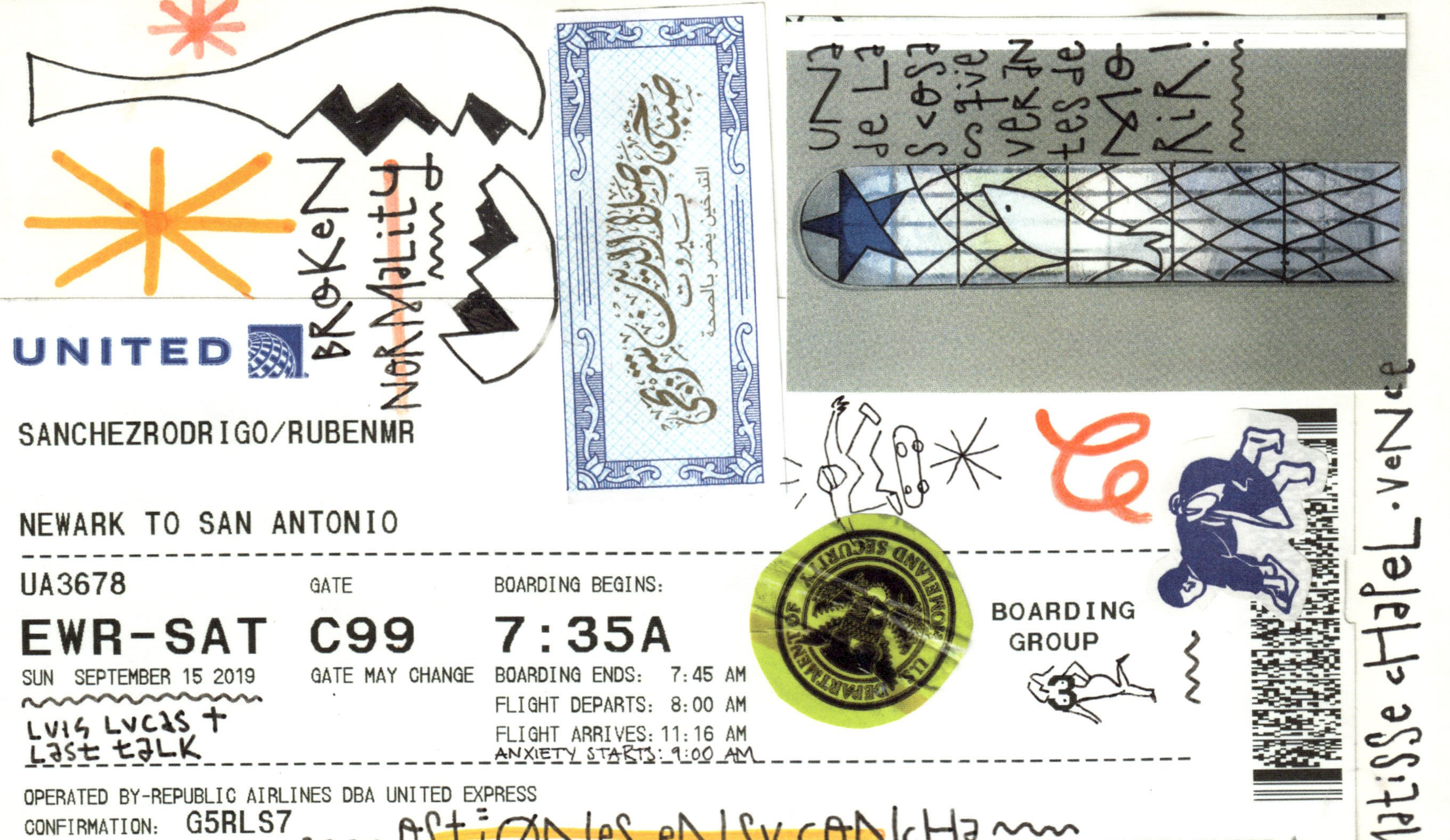

UNITED
BROKEN NORMALITY
SANCHEZRODRIGO/RUBENMR
NEWARK TO SAN ANTONIO
UA3678
GATE
BOARDING BEGINS:
EWR-SAT   C99   7:35A
SUN SEPTEMBER 15 2019
GATE MAY CHANGE
BOARDING ENDS: 7:45 AM
FLIGHT DEPARTS: 8:00 AM
FLIGHT ARRIVES: 11:16 AM
ANXIETY STARTS: 9:00 AM
LUIS LUCAS +
LAST TALK
OPERATED BY-REPUBLIC AIRLINES DBA UNITED EXPRESS
CONFIRMATION: G5RLS7
TICKET: 0165074374117
BOARDING GROUP
3
A STAR ALLIANCE MEMBER
canciones en su concha
una de las cosas que ver antes de morir!
Matisse chapel · Vence

~~~~~ –

MUSHKILA : PROBLEM

MAFI MUSHKILA : NO PROBLEM

WALLAH LENKEIAF : LET'S HAVE FUN

YO : ANA'
TU : ~~ENTZA~~ EÍNTA
EL : WHDA NRC : HIA
AHORA : HESSA   TODAY : LIOM
MAÑANA : BUKRAN
RINTAR : ORSOM
BIN TÉKTURSOM ? : WANNA PAINT ?
CAR : SAYARA   AVION : TAYARA
ASIR : ANDAR
HOT : SCHOB / SAHJEN
COLD : BERT / BÆRET
WEATHER : YOW
LET'S PLAY : YALLAH NELÁB !
NO : LA   HERE : HON
YES : A   THERE : HUNÁ
VERY : TÍIER
SWAY : SLOWLY

EID
MUBARAK

BLACK : ESWED
WHITE : APIAT
BLUE : ESDRÁ
RED : AHMAR
GREEN : AHDER
ORANGE : BORTOKALI
YELLOW : ASFER
PINK : SAHARI
GRAY : REMETI

ASSIF : SORRY
GIDISH : HOW MUCH !

BÁDEN : LATER
MAI : WATER

COME : TÁL
COME HERE : TÁL HON

FORGA SAID'E : NICE TO MEETU
YSU·HAN : HUNGRY
YVÁN'
NAÁSAN : SLEEPY
~~~~~

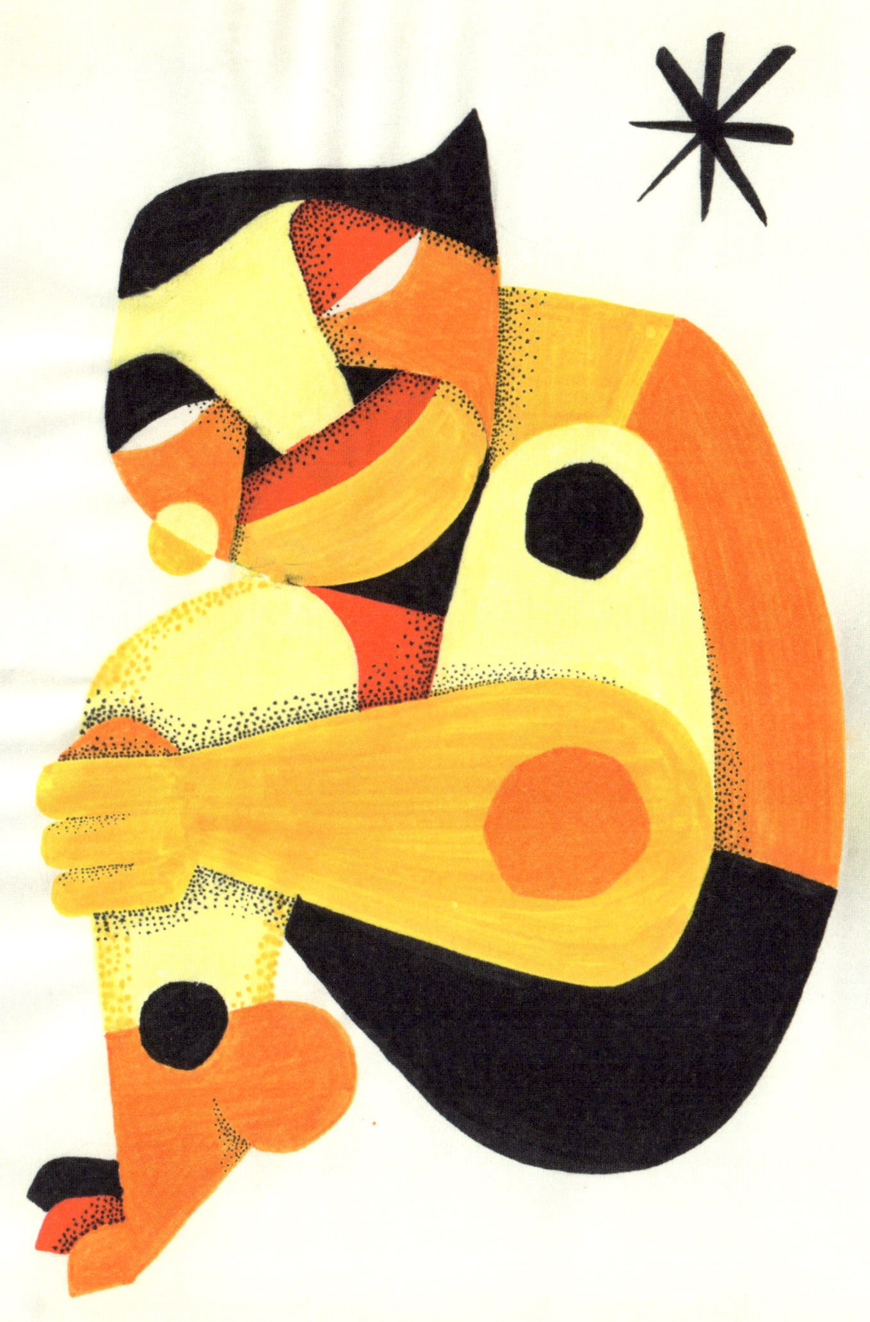

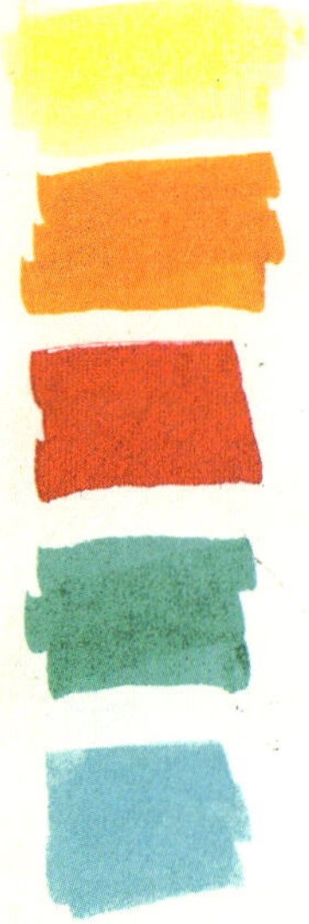

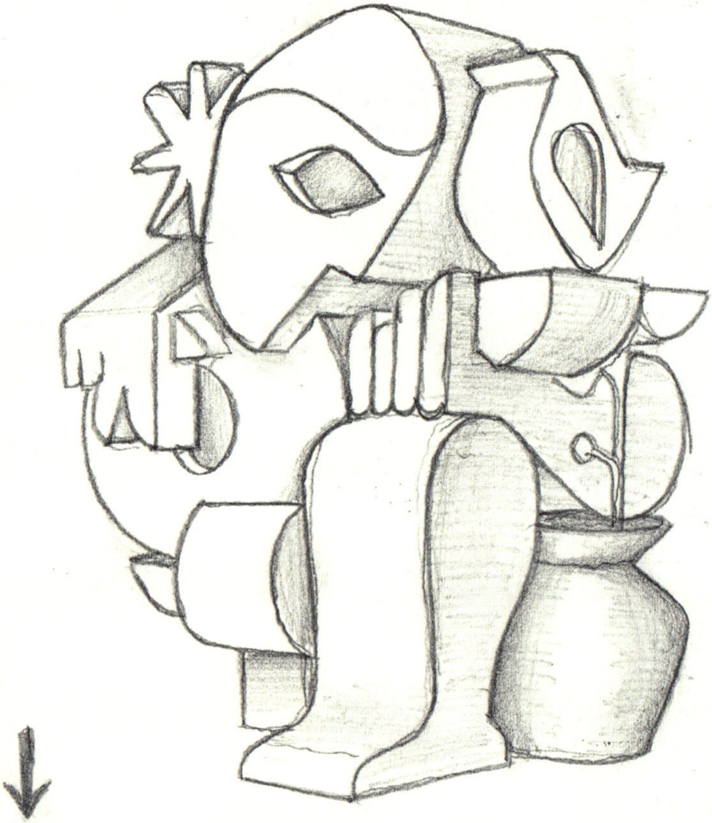

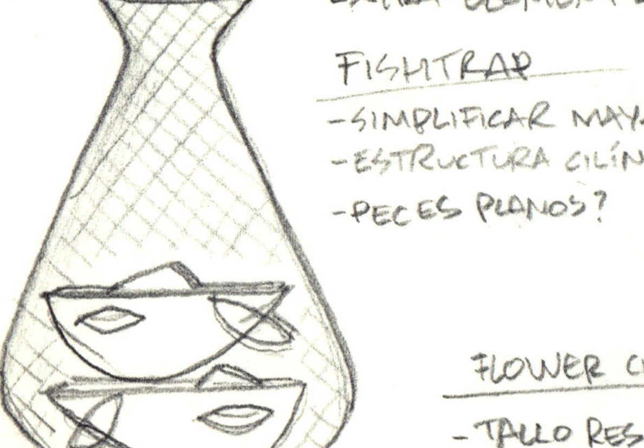

EXTRA ELEMENTS ?

FISHTRAP

- SIMPLIFICAR MAYA
- ESTRUCTURA CILÍNDRICA
- PECES PLANOS?

FLOWER CULTURE

- TALLO RESISTENTE
- NO MUY CURSI
- FLORES LOCALES
- SOBREDIMENSIONADA

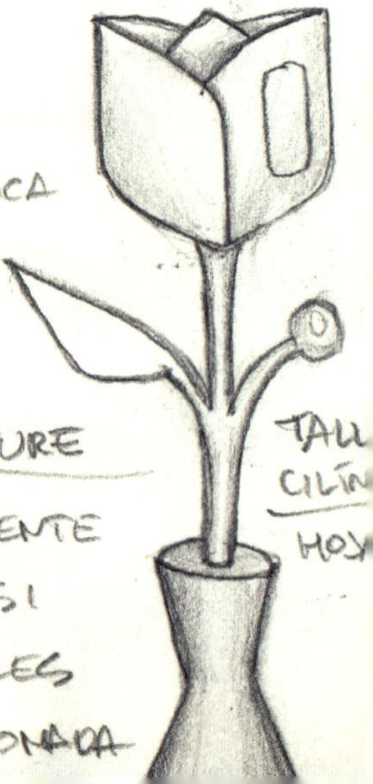

LOCALFISH PERCH

TALL
CILÍN
HOJ

PESCADOR NOSTÁLGICO CON GUITARRA

LAKE ISSUES / MENOS ES MAS
SIEMPRE SÍNTESIS / MOFLETE SÍ? CONFUSIÓN
RELAJA CON DETALLES / BLOCKY SHIT / NOCTURNIDAD
ESTUDIA PUNTOS DEBILES – INTERACTIVO,

↓
ESTRELLA
LUNA?

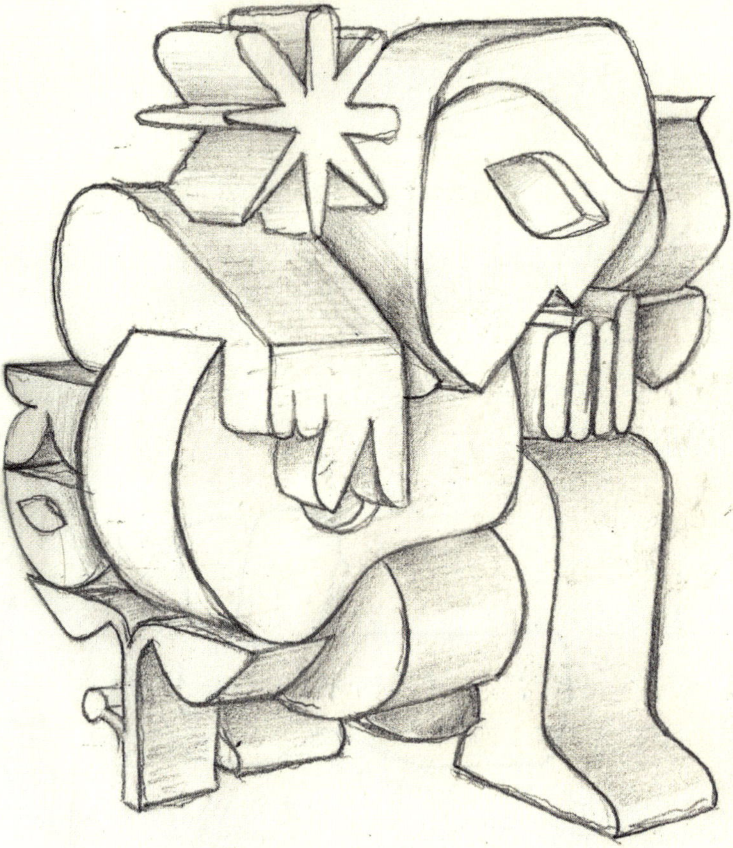

PROYECTO EXCENEVEX / BRONCE / STAINLESS STEEL
HERON

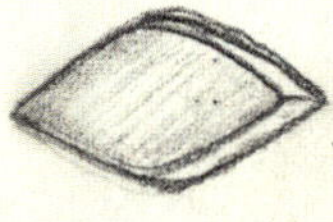
EYE OPT 1
CLEAN / SCARY?

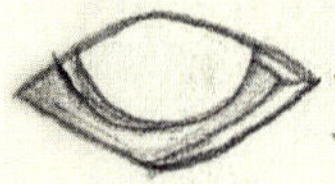
EYE OPT 2
PUPILA / NORMAL

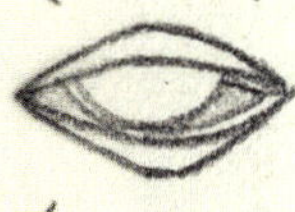
EYE OPT 3
PUPILA + PARPADOS
CHILLING!

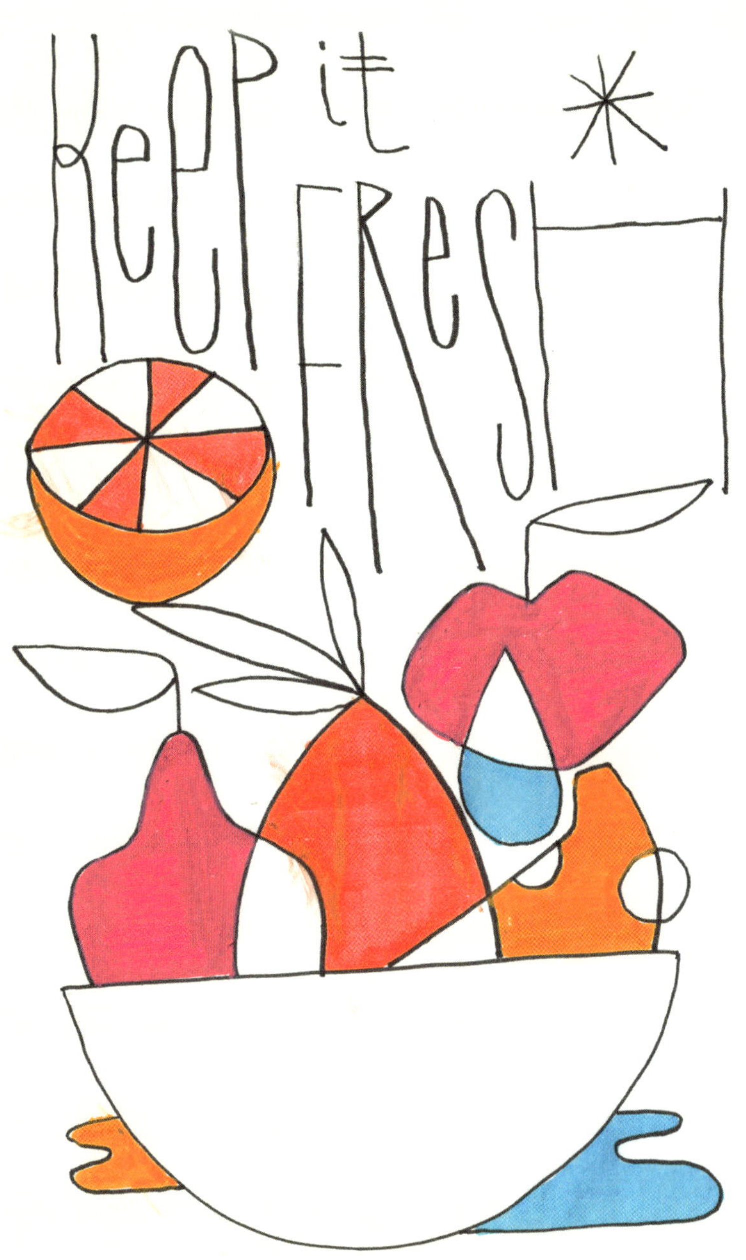

KEEP it
FRESH

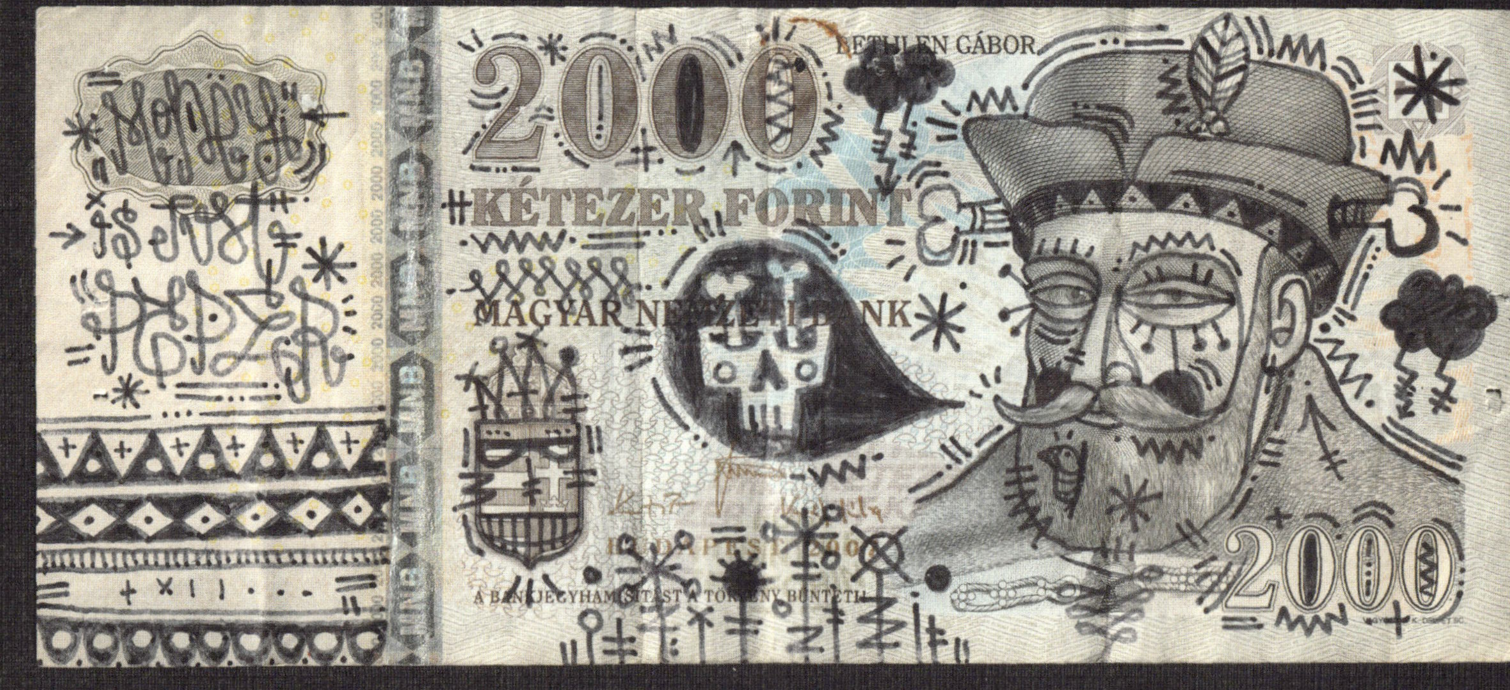
2000
KÉTEZER FORINT
MAGYAR NEMZETI BANK
BETHLEN GÁBOR
A BANKJEGYHAMISÍTÁST A TÖRVÉNY BÜNTETI
BUDAPEST 2000
2000

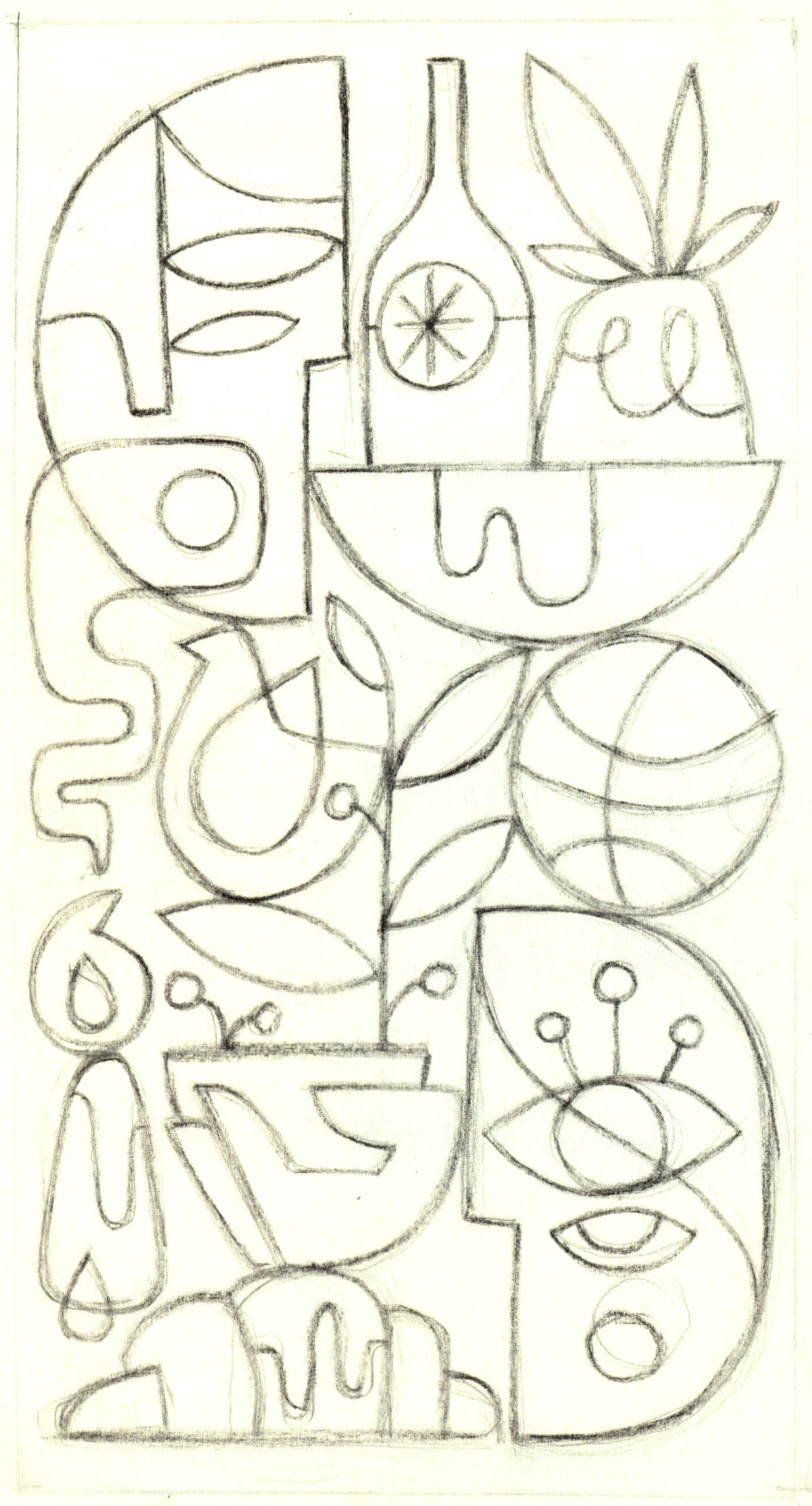

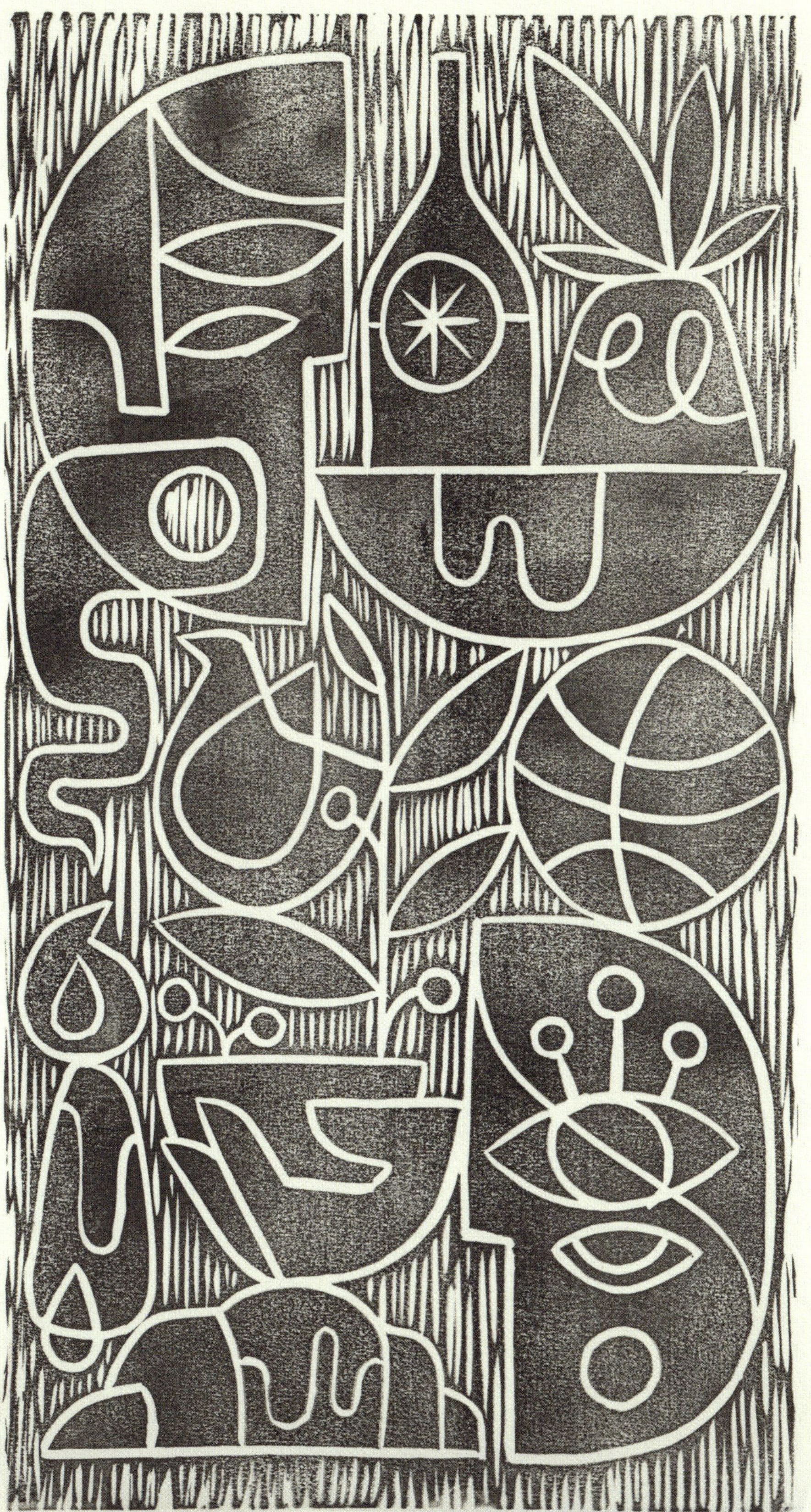

EQUILIBRIO
SUEÑOS LUCIDOS
INTERACCION
CONECTIVIDAD
JUEGO HUMOR
CAPAS & SOMBRAS
COMO NOS COMUNICAMOS
COMO CONECTEIXAR?
COTIDIANIDAD
MEDITERRANEO
INESTABILIDADE
POSTURAS IMPOSIBLES
IGUALDAD PERPETUA
FANTASIA VS REALIDAD
MIEDOS
TODOS
ESPACIOS CERRADOS
TRASLUCIDEZ + INTERSECCIÓN
ELLA

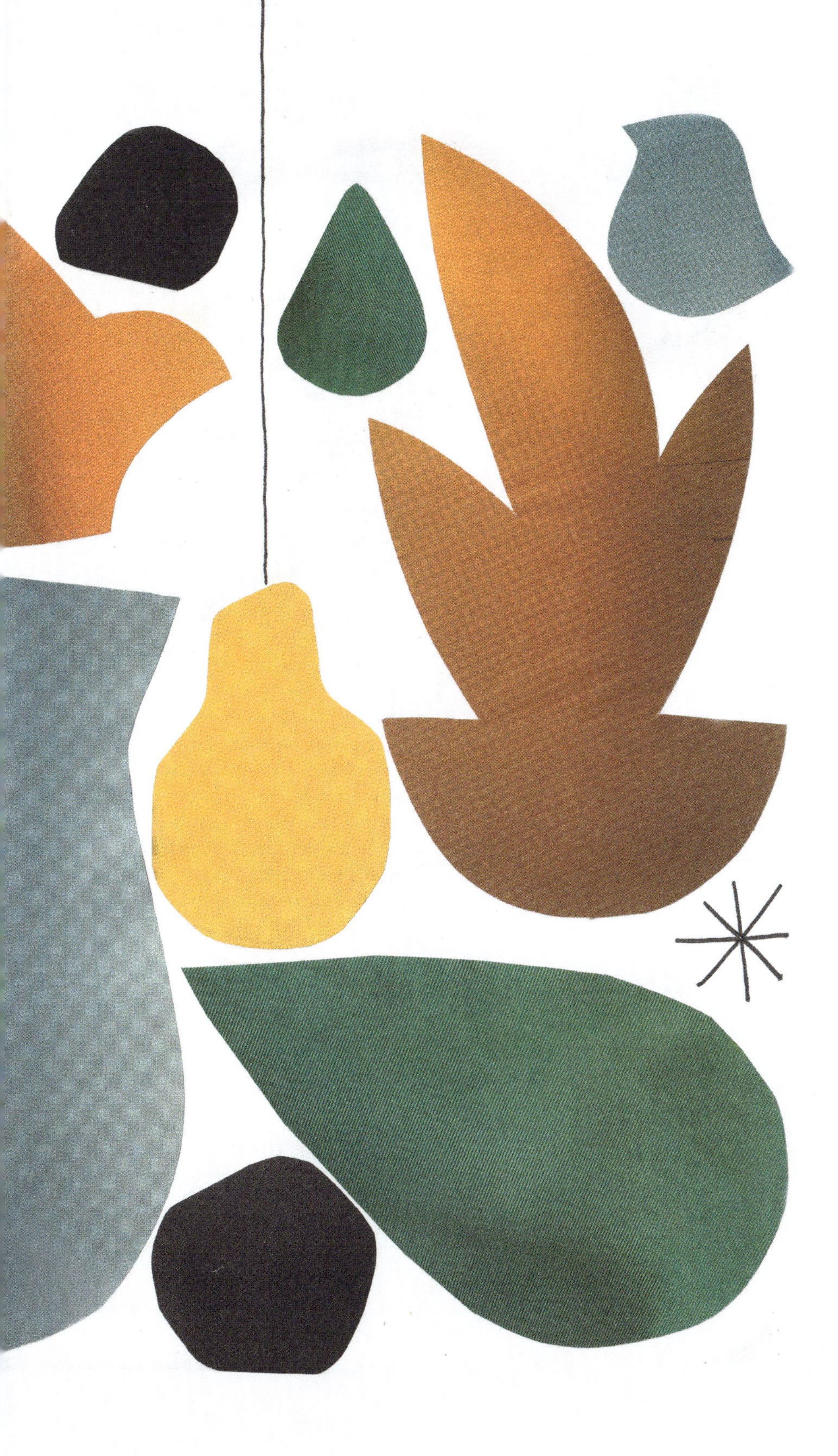

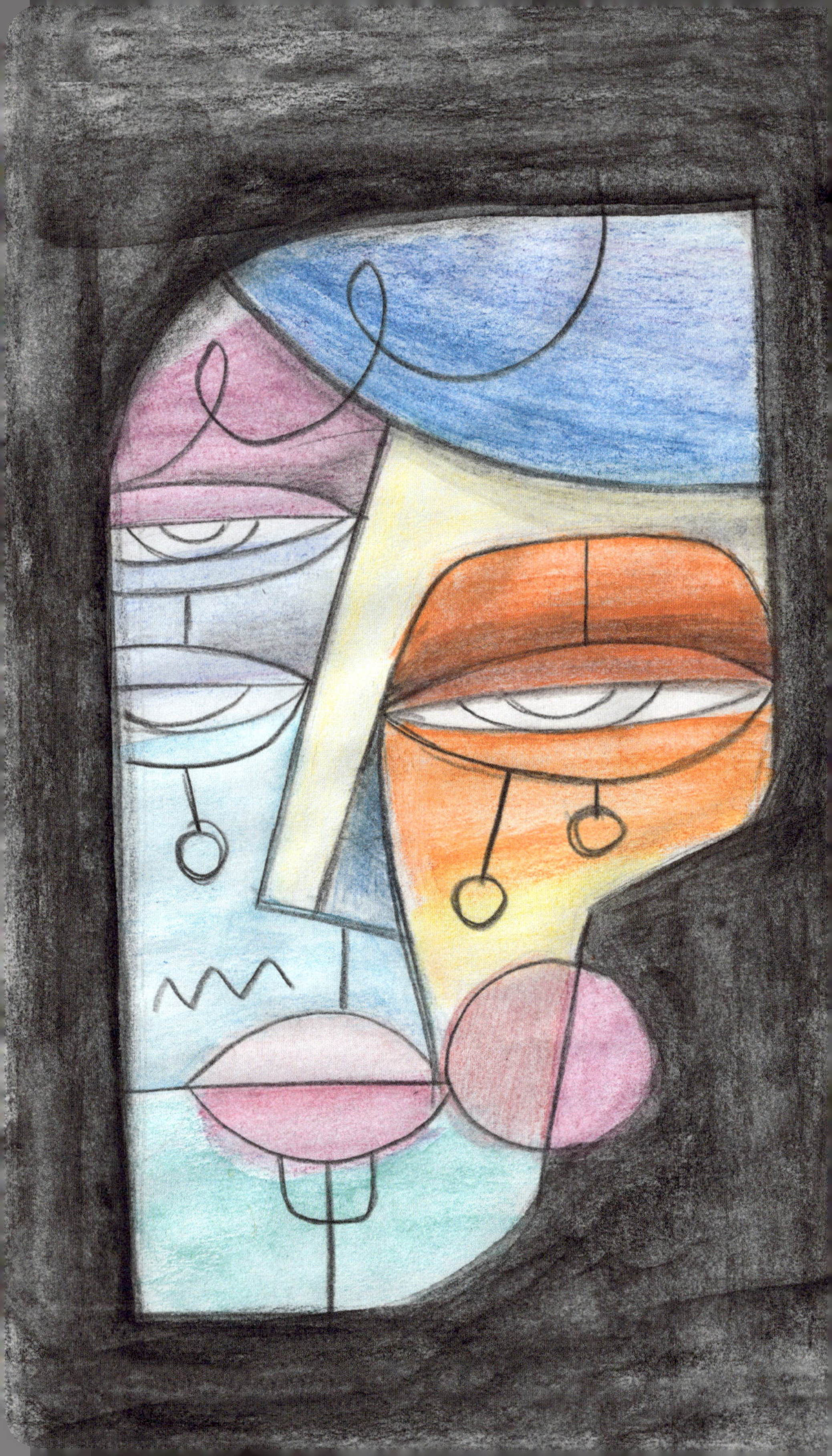

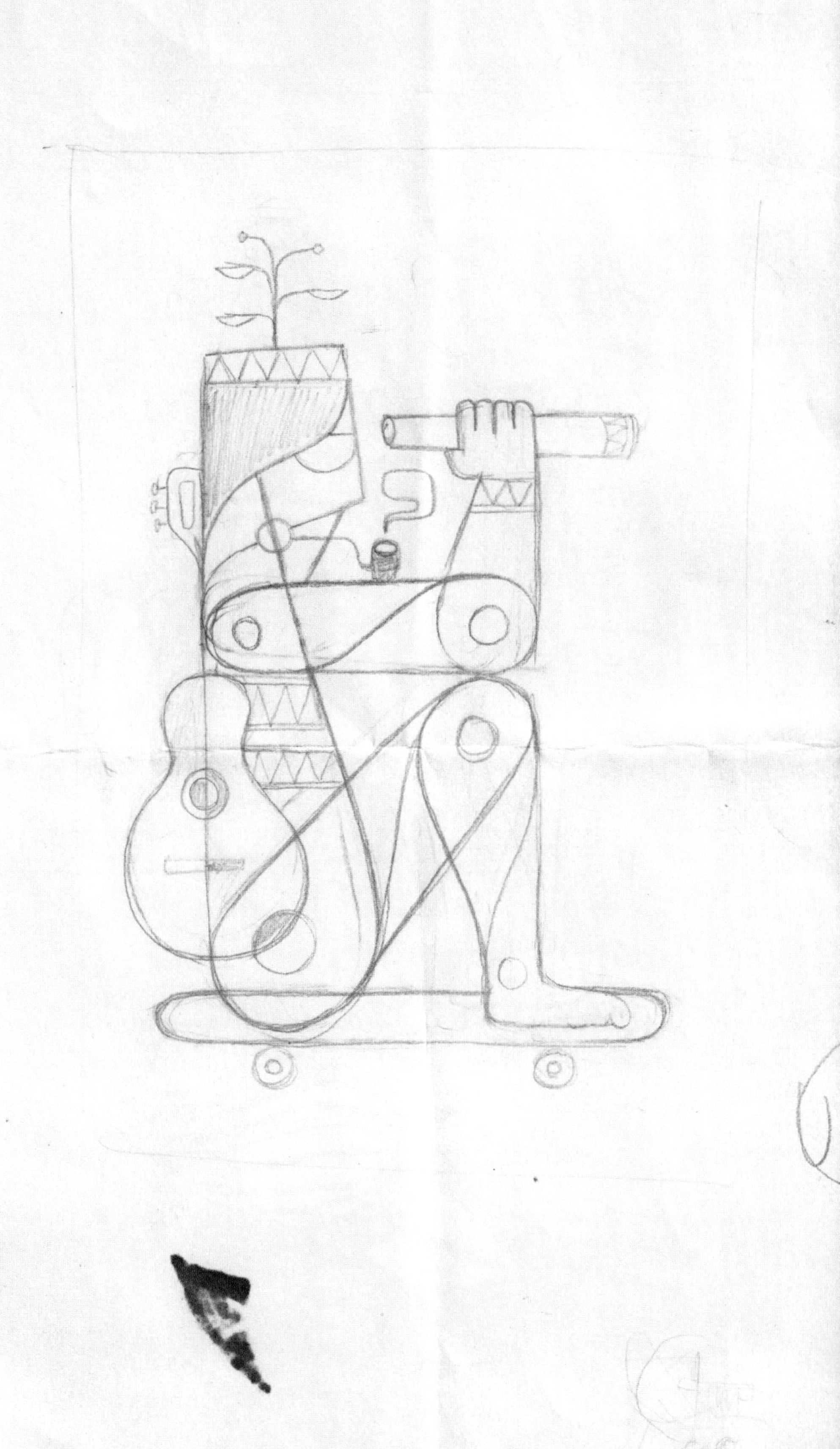

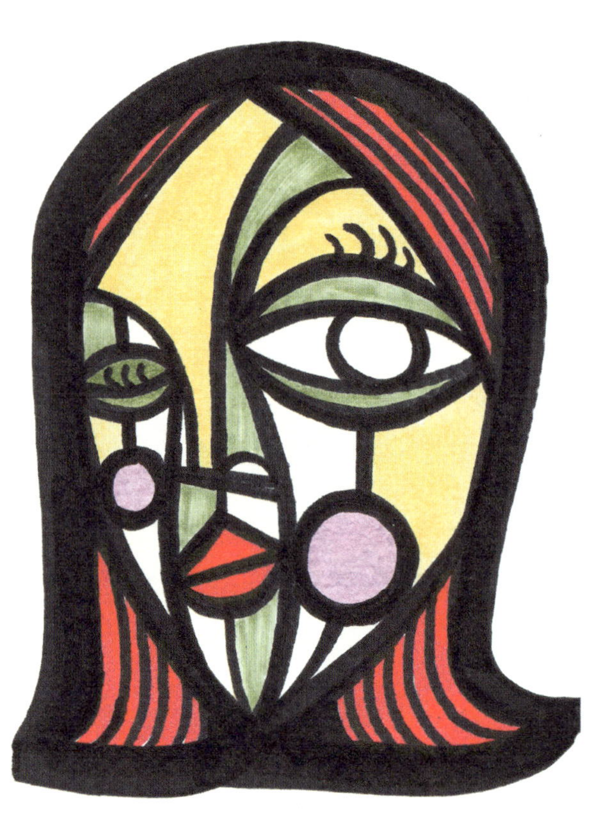

OLD
BOOKS
i didn't
REaLLy waNt to
add

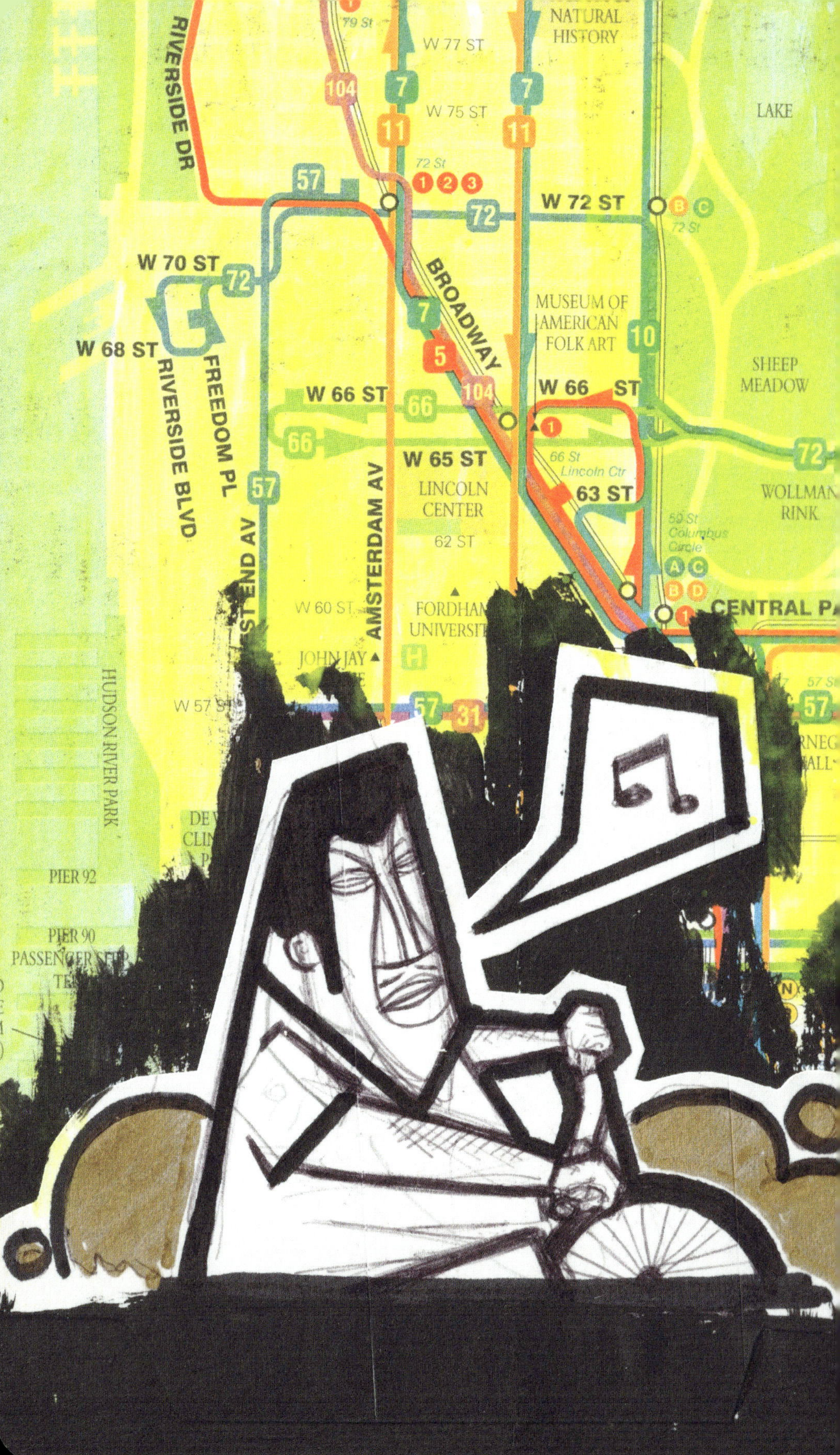

RIVERSIDE DR
79 St
W 77 ST
W 75 ST
NATURAL HISTORY
LAKE
104
7
7
11
11
57
72 St
1 2 3
72
W 72 ST
B C
72 St
BROADWAY
W 70 ST
72
7
MUSEUM OF AMERICAN FOLK ART
10
W 68 ST
5
SHEEP MEADOW
FREEDOM PL
RIVERSIDE BLVD
W 66 ST
66
104
W 66 ST
1
W 65 ST
66
66 St
Lincoln Ctr
63 ST
WOLLMAN RINK
72
57
AMSTERDAM AV
LINCOLN CENTER
62 St
END AV
59 St
Columbus Circle
W 60 ST
FORDHAM UNIVERSITY
A C
B D
1
CENTRAL PA
JOHN JAY
H
57 St
57
HUDSON RIVER PARK
W 57 ST
57
31
RNEG
ALL
PIER 92
DE
CLIN
P
PIER 90
PASSENGER SE
TE

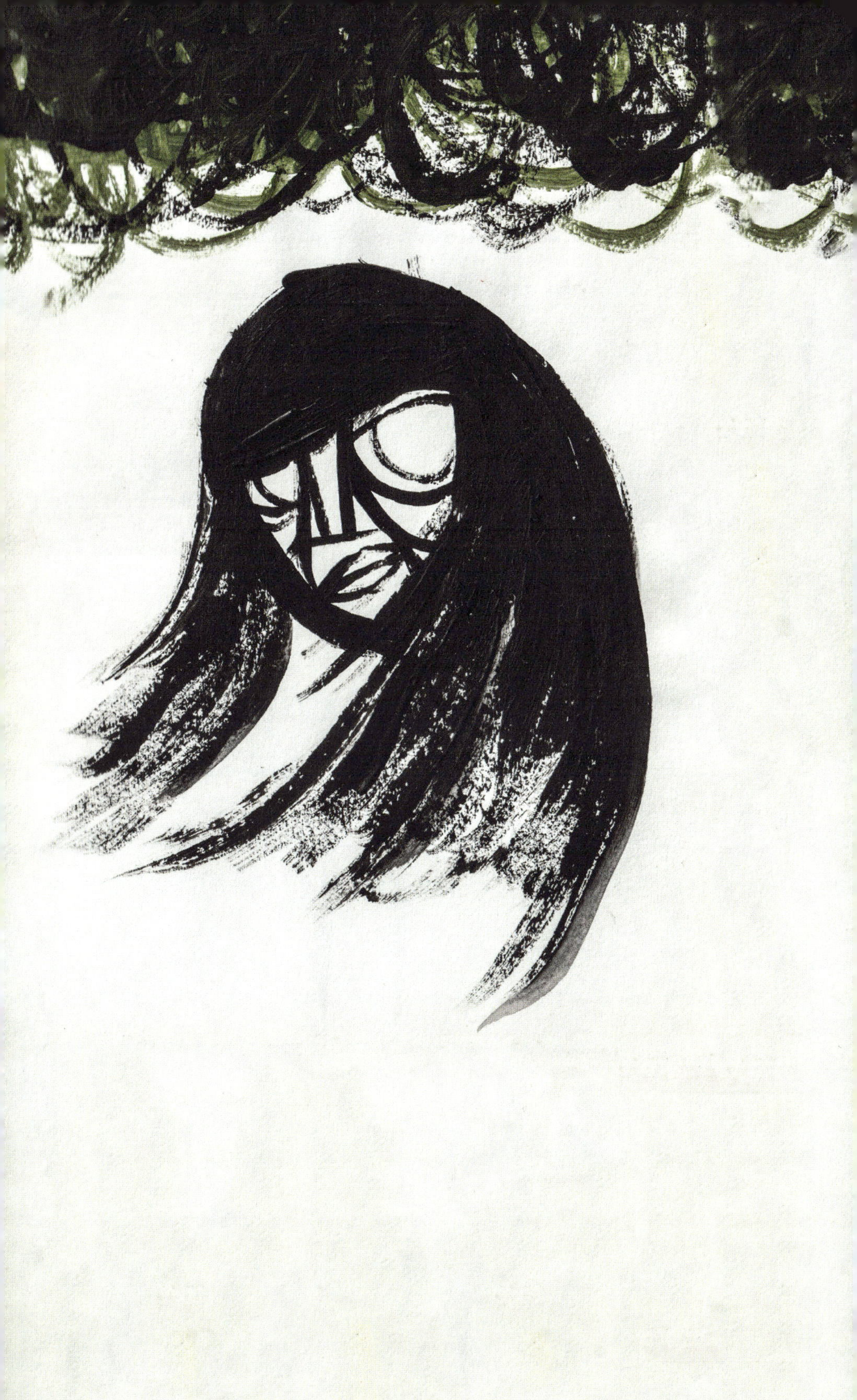

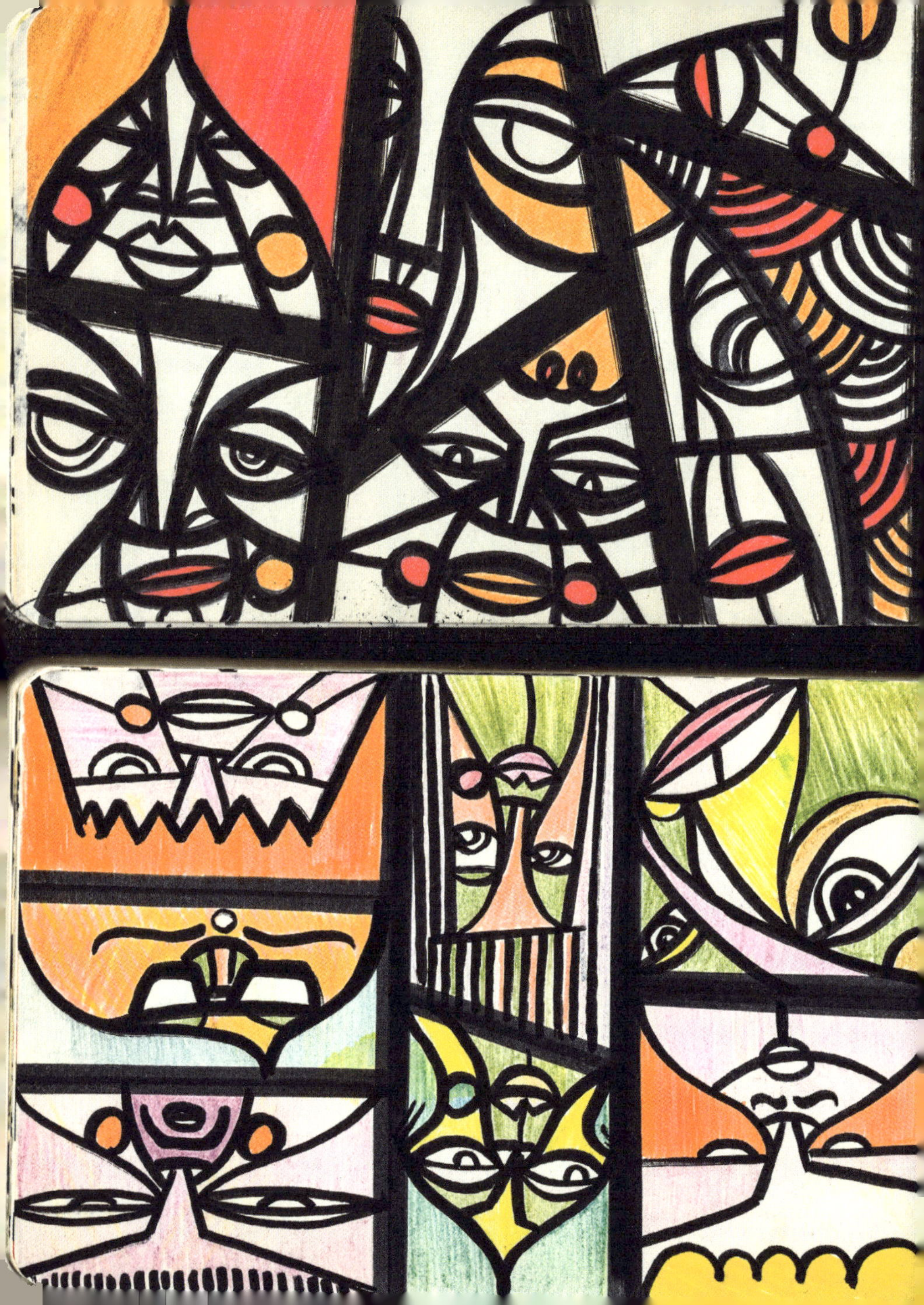

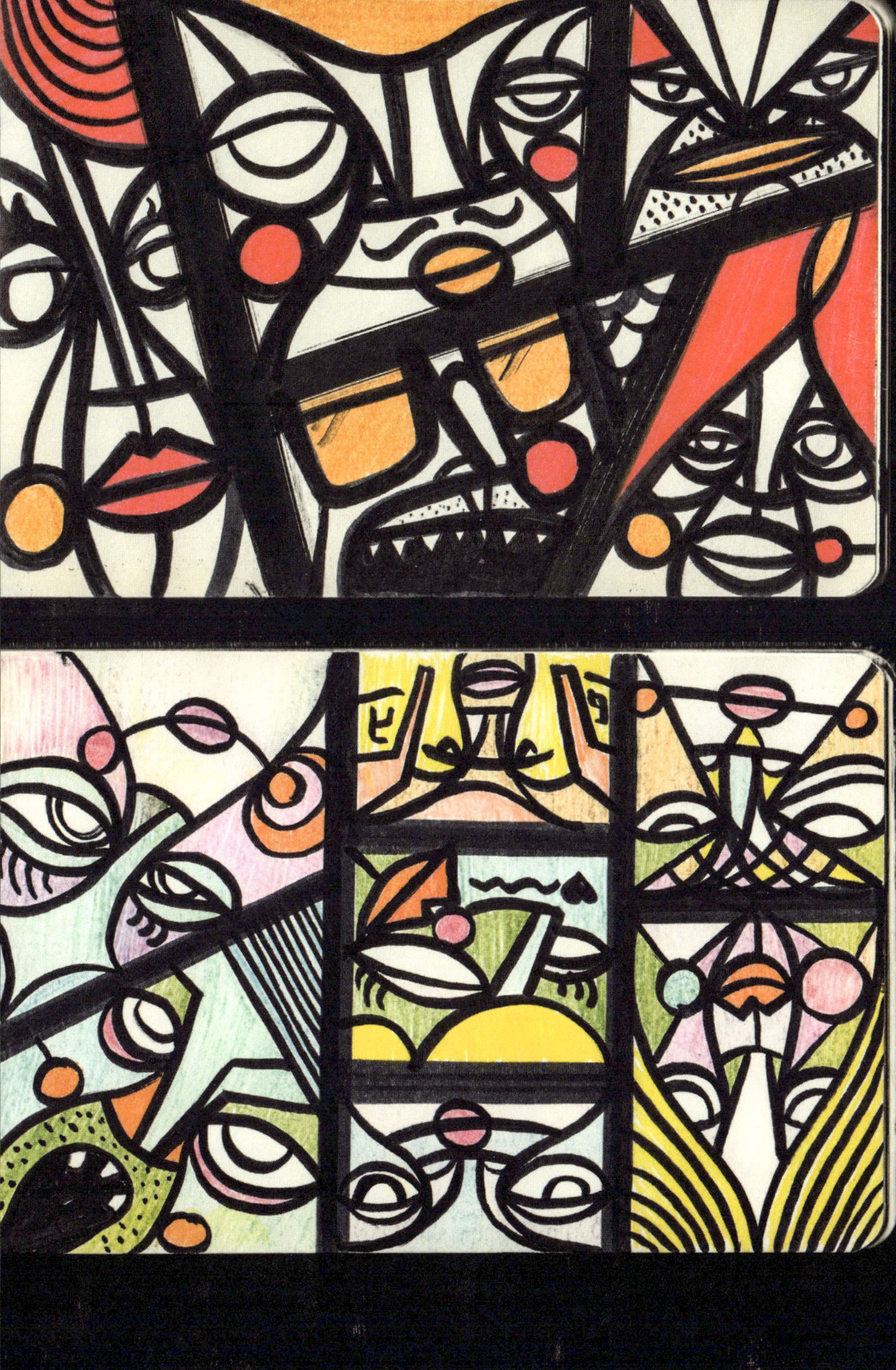

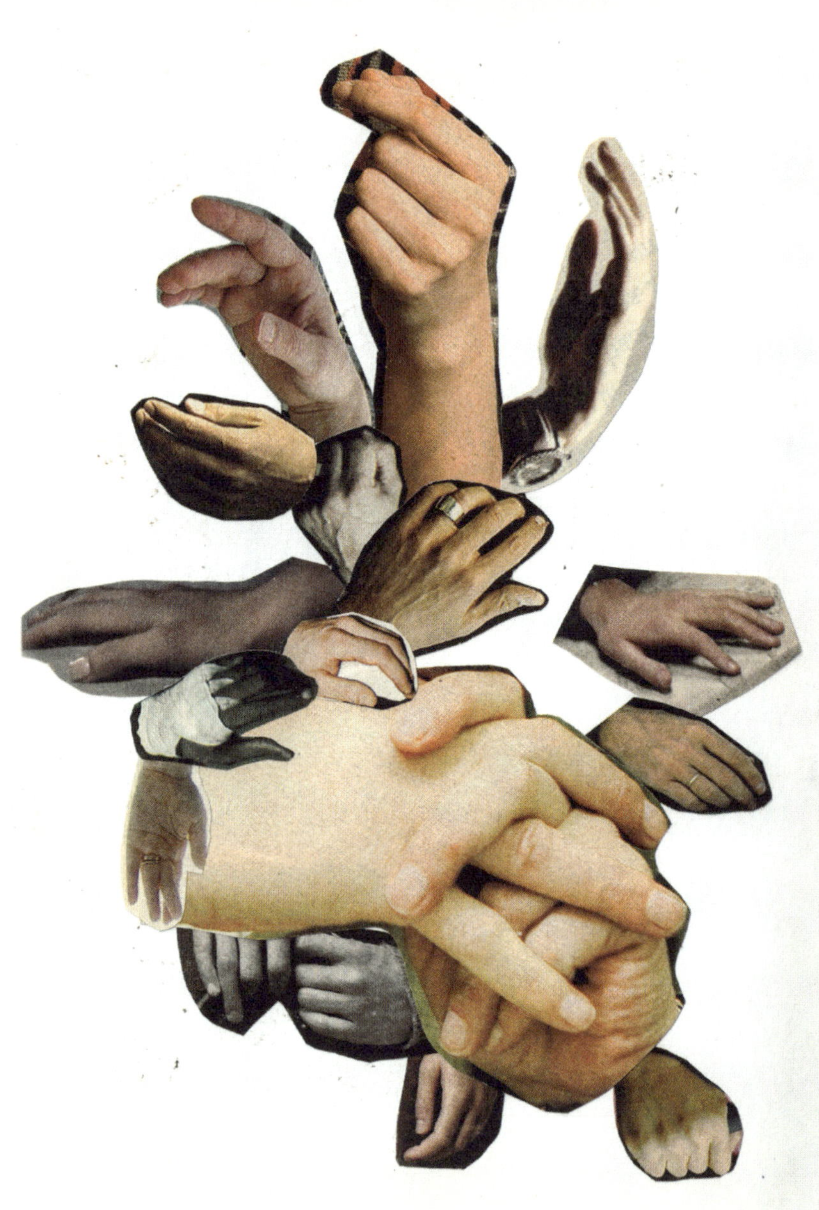

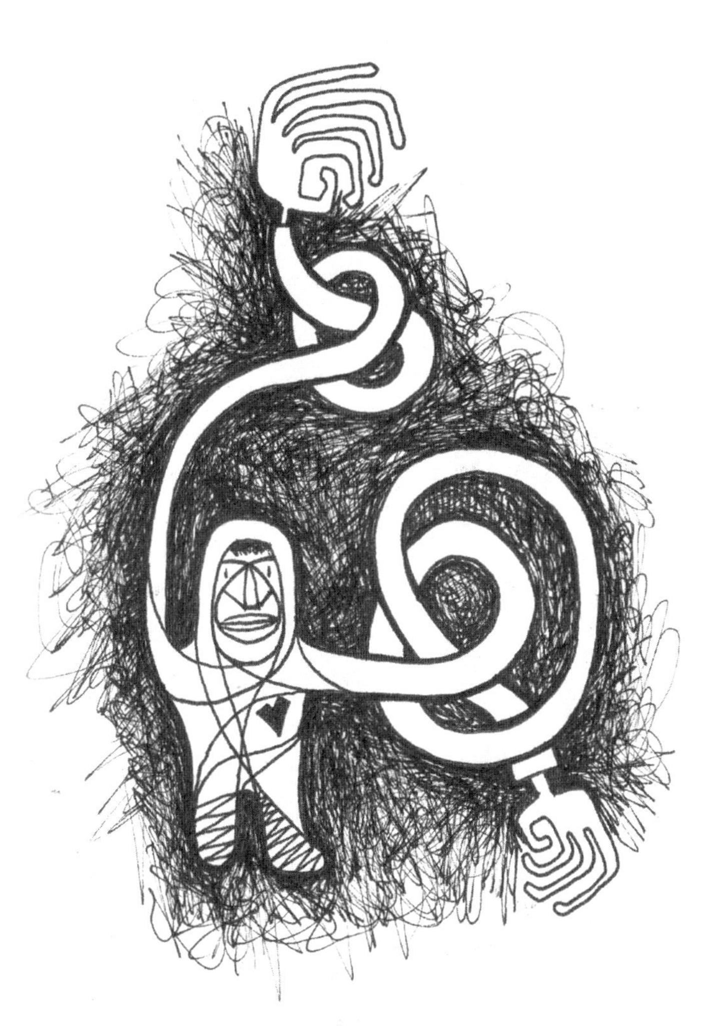

SEPR
OHiB
E TERM
inant
eMenTe

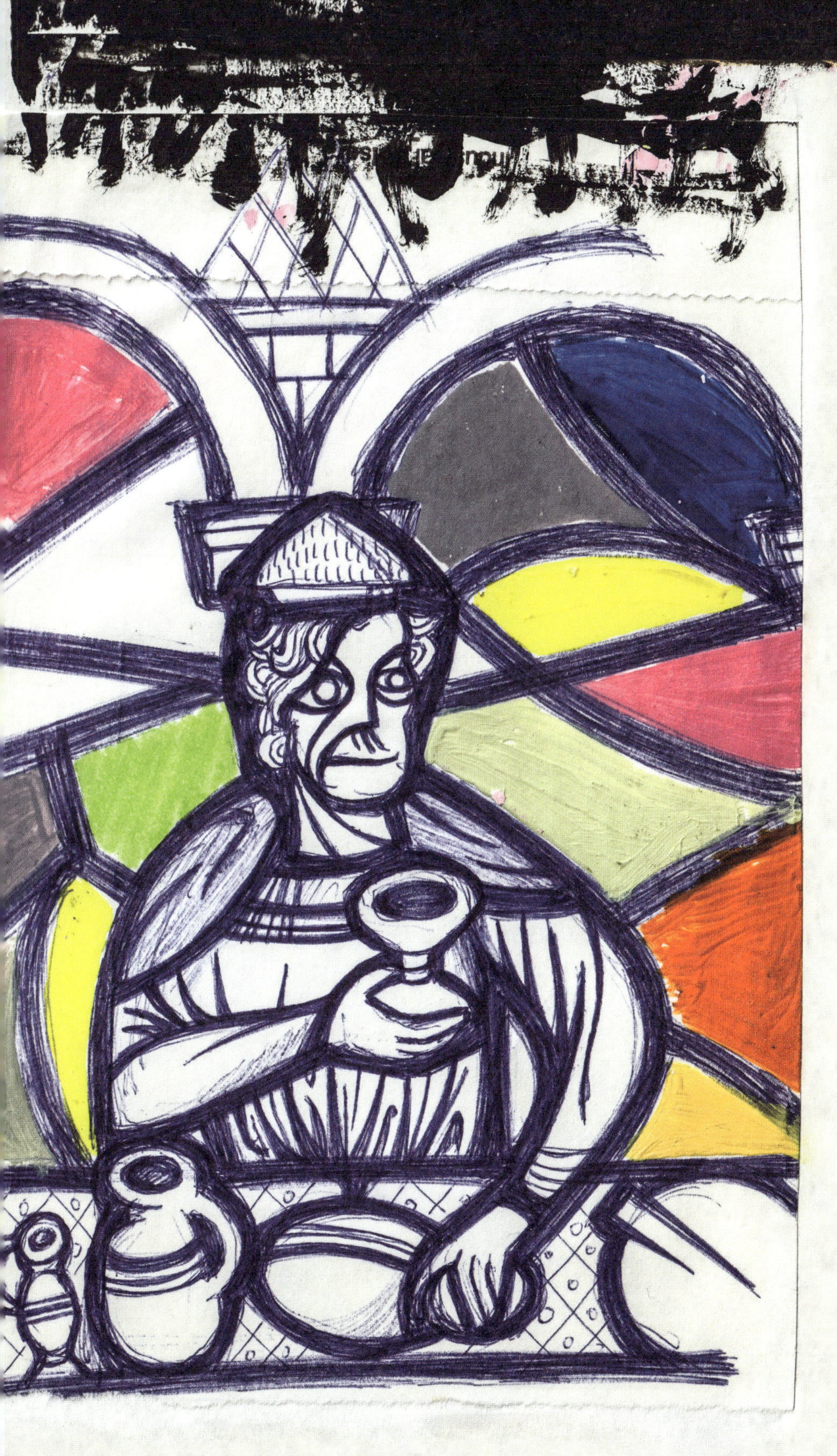

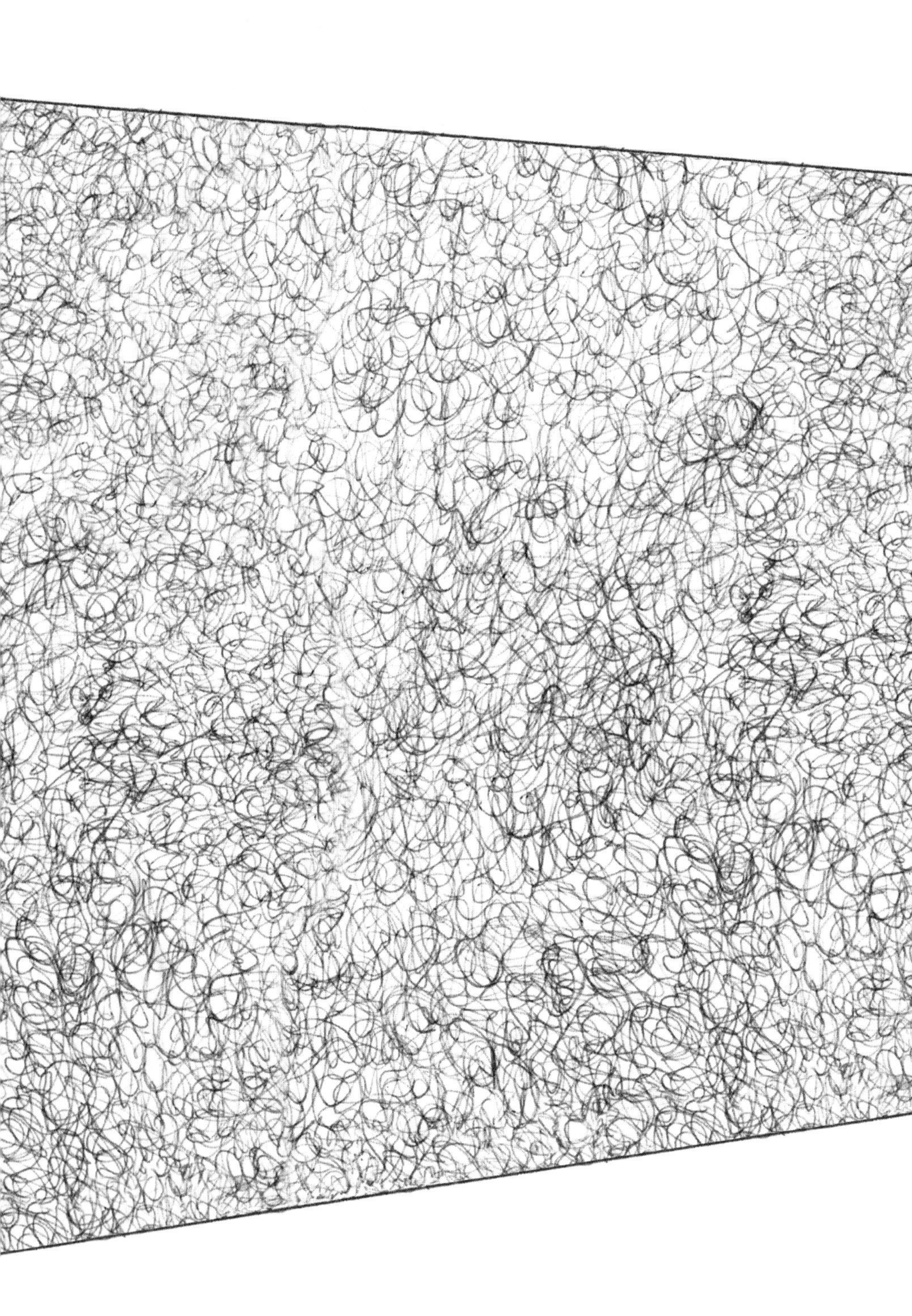

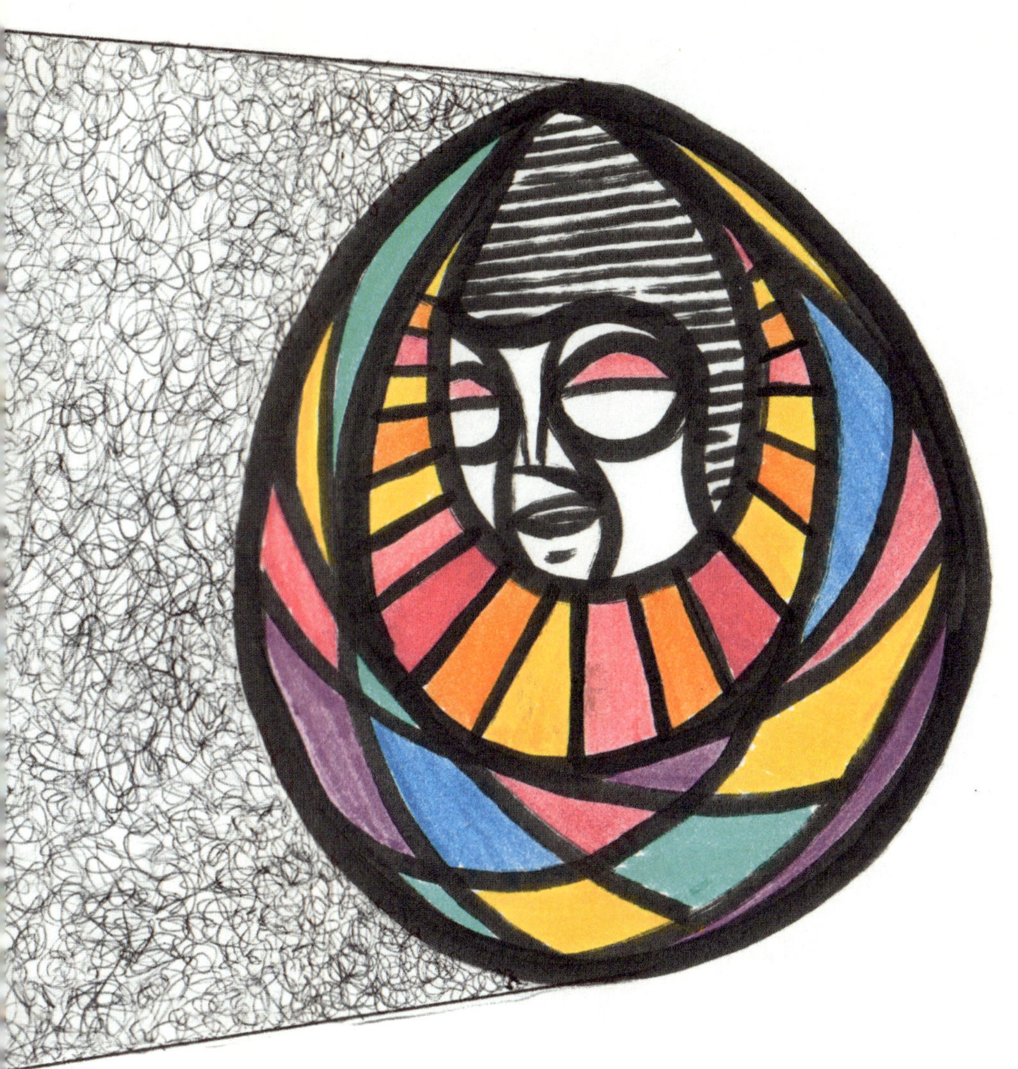

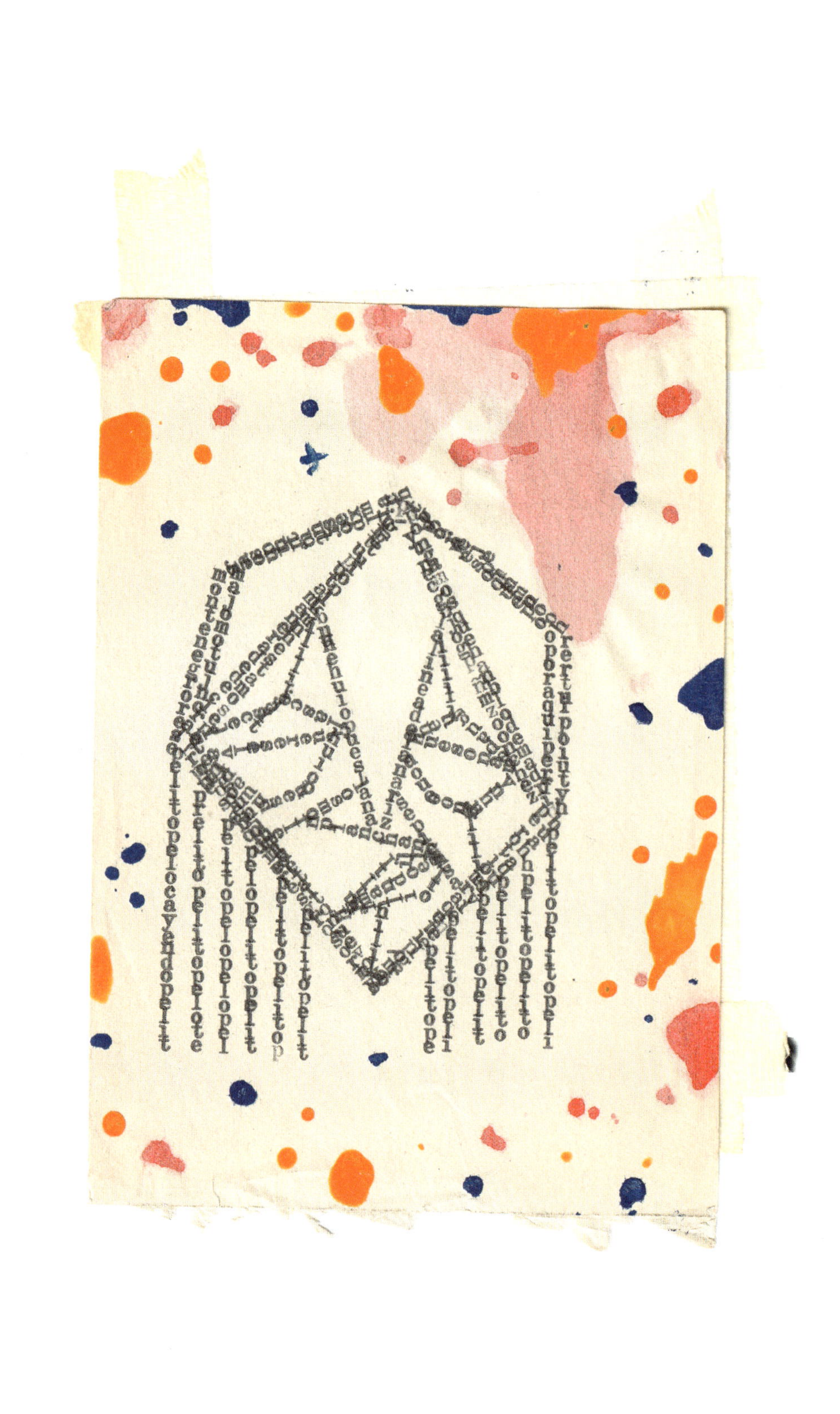

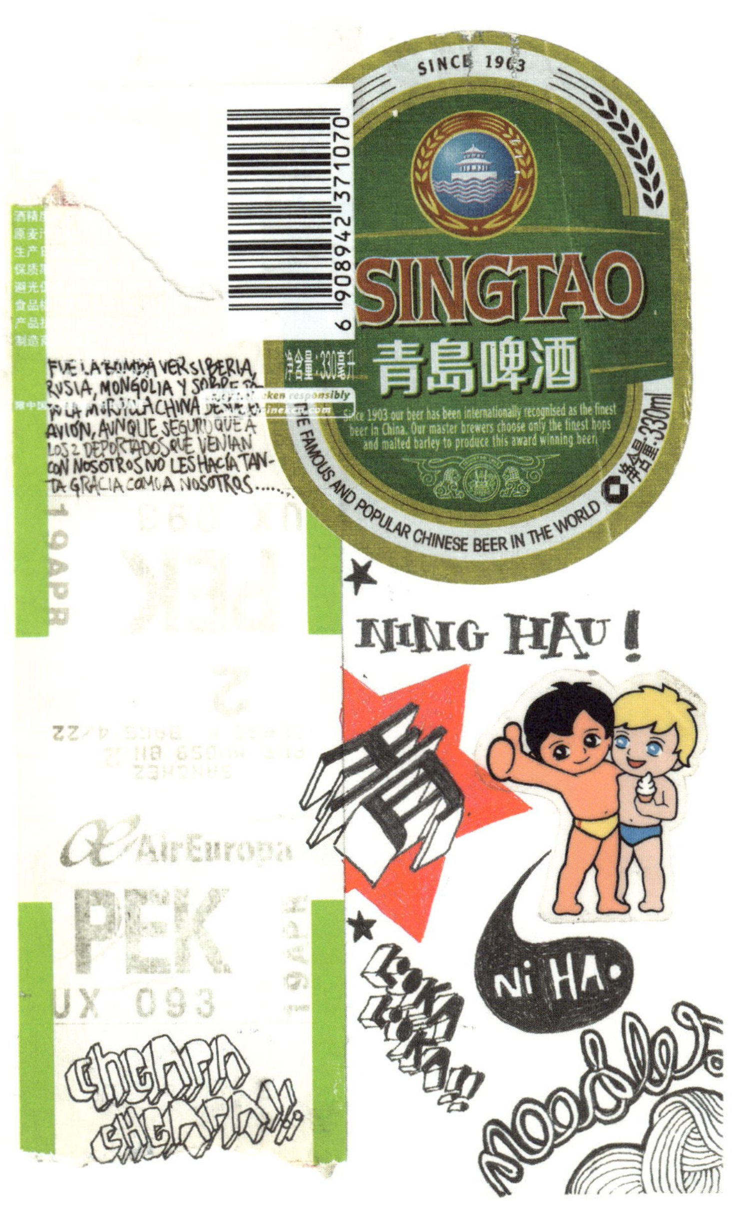

SINCE 1903
SINGTAO
青島啤酒
净含量：330毫升
330ml
净含量：330ml
Since 1903 our beer has been internationally recognised as the finest beer in China. Our master brewers choose only the finest hops and malted barley to produce this award winning beer.
THE FAMOUS AND POPULAR CHINESE BEER IN THE WORLD
FUE LA BOMBA VER SIBERIA, RUSIA, MONGOLIA Y SOBRE TODO LA MÚSICA CHINA DESDE EL AVIÓN, AUNQUE SEGURO QUE A LOS 2 DEPORTADOS QUE VENÍAN CON NOSOTROS NO LES HACÍA TANTA GRACIA COMO A NOSOTROS......
NING HAU !
Ni HAO
LOOKA LOOKA !!
noodle.
CHEAPA CHEAPA !!
AirEuropa
PEK
UX 093
19APR

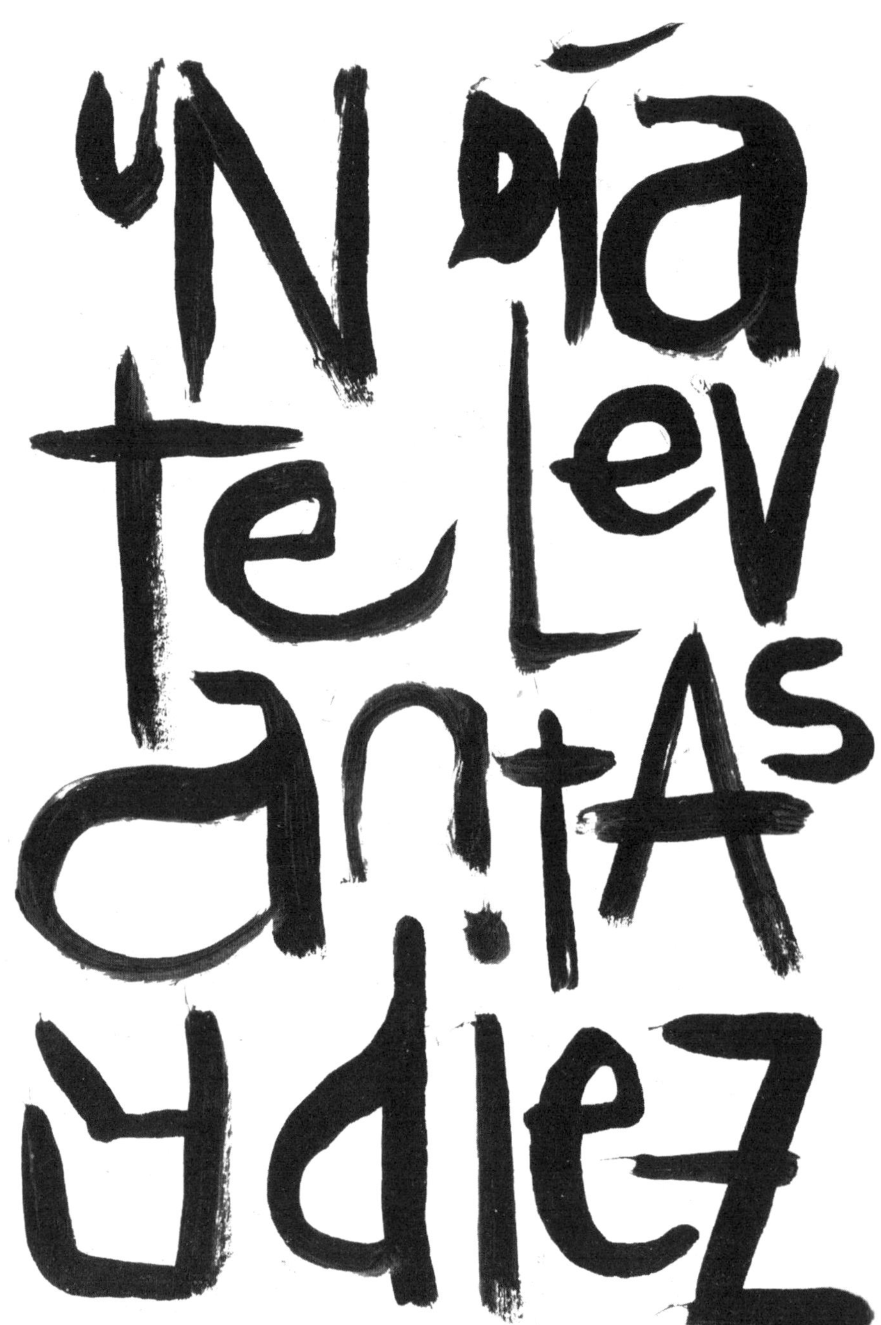

UN DÍA
TE LEV
ANTAS
Y DIEZ

minutos
más t
arde vu
elvesa
la cama.

Ajuntament ✠ de Barcelona

INSTITUT MUNICIPAL D'HISENDA
www.bcn.es/hisenda

IDENTIFICACIÓ / IDENTIFICACIÓN

Núm. rebut / Núm. recibo	Data emissió document / Fecha emisión documento	Núm. Núm
EI-2007-6-05-19553690	**08/03/07**	
Núm. provisió / Núm. providencia	Data provisió de constrenyiment / Fecha providencia de apremio	
14/06	**6/3/2006**	5

OBLIGAT AL PAGAMENT / OBLIGADO AL PAGO

NIF:	INFRACTOR: SANCHEZ RO

DEUTE / DEUDA

CONCEPTE / CONCEPTO   MULTES / MULTAS

Objecte	Infracció/Lloc infracc.	Data Infr/Expe
Objeto	Infracción/Lugar infracc.	Fecha Infr/Expe

EFECTUAR NECESSITATS BIOLOGIQUES VIA PUB

EFECTUAR NECESIDADES BIOLOGICAS VIA PUBL

HEURES 0002   02-10-05

2005/70186

Import a pagar /
Importe a pagar

EUR**********99,17

TIFICACIÓ   1091077125   **IMPORT**   99,17

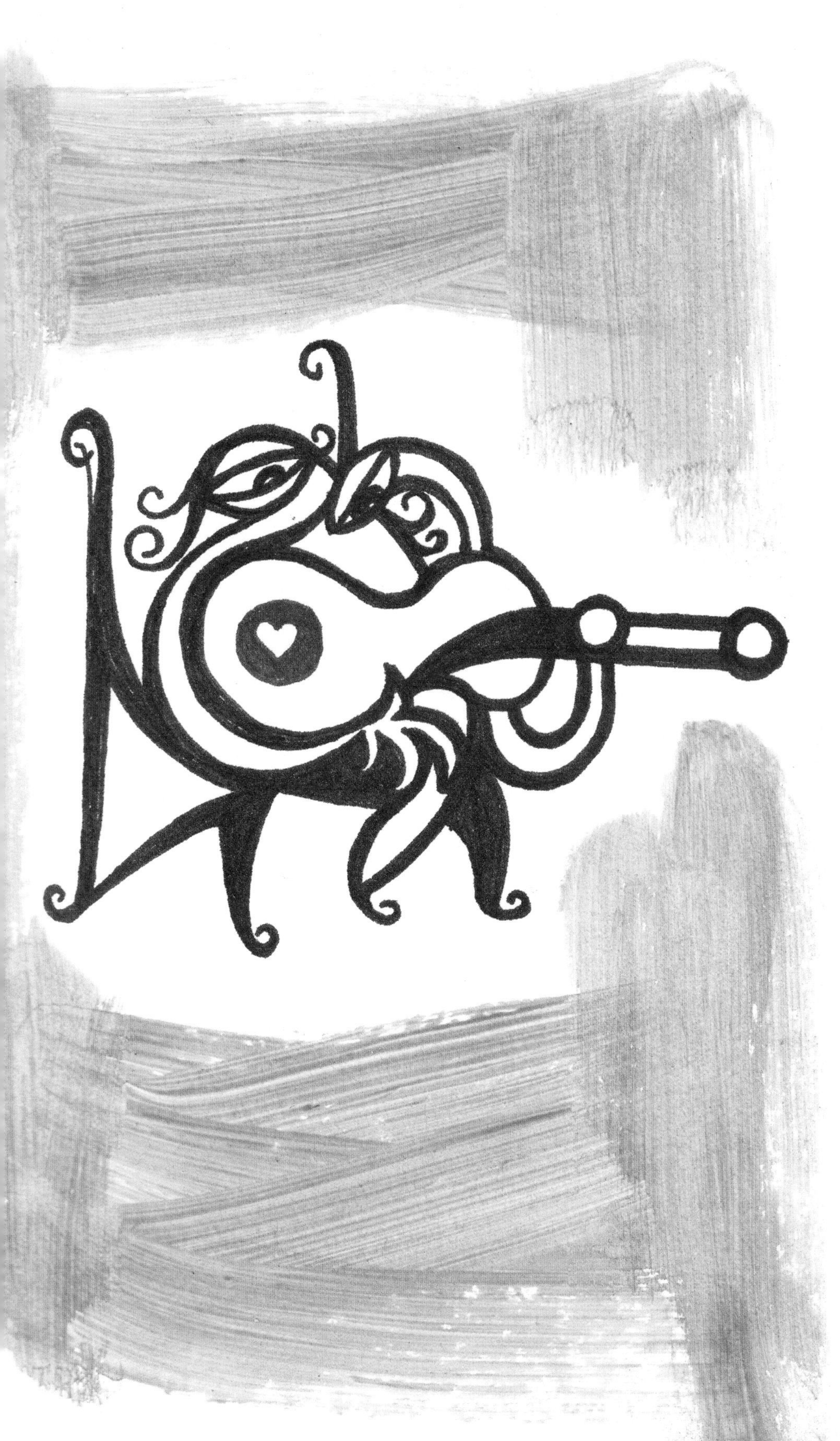

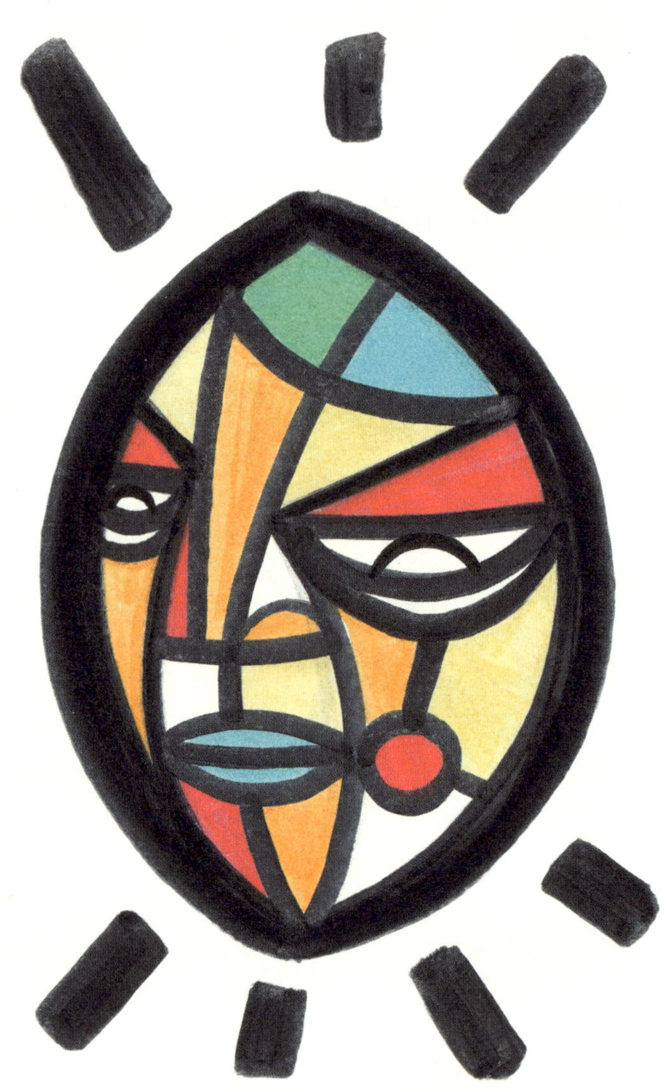

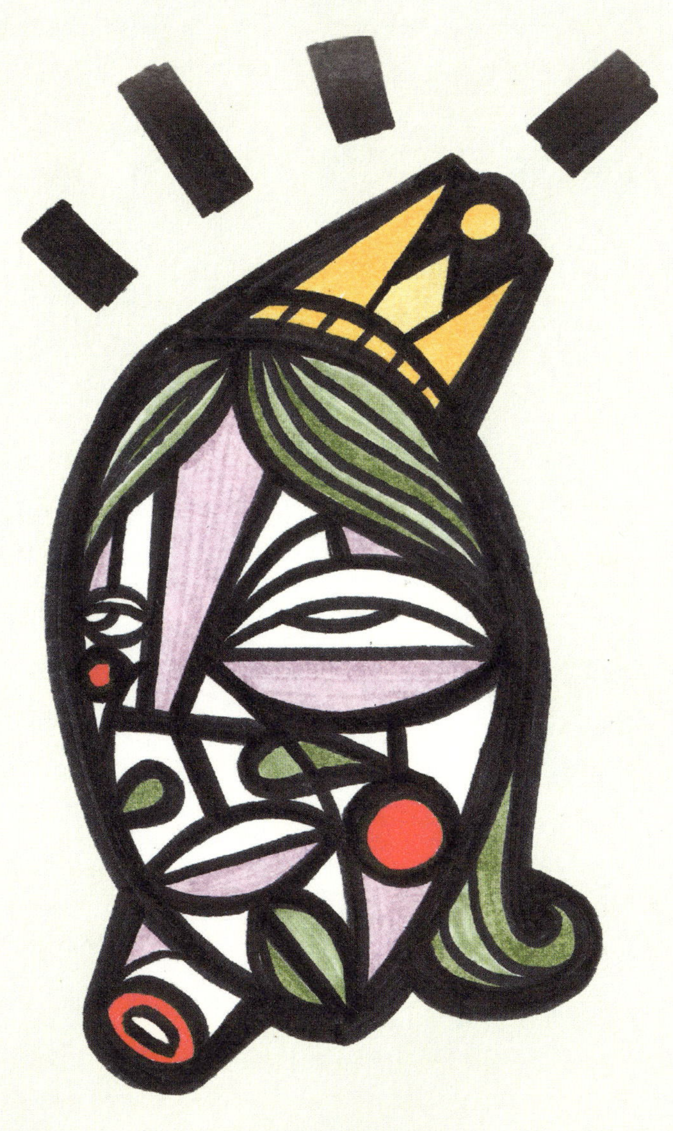

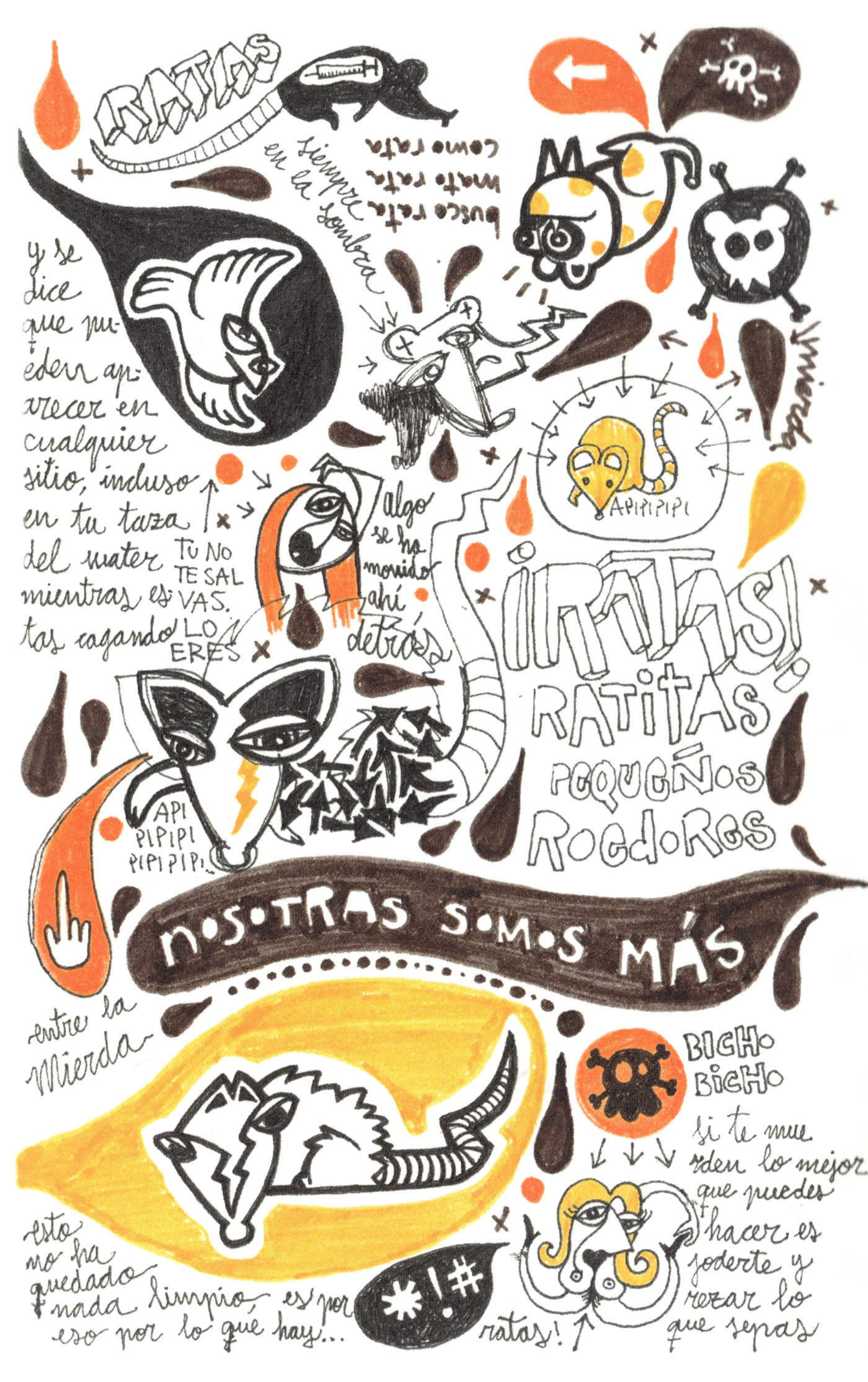

RATAS
Siempre en la sombra
busca rata / mata rata / como rata
y se dice que pueden aparecer en cualquier sitio, incluso en tu taza del water mientras estás cagando
TU NO TE SALVAS. LO ERES
Algo se ha movido ahí detrás
mierda
APIPIPIPI
¡RATAS! RATITAS pequeños roedores
API PIPIPI PIPI PIPI
entre la mierda
NOSOTRAS SOMOS MÁS
esto no ha quedado nada limpio, es por eso por lo que hay...
*!#
ratas!
BICHO BICHO
si te muerden lo mejor que puedes hacer es joderte y rezar lo que sepas

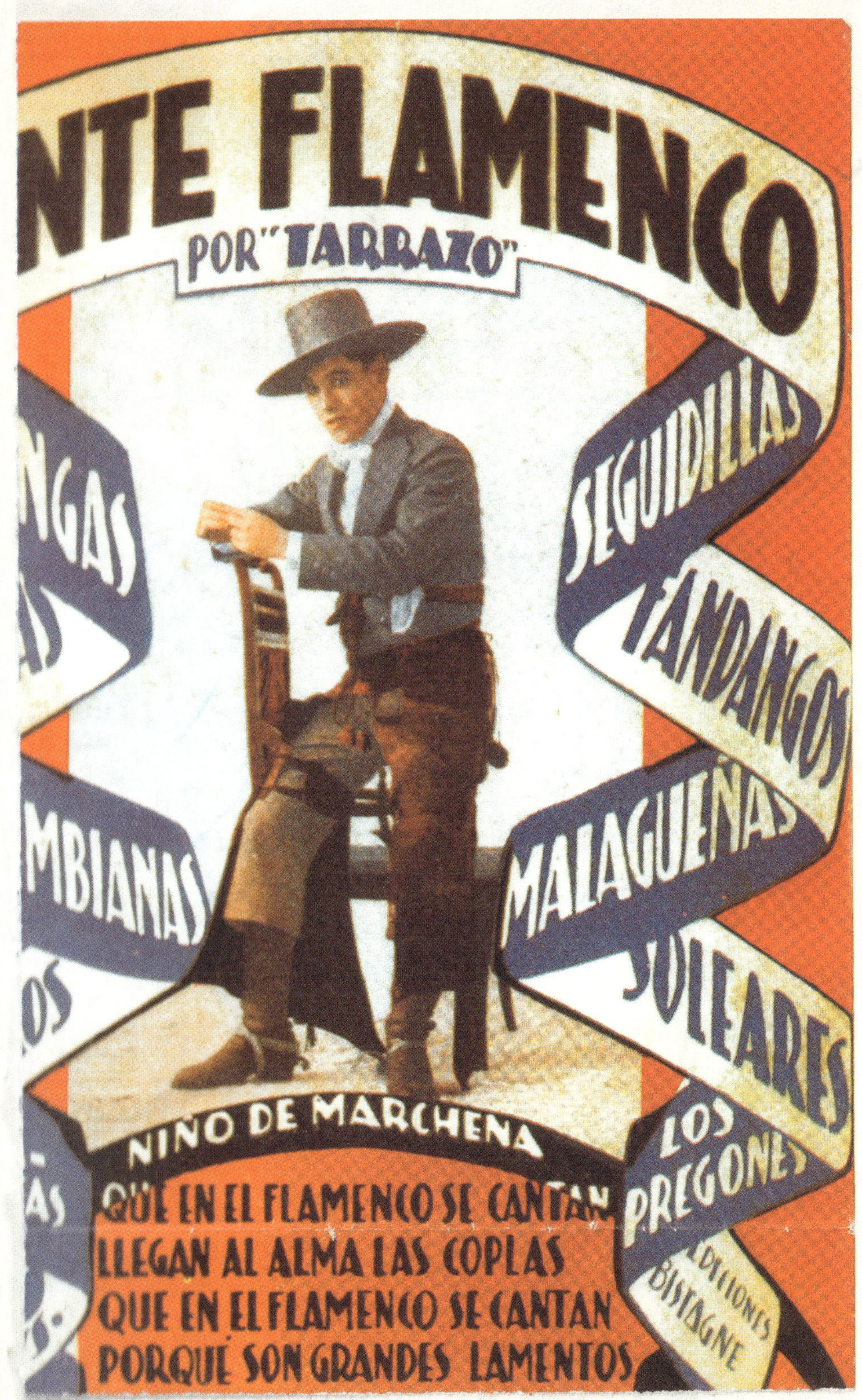
NTE FLAMENCO
POR "TARRAZO"
SEGUIDILLAS
NGAS
FANDANGOS
BIANAS
MALAGUEÑAS
OS
SOLEARES
NIÑO DE MARCHENA
LOS PREGONES
ÁS
QUE EN EL FLAMENCO SE CANTAN
LLEGAN AL ALMA LAS COPLAS
QUE EN EL FLAMENCO SE CANTAN
PORQUÉ SON GRANDES LAMENTOS
EDICIONES BISTAGNE

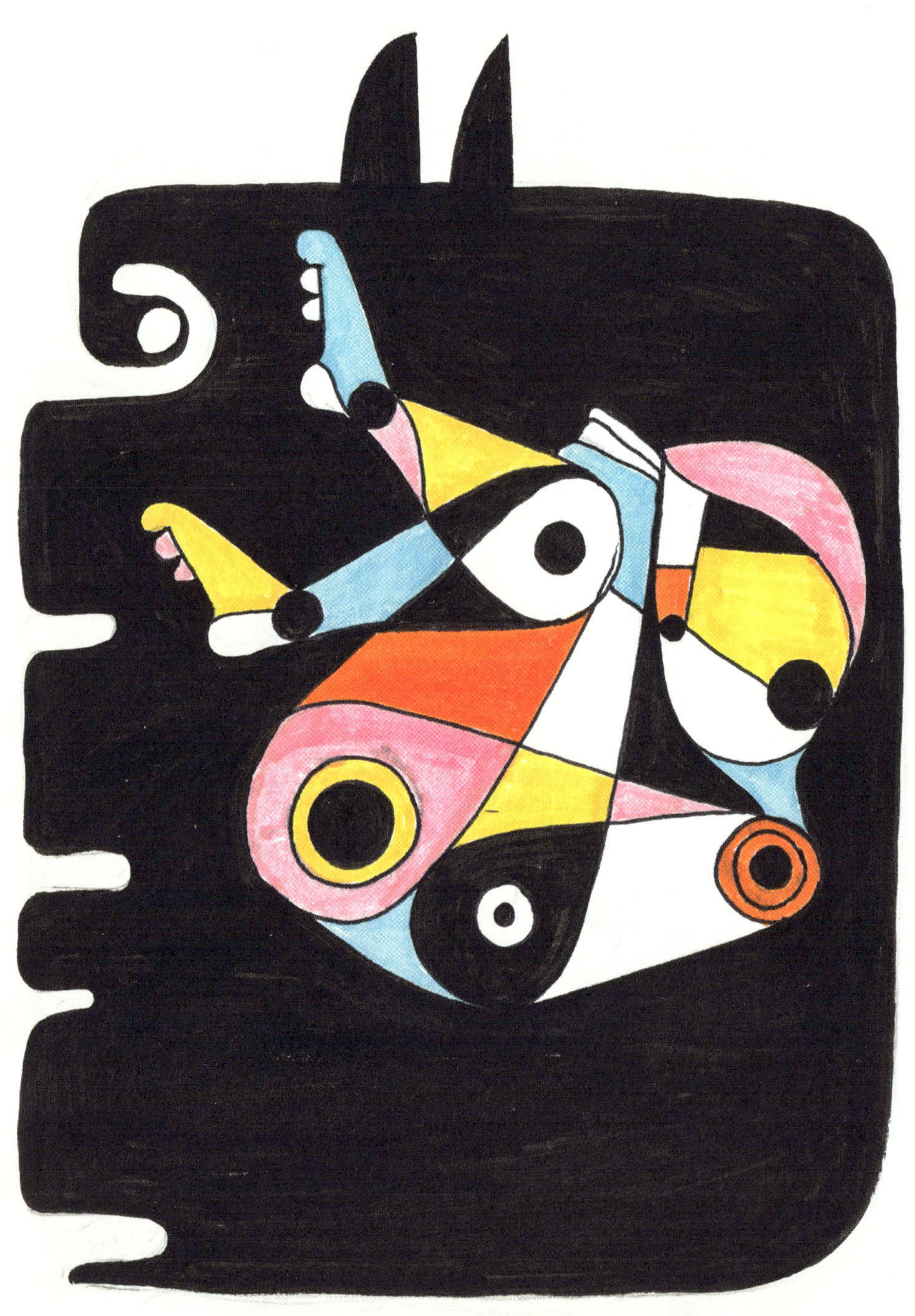

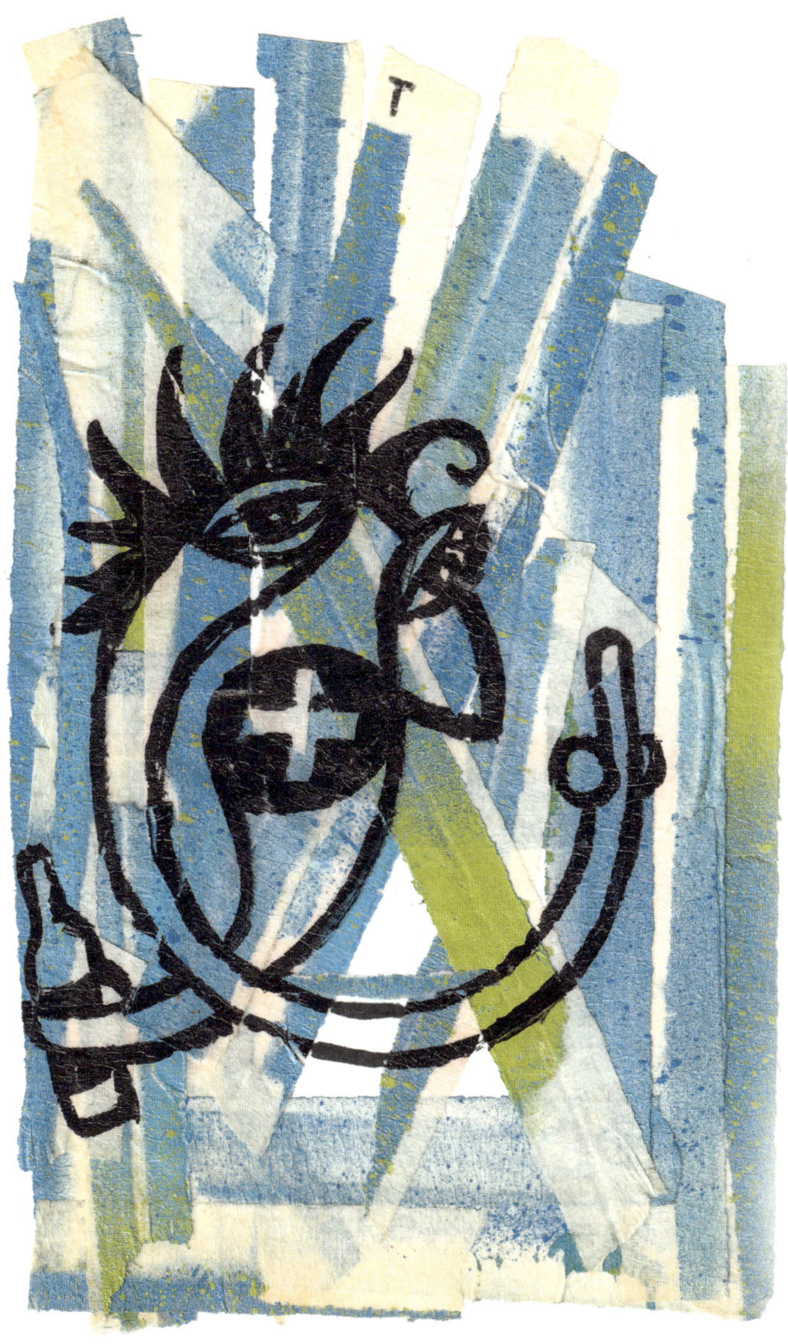

T

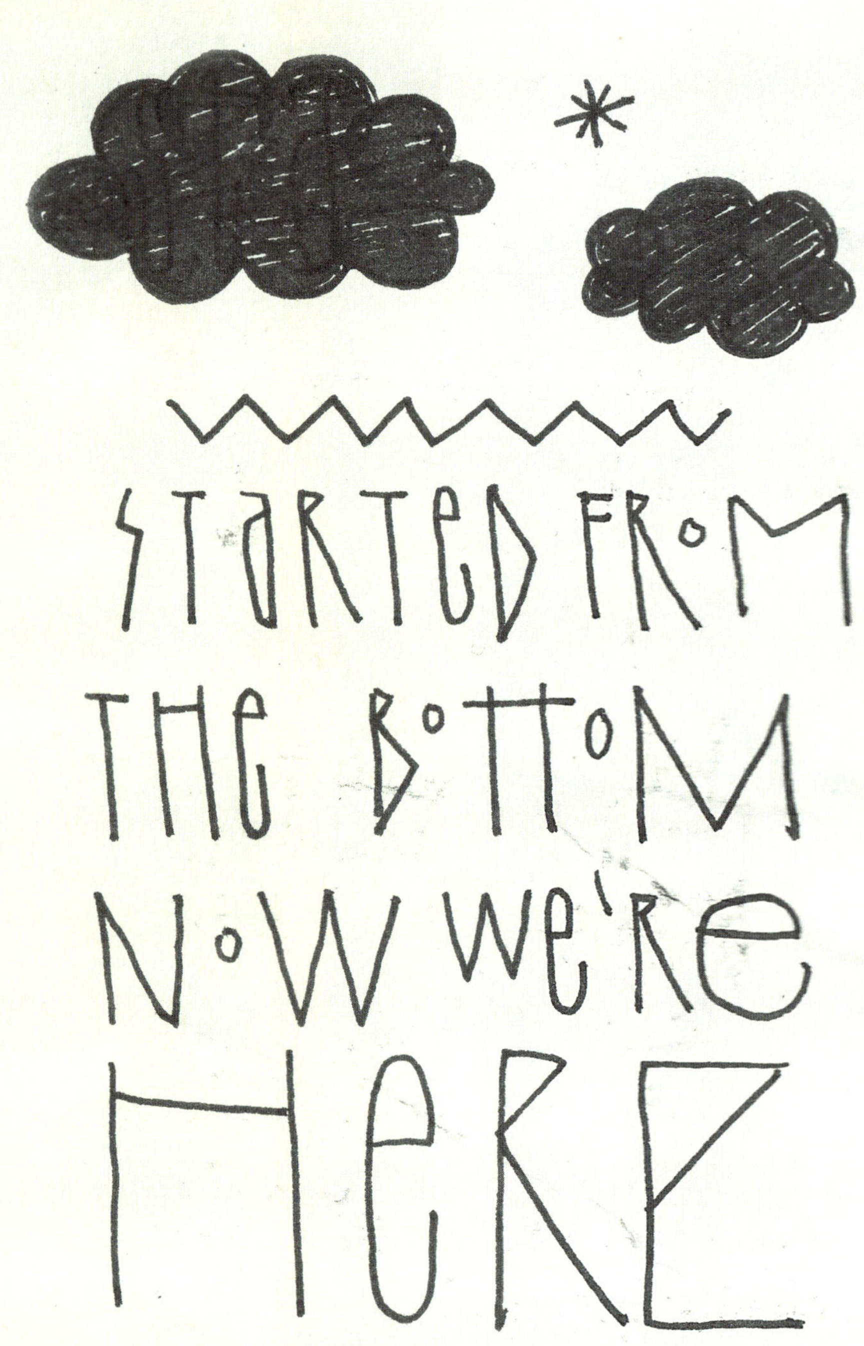

STARTED FROM
THE BOTTOM
NOW WE'RE
HERE

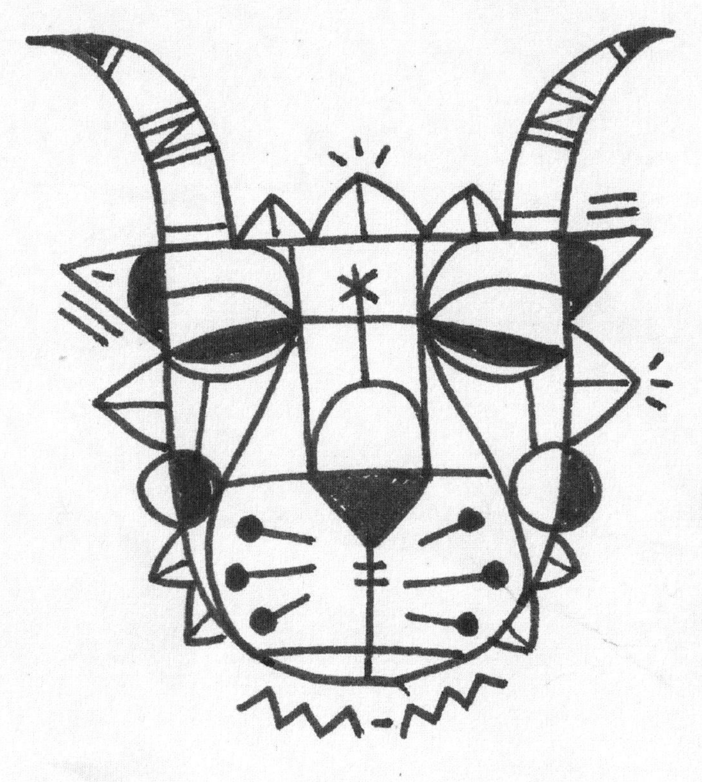

Goatiger *

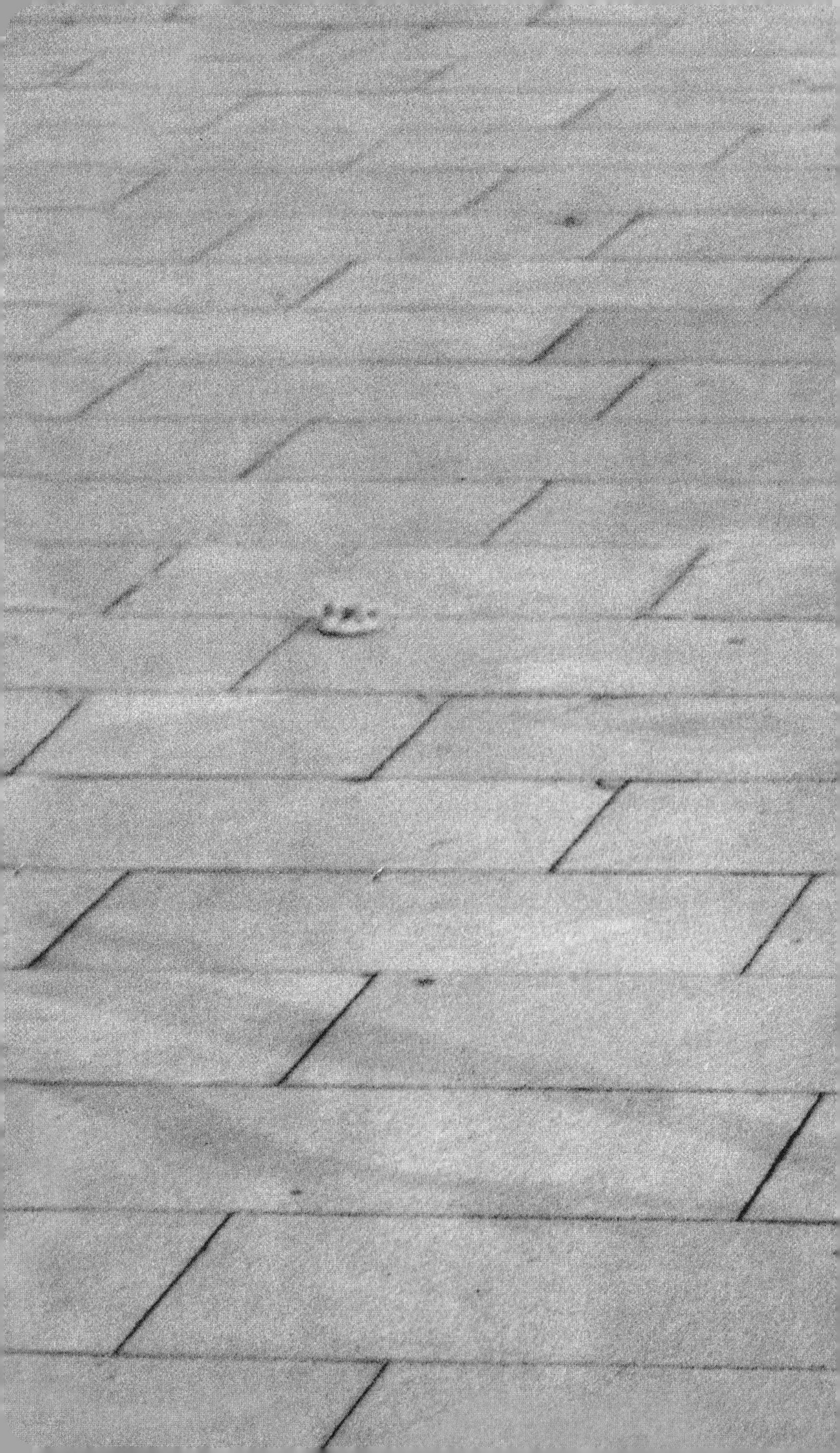

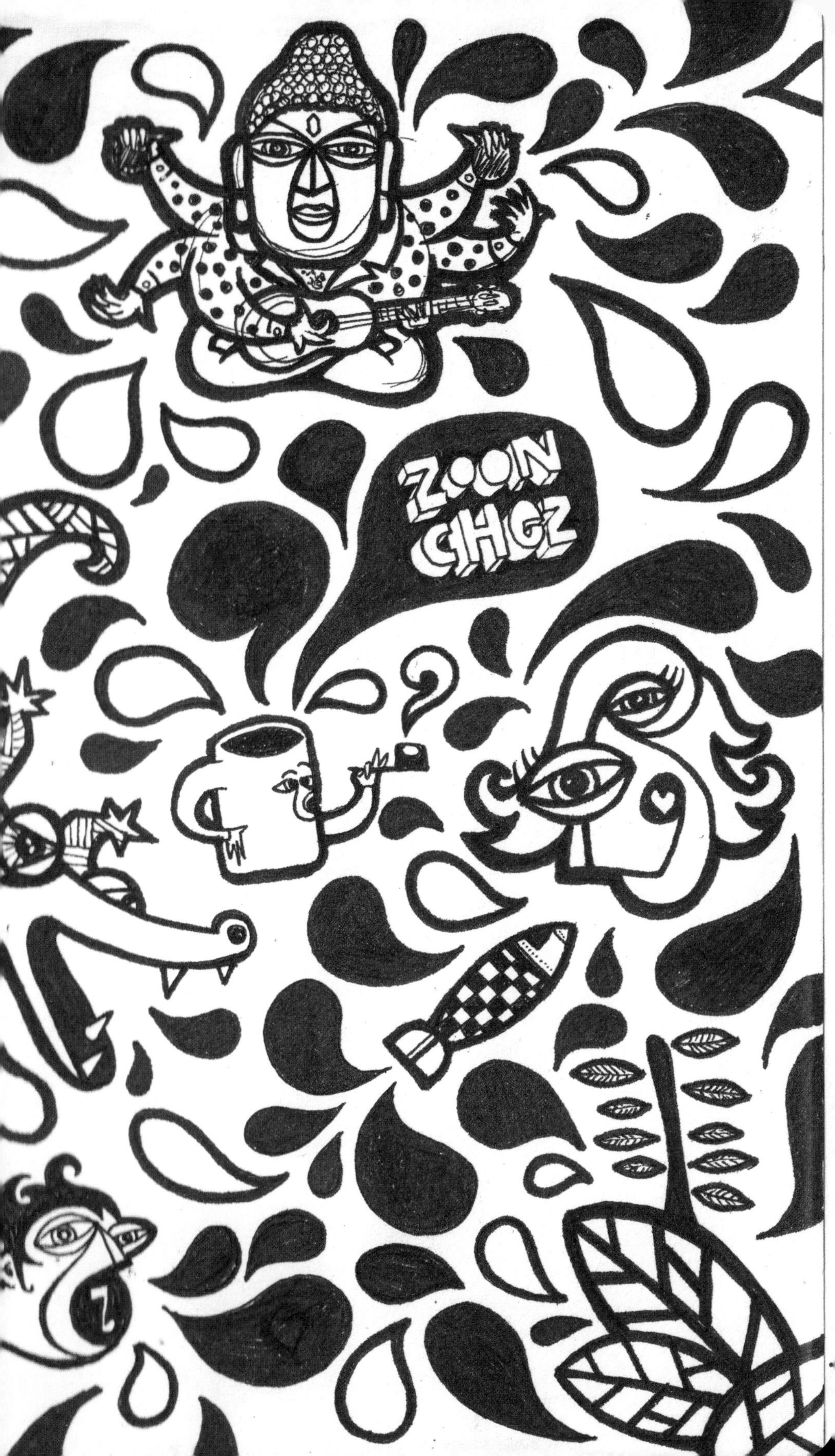
ZOON
CHGZ

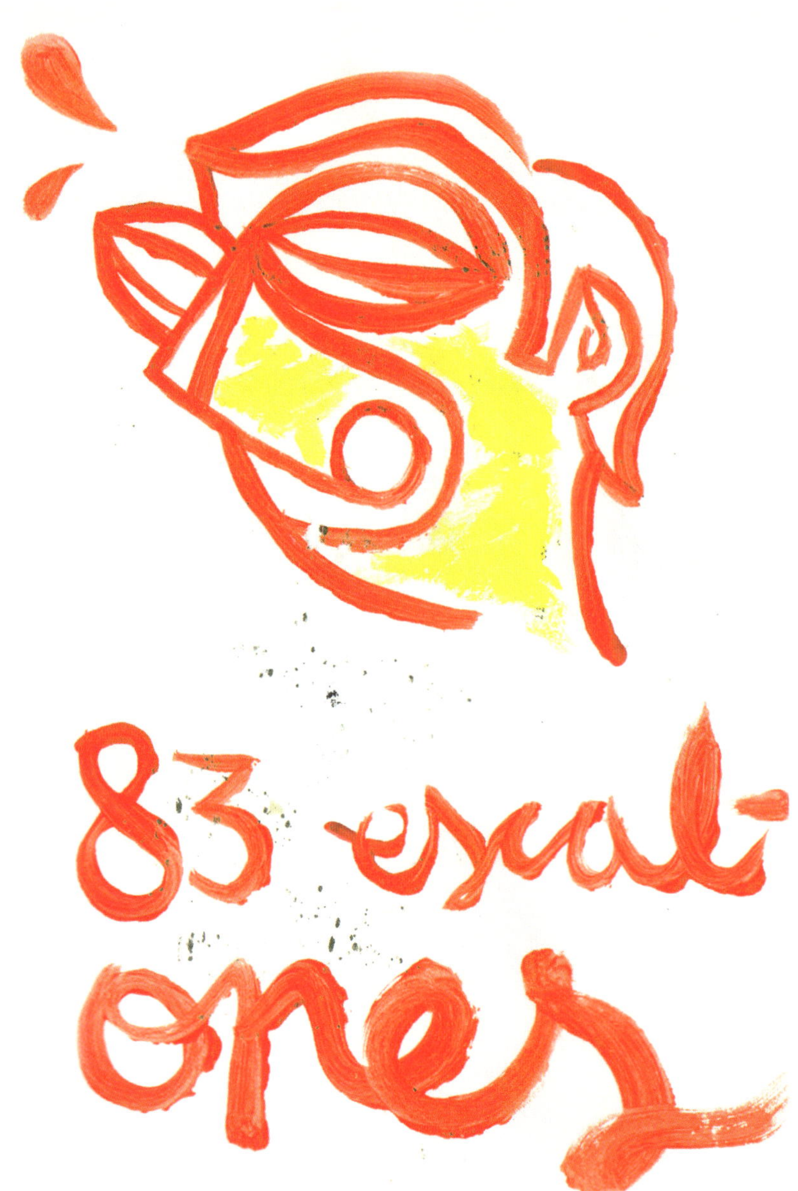

83 escal-
ones

From: Ruben Sanchez <iamrubensanchez@gmail.com>
Date: 12 August 2016 at 10:19:05 GMT+2
To: Ruben Sanchez <iamrubensanchez@gmail.com>
Subject: Ilustración_sin_título.jpg

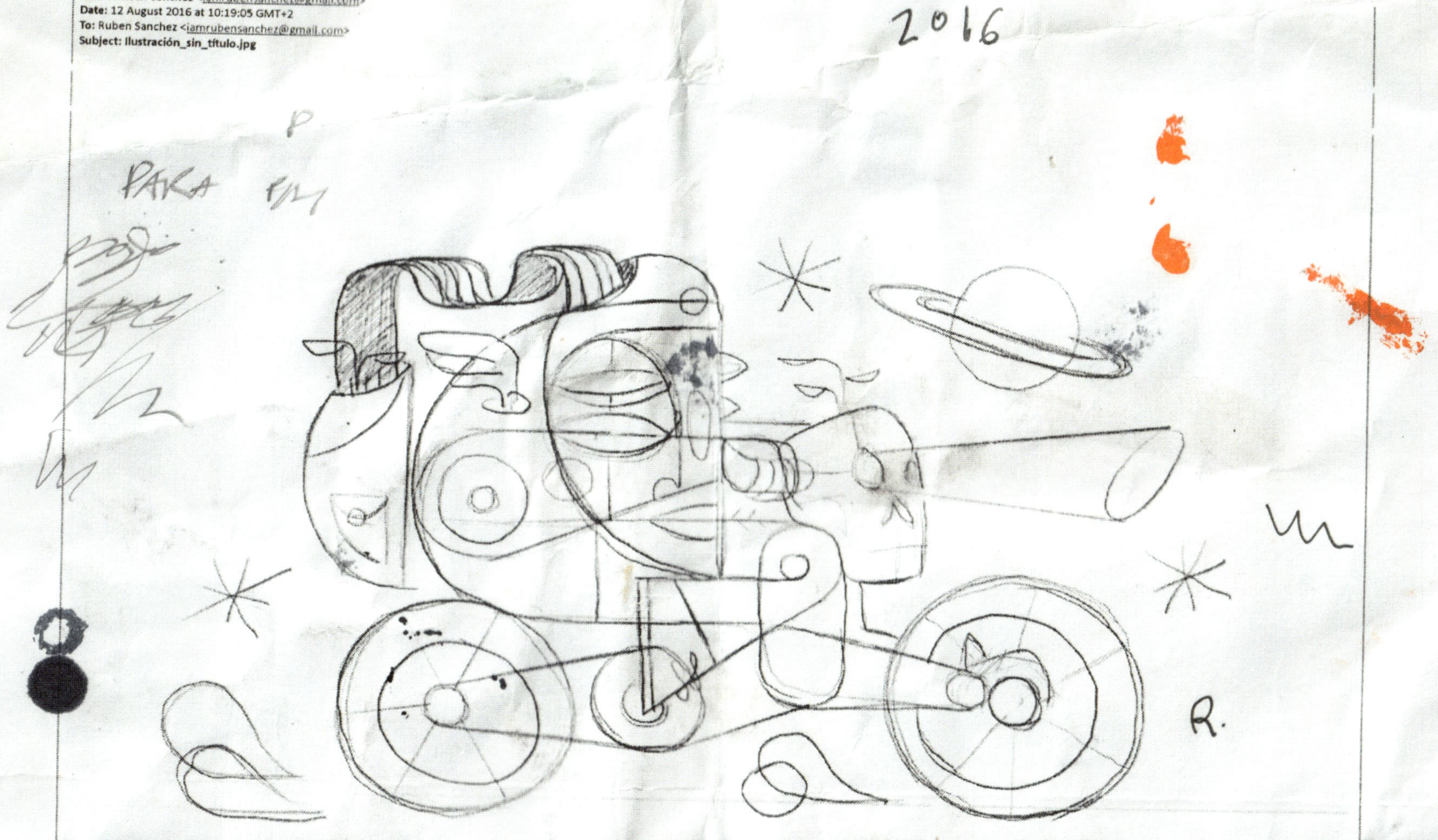

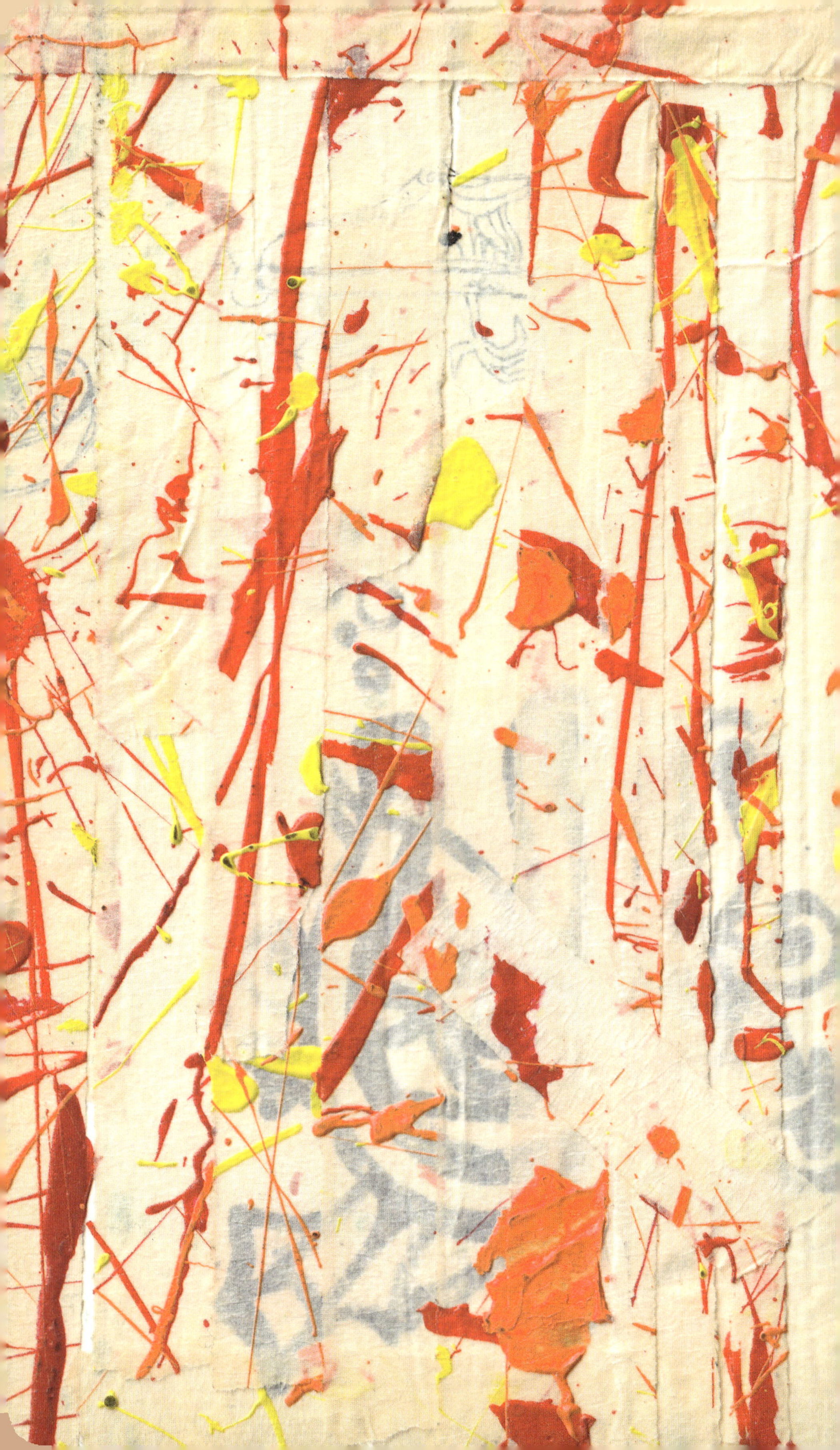

JALIEN À KEBAB

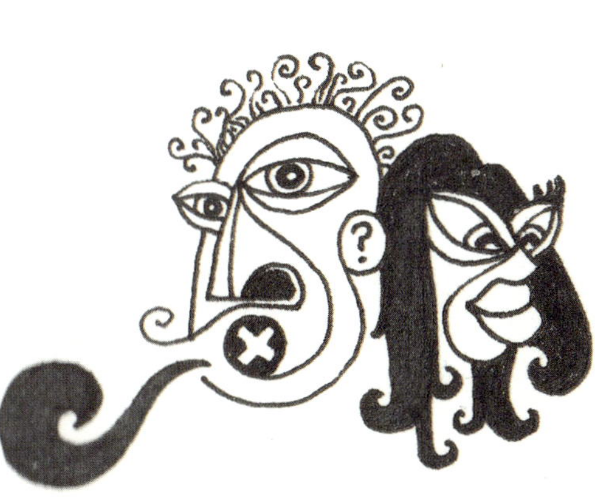

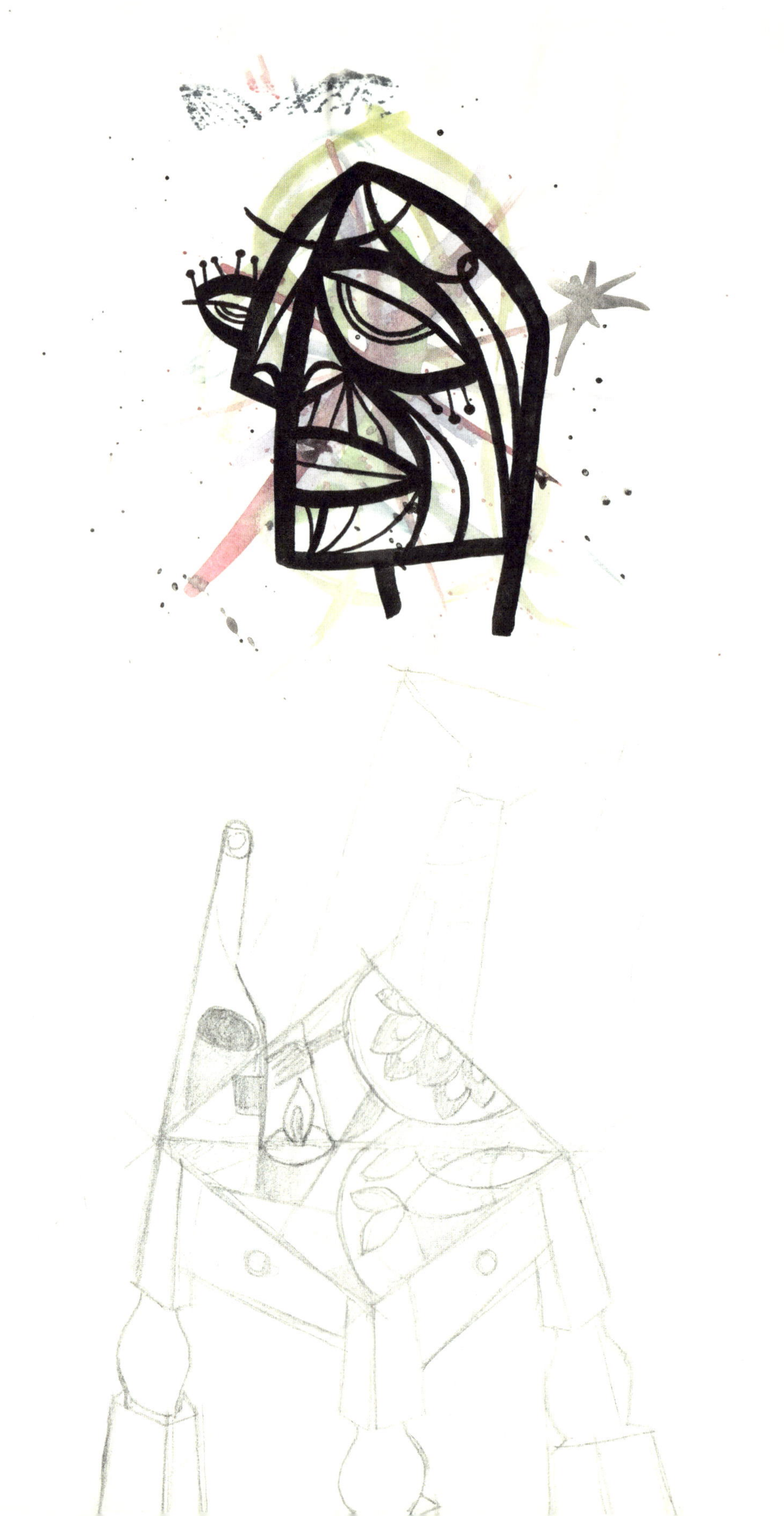

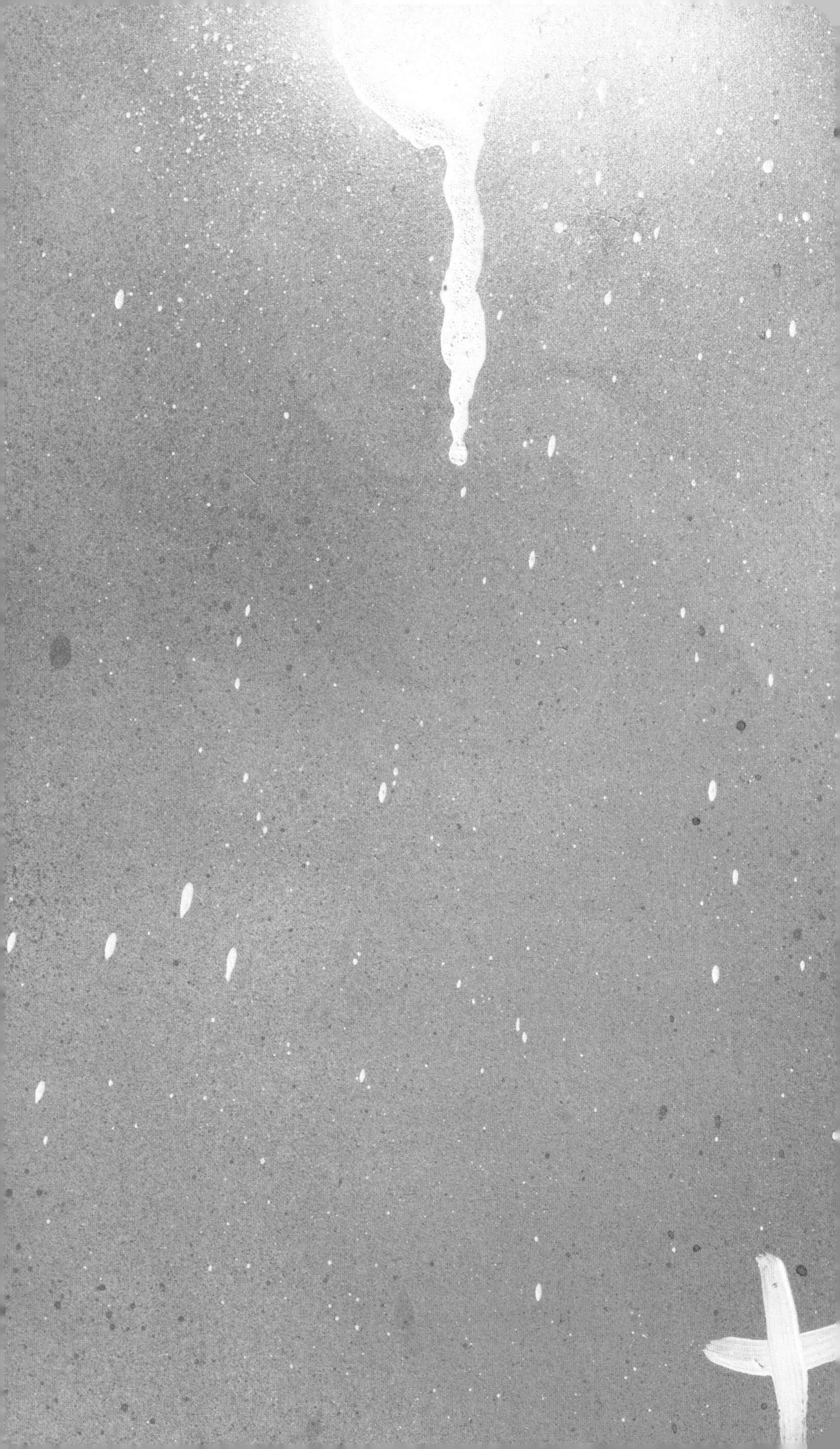

BADALONA
SARDANISTA

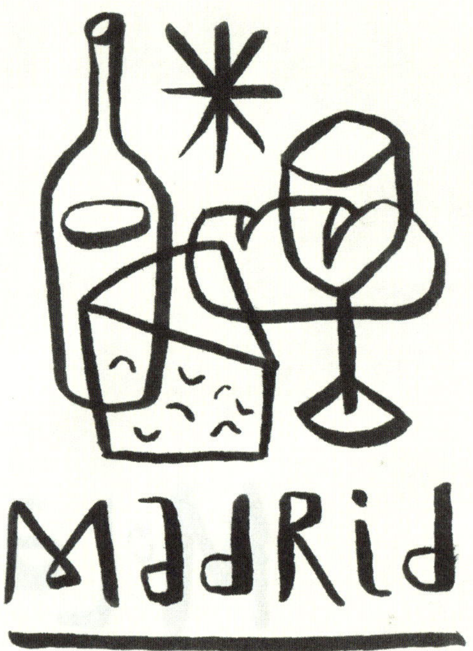
MadRid

PERO FIJO,
OK VENGA VAMOS
¿NOS QUEDAMOS?

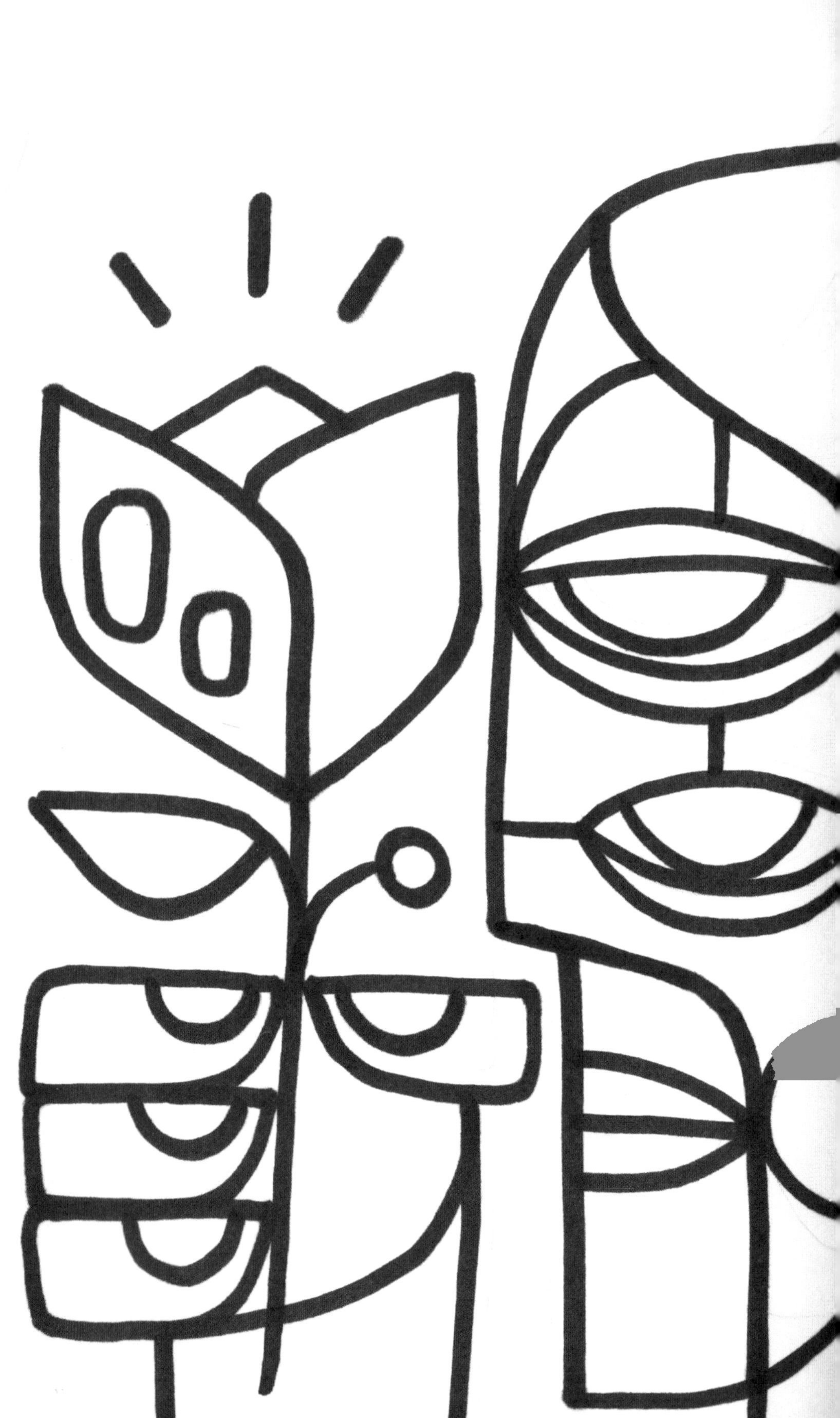

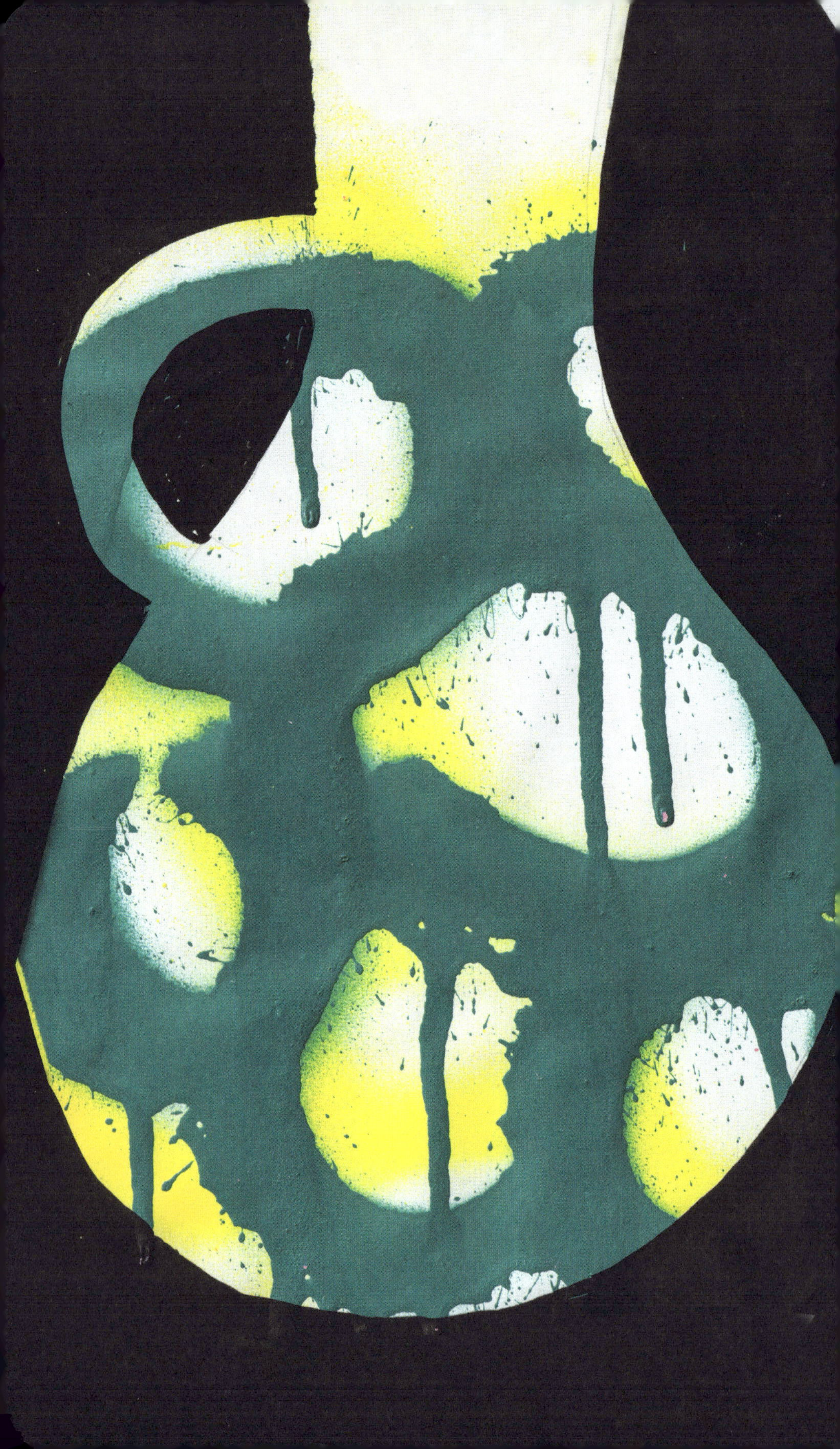

SYMMETRY SUCKS

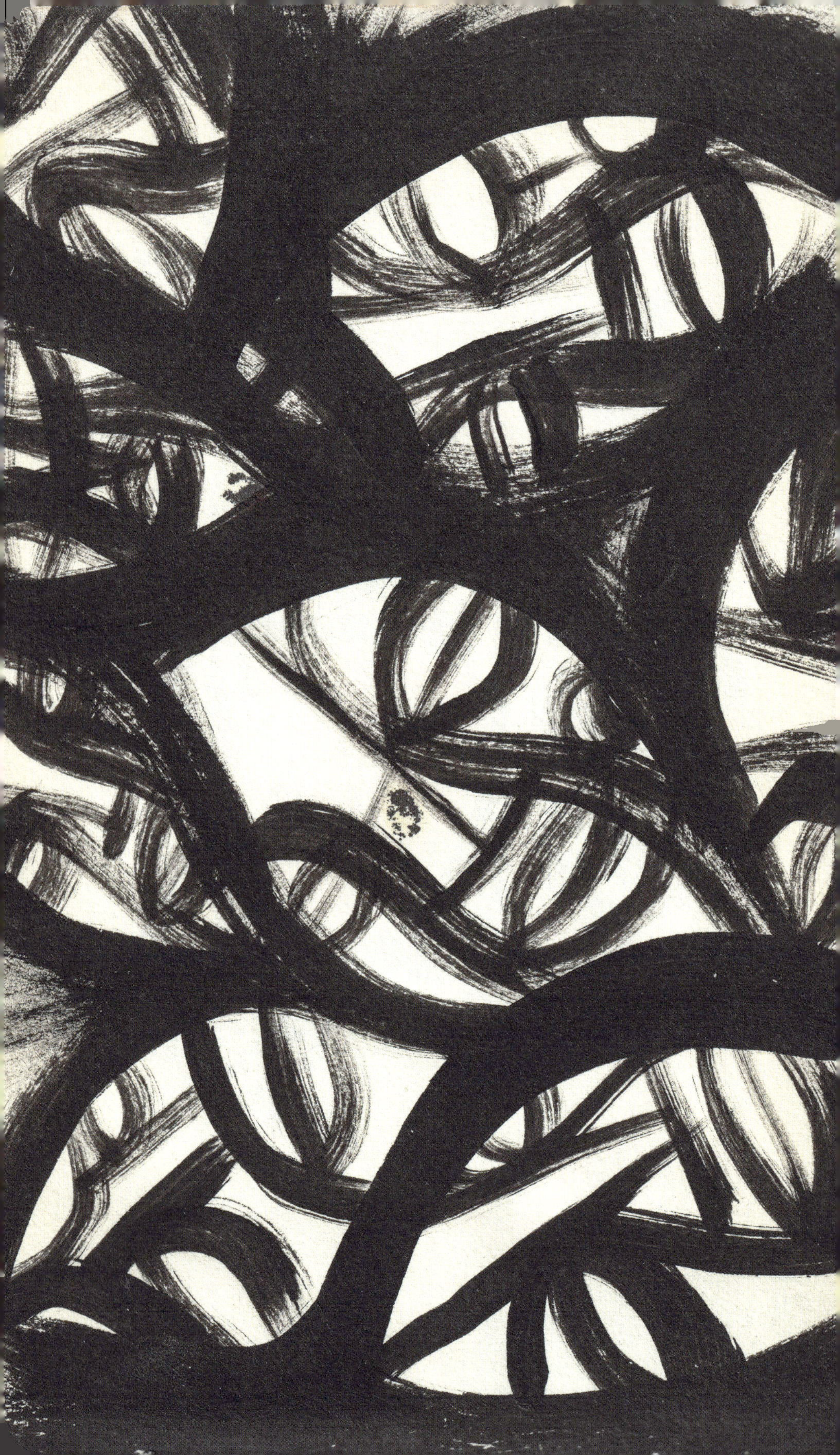

Lo que Hago
No vieNe de La
RaZóN,
vieNe de La
vida MisMa.
La RaZóN La
dejó PaRa La
tēcNica

Xavier Corberó

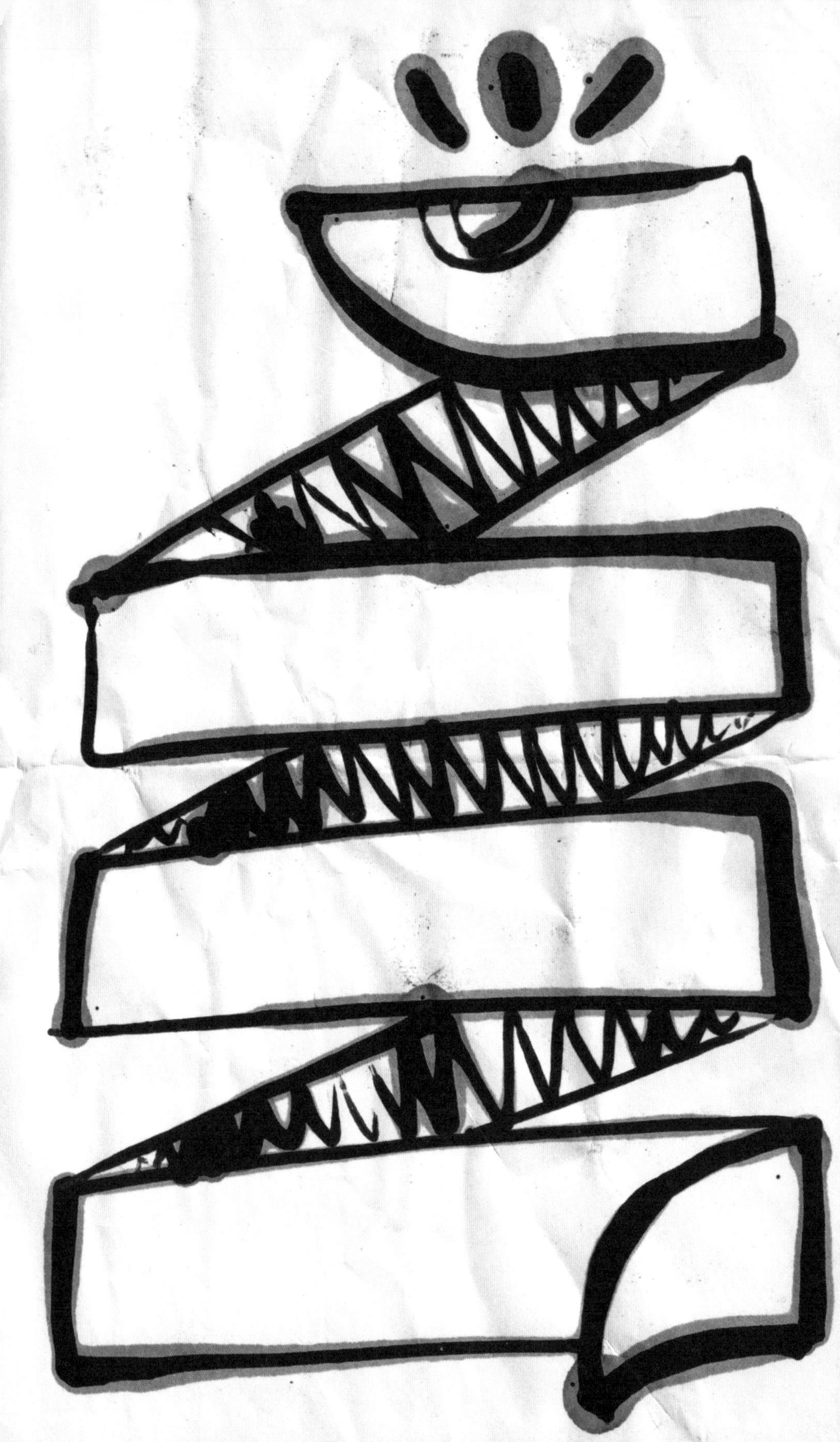

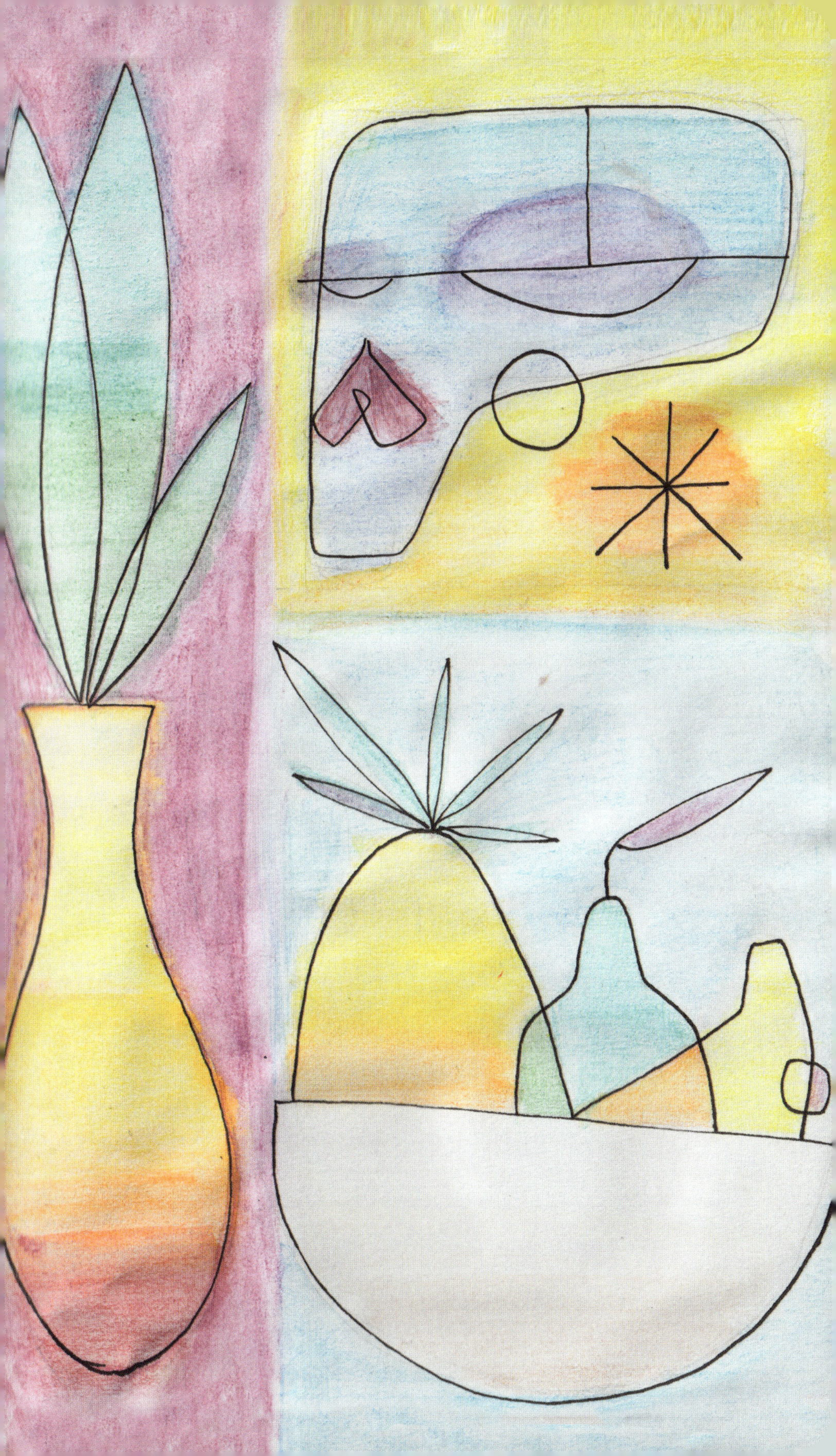

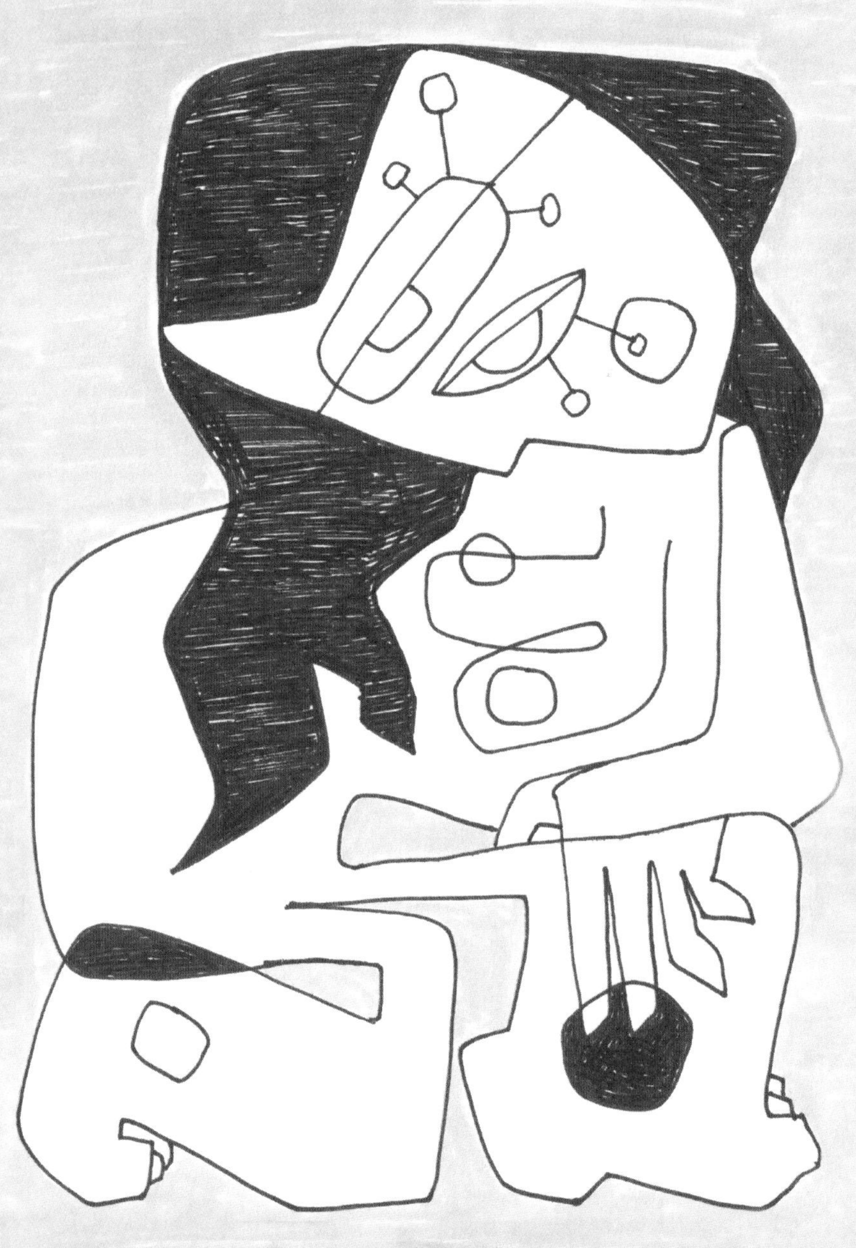

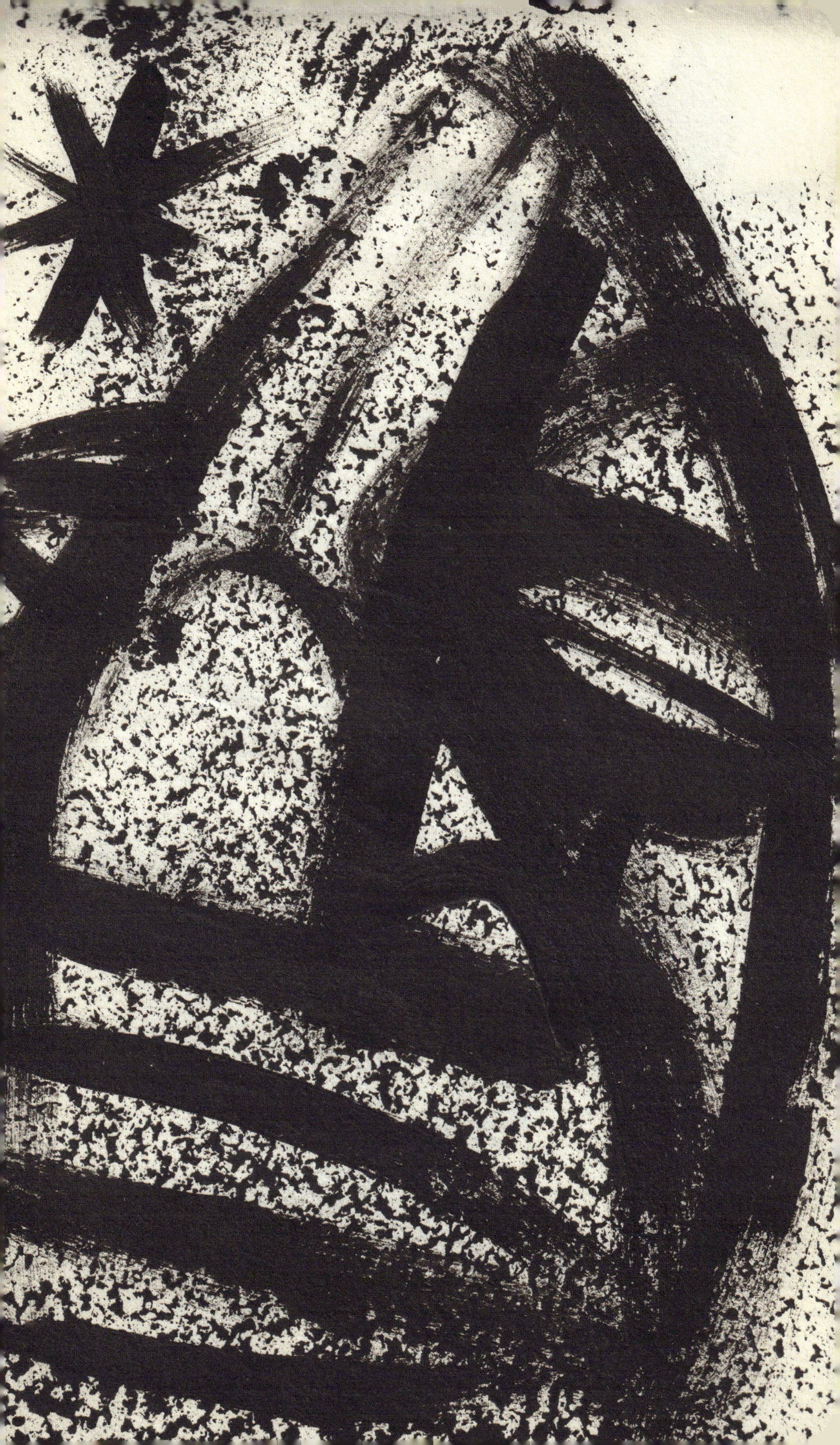

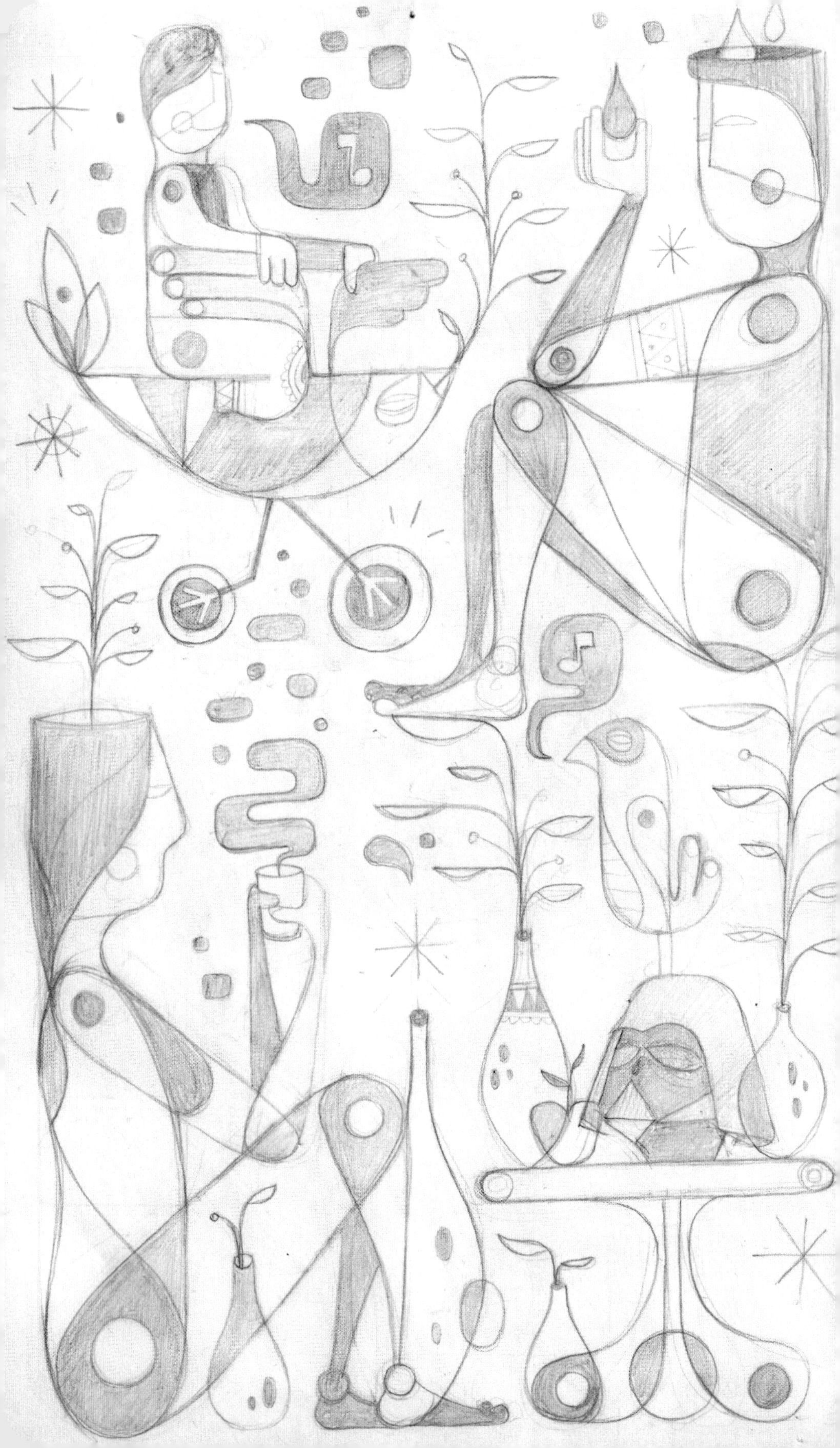

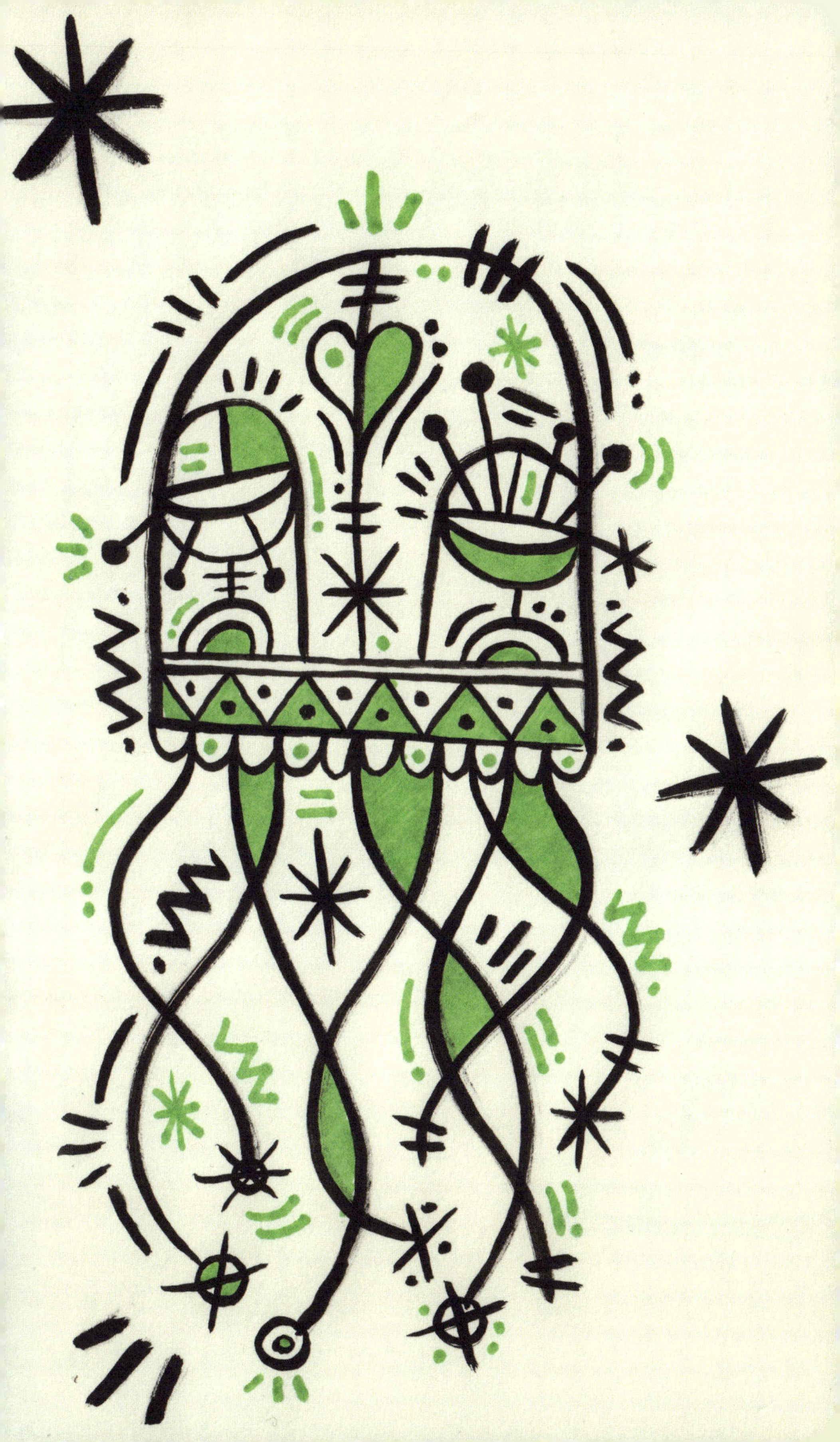

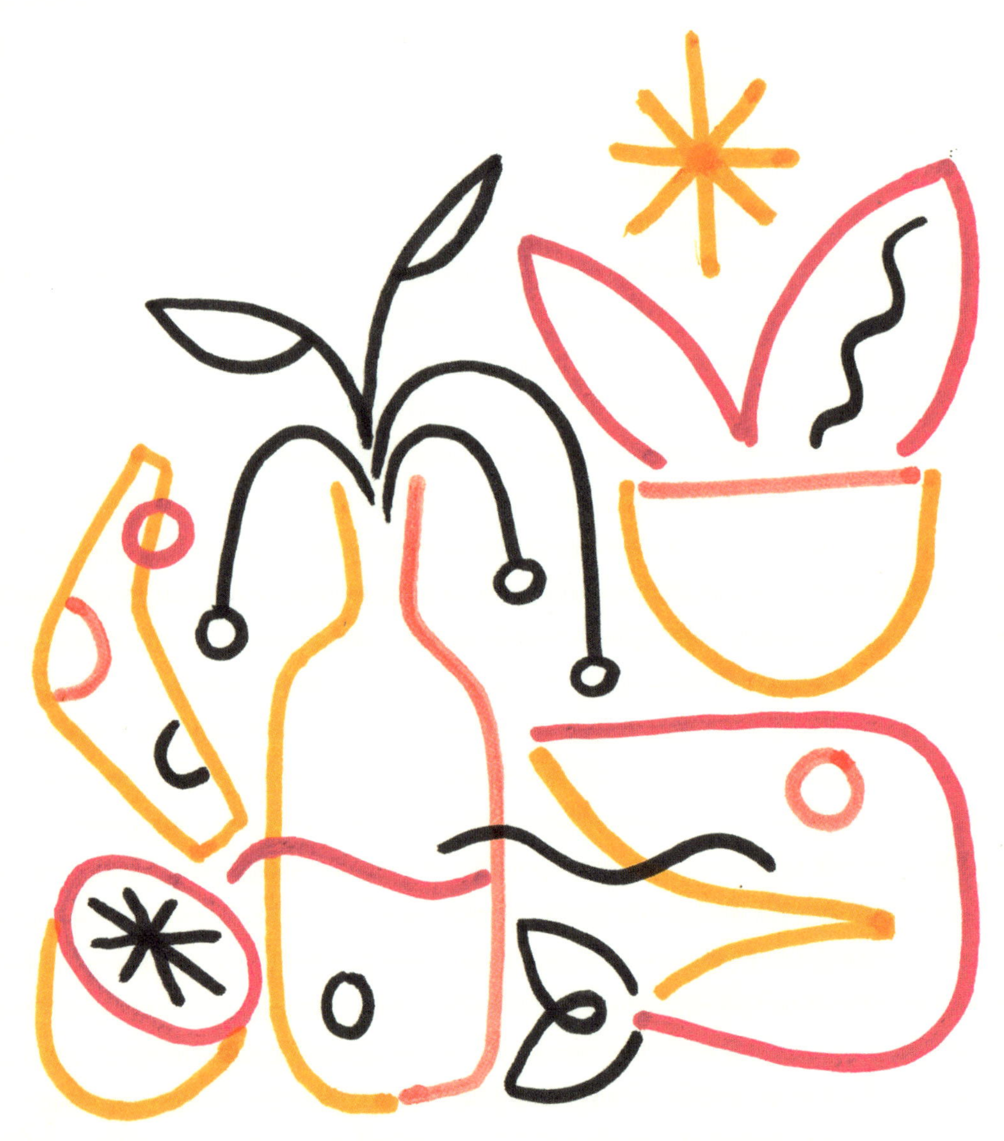

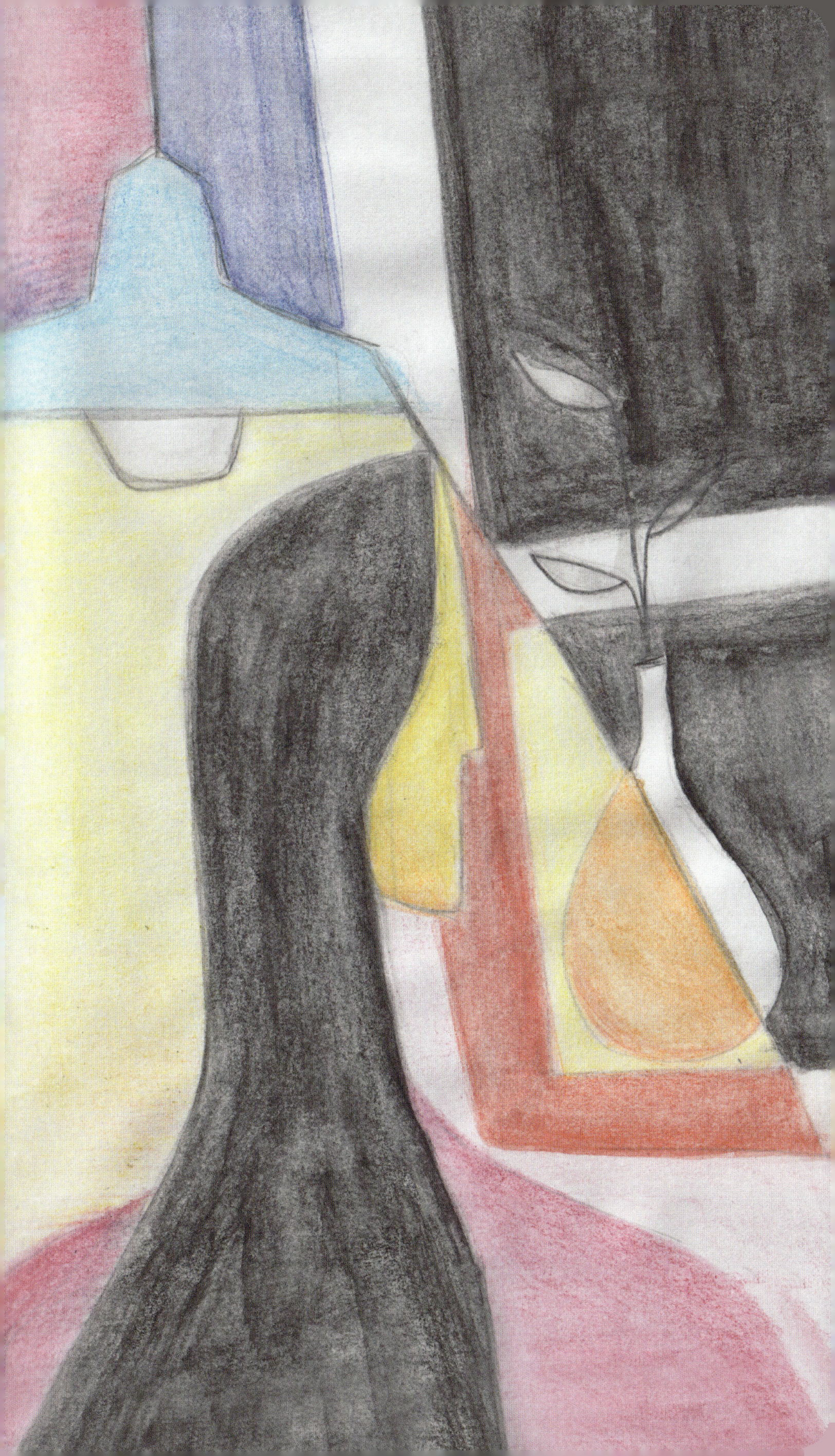

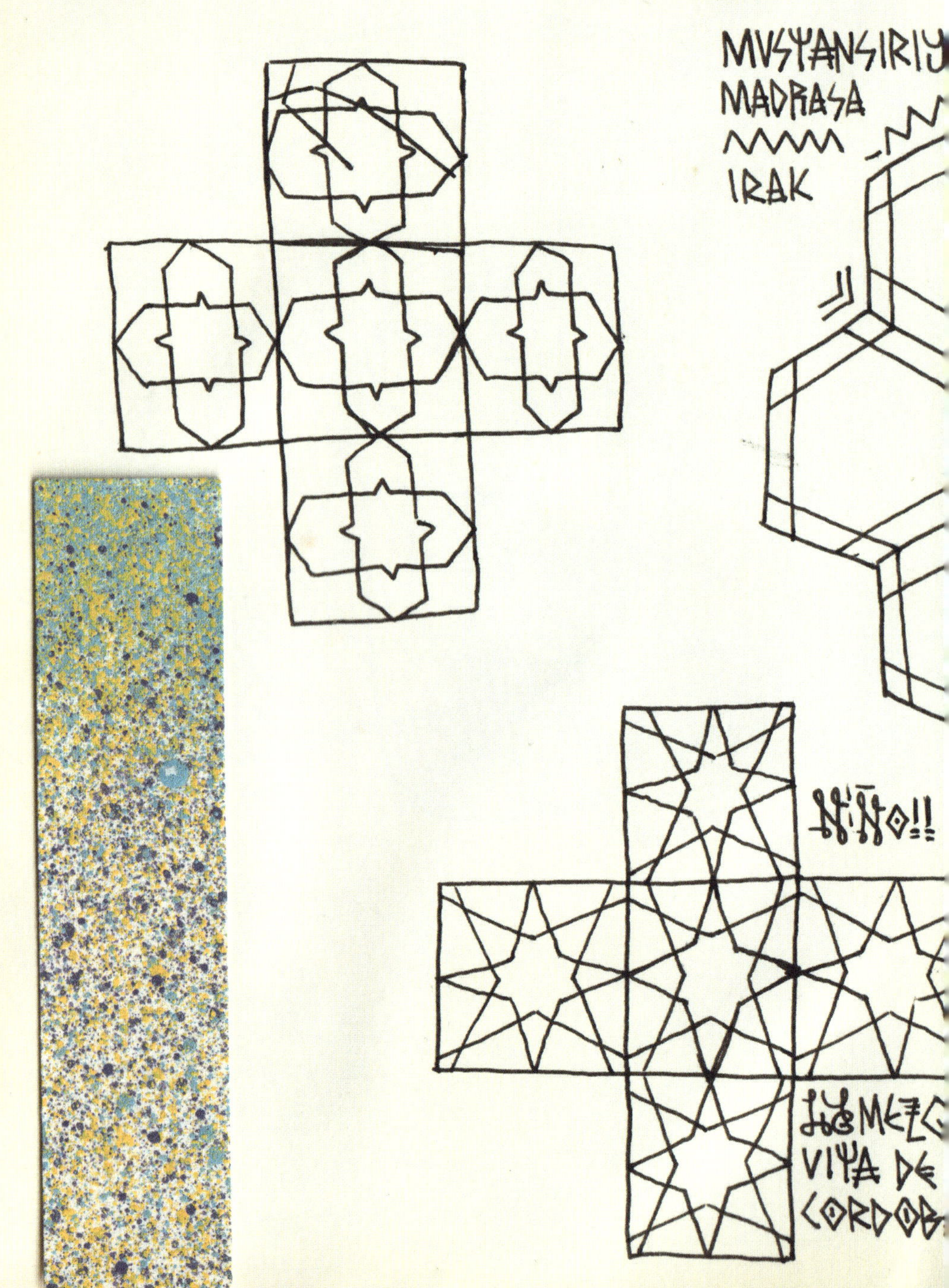
ISLAMIC PATTERNS
MUSTANSIRIYA
MADRASA
IRAK
NIÑO!!
MEZQUITA
VIYA DE
CORDOBA

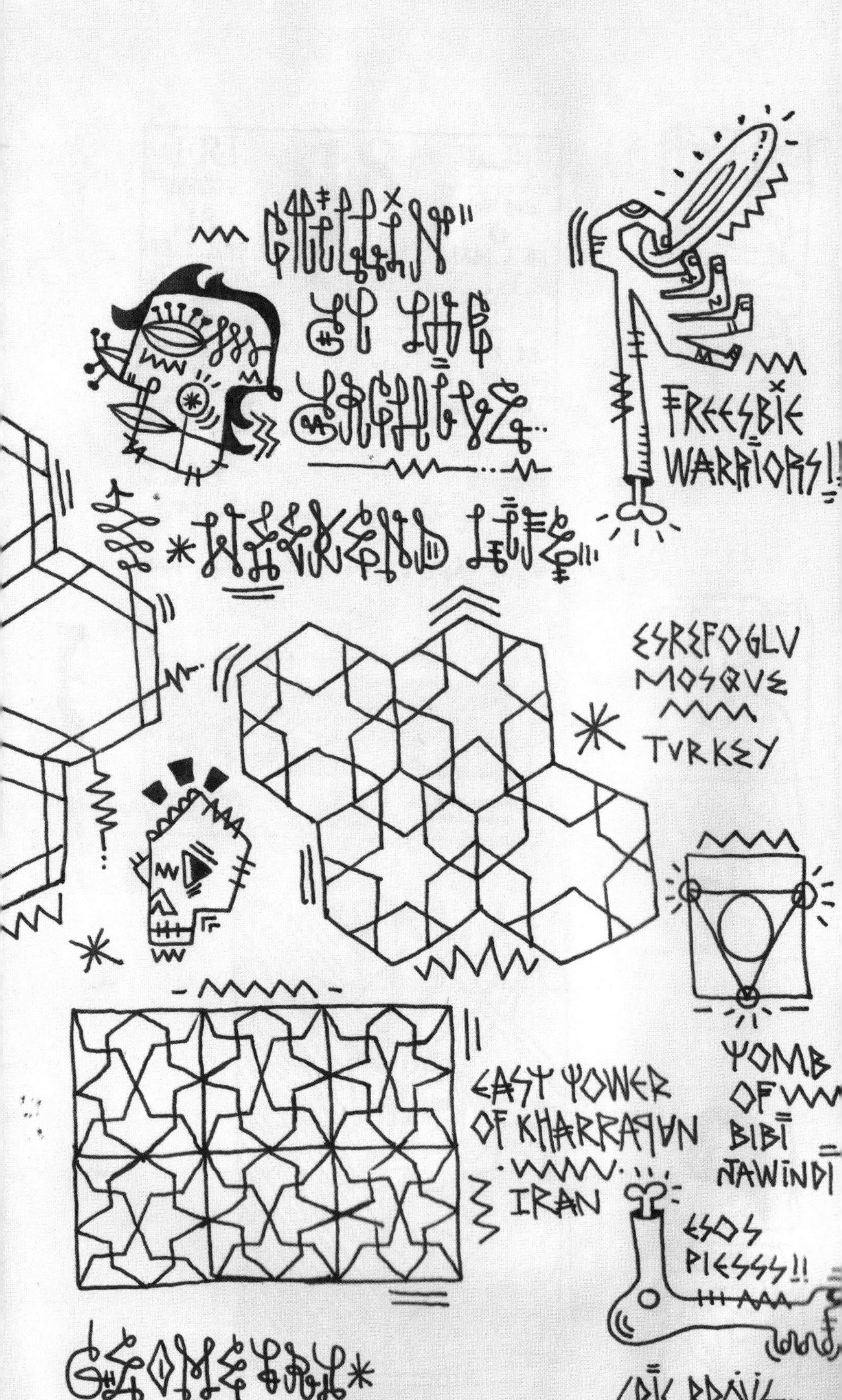
CHILLIN AT THE ARCHIVE...
FREESBIE WARRIORS!!
WEEKEND LIFE
ESREFOGLU MOSQUE TURKEY
EAST TOWER OF KHARRAQAN IRAN
TOMB OF BIBI JAWINDI
SOS PLESSS!!
GEOMETRY
ERIC BROUG...

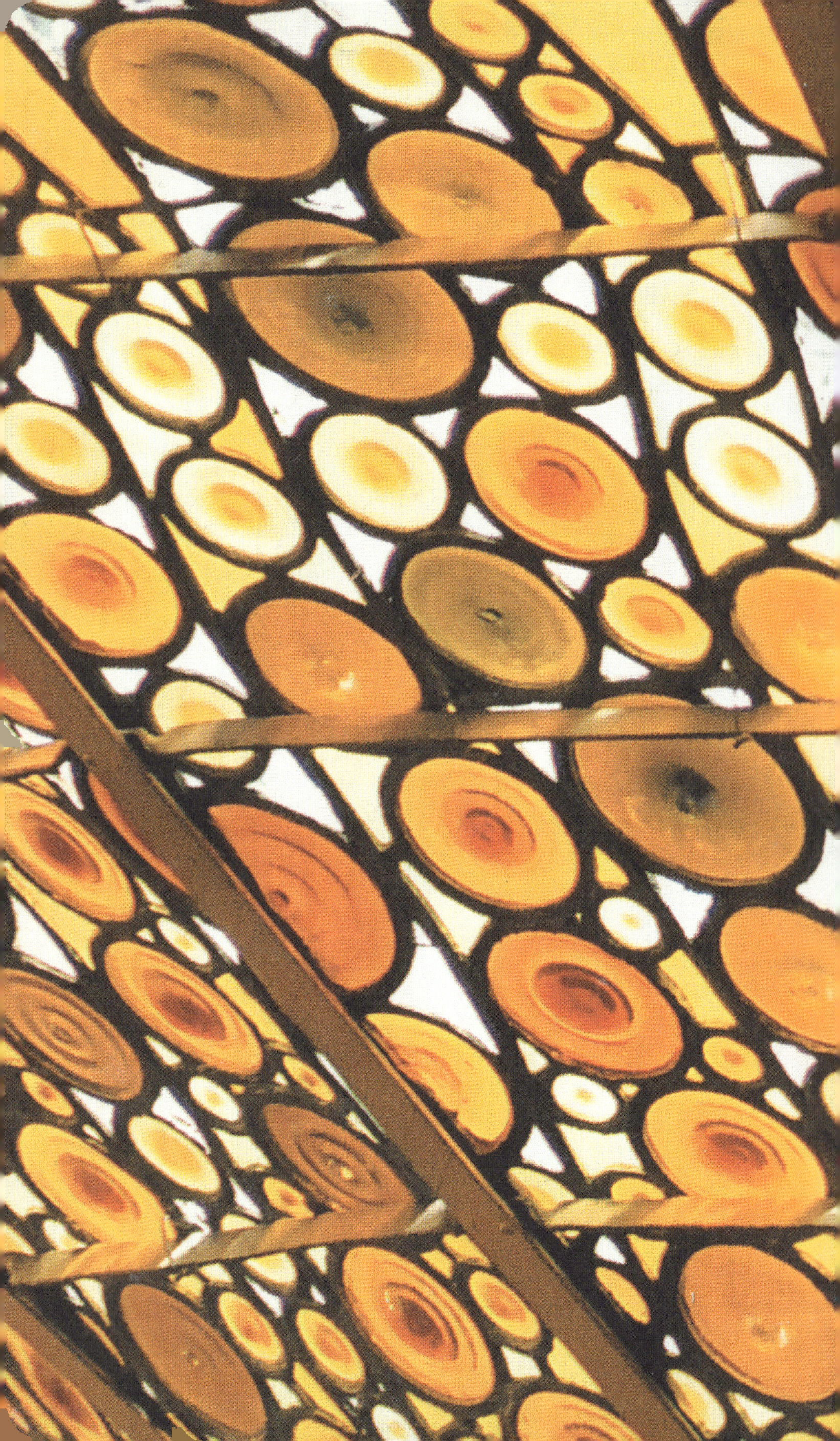

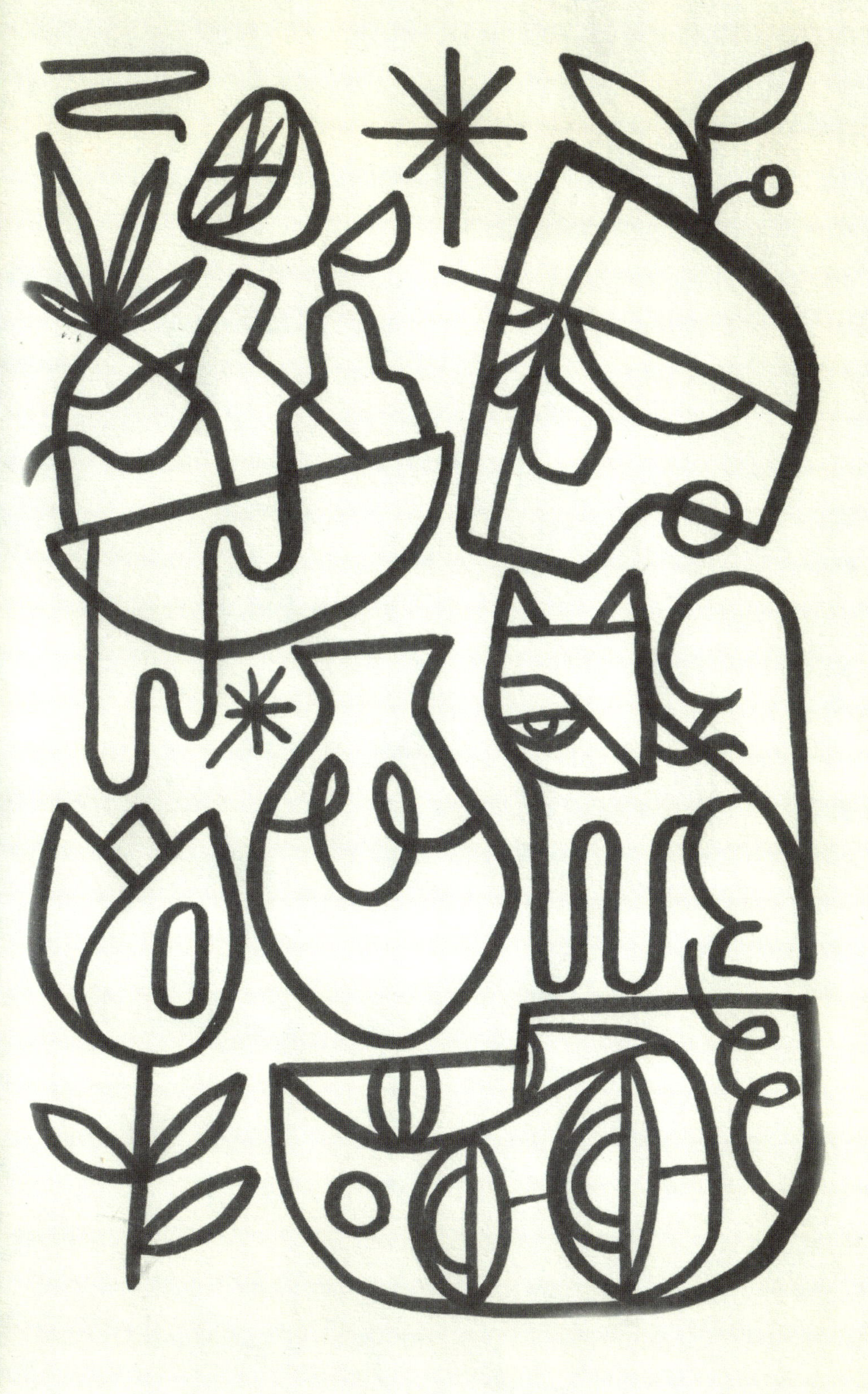

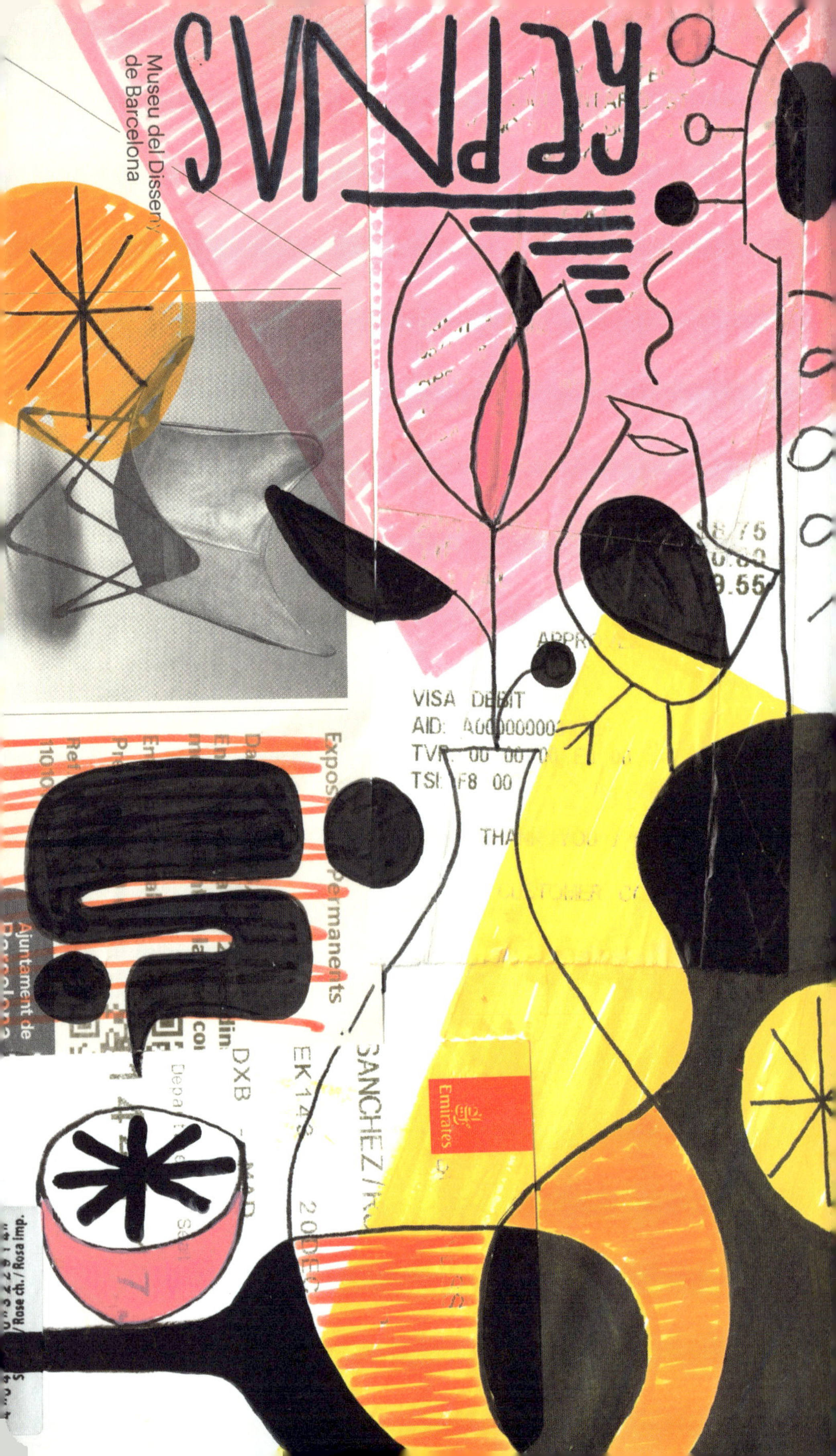

Museu del Disseny
de Barcelona
VISA DEBIT
AID: A00000000
TVR: 00 00
TSI: F8 00
APPR
THANK YOU
Exposicions Permanents
EK 14
DXB
SANCHEZ/R
Emirates
Ajuntament de Barcelona
08.75
9.55

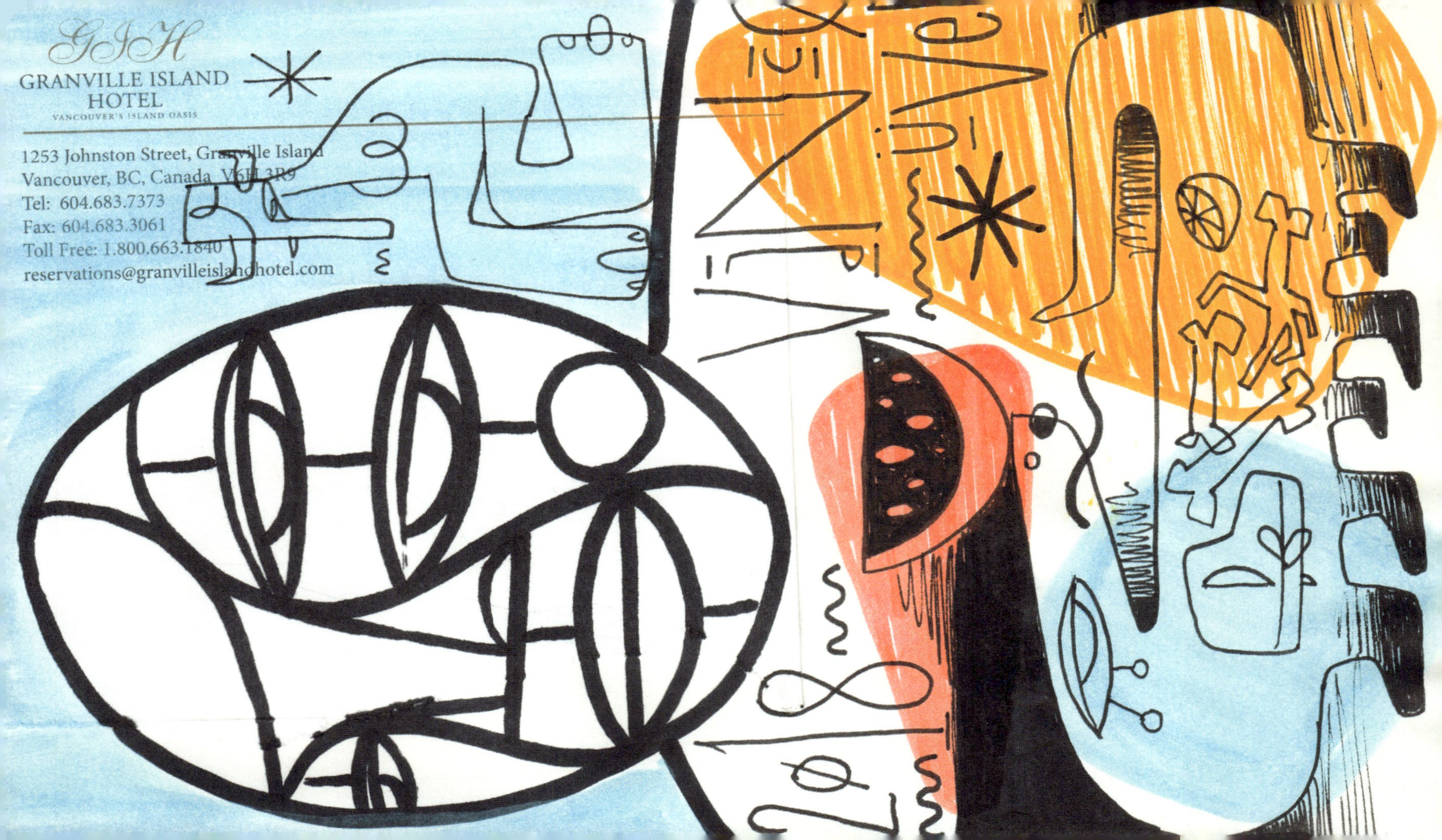
GIH
GRANVILLE ISLAND
HOTEL
VANCOUVER'S ISLAND OASIS
1253 Johnston Street, Granville Island
Vancouver, BC, Canada V6H 3R9
Tel: 604.683.7373
Fax: 604.683.3061
Toll Free: 1.800.663.1840
reservations@granvilleislandhotel.com

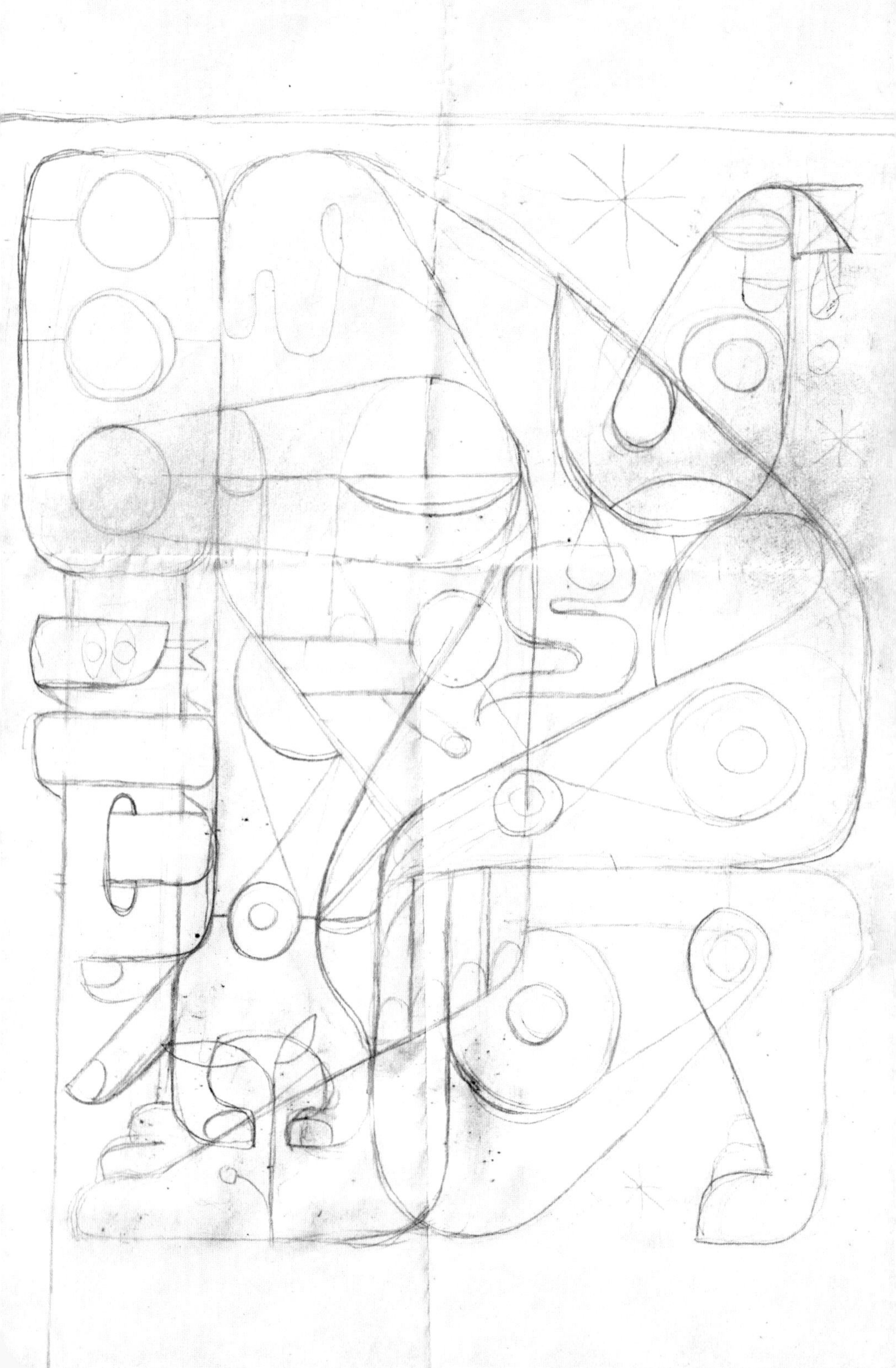

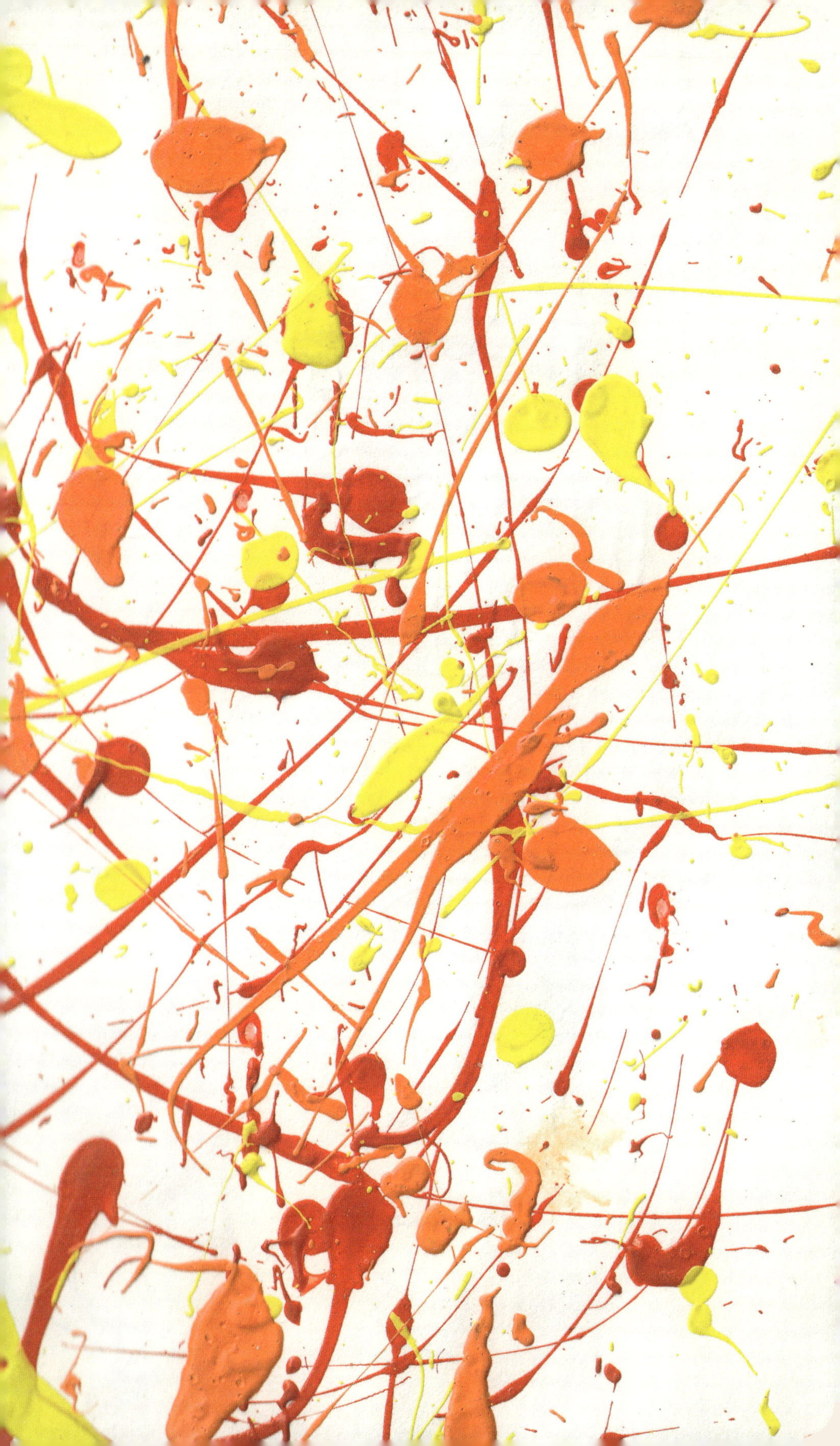

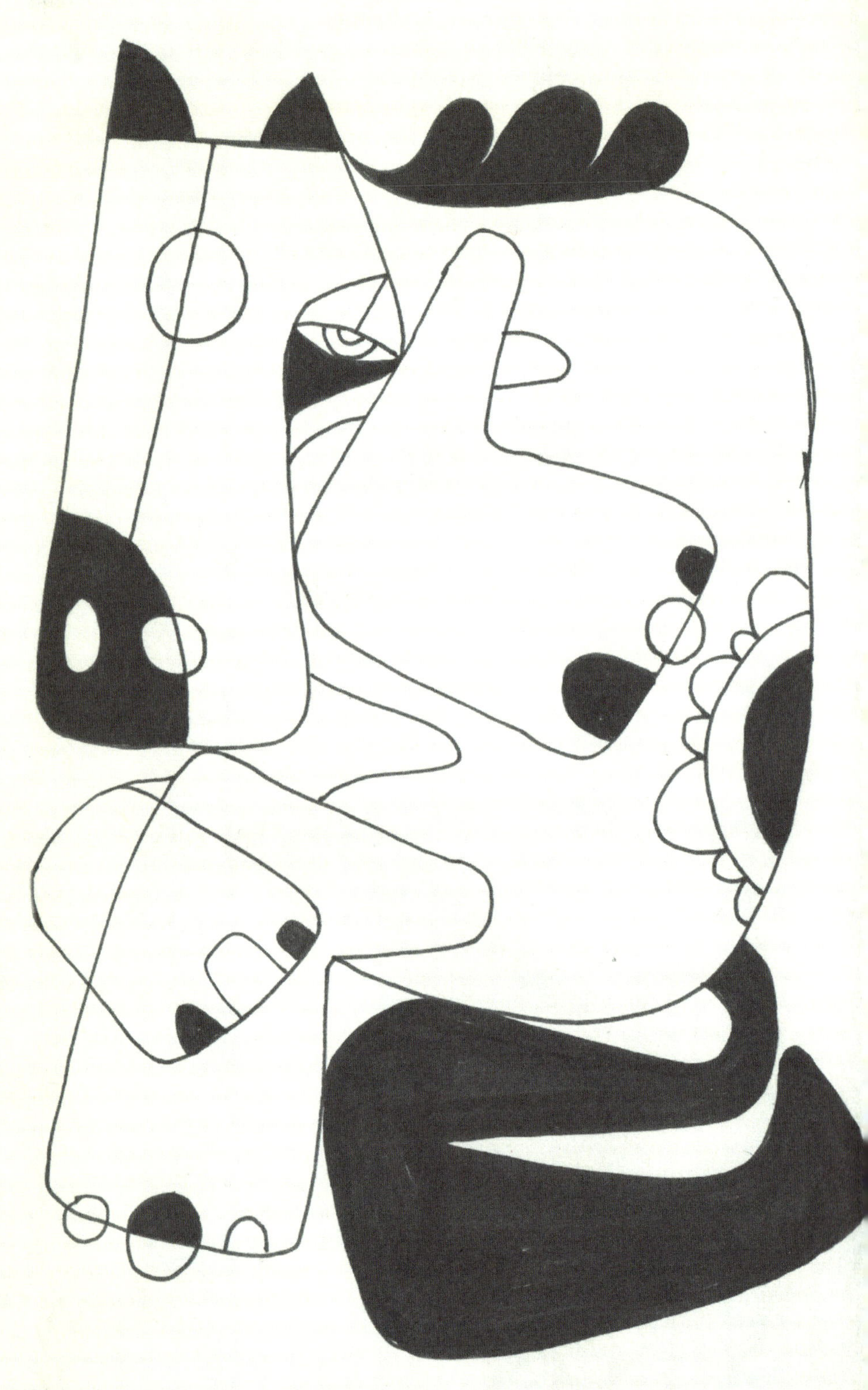

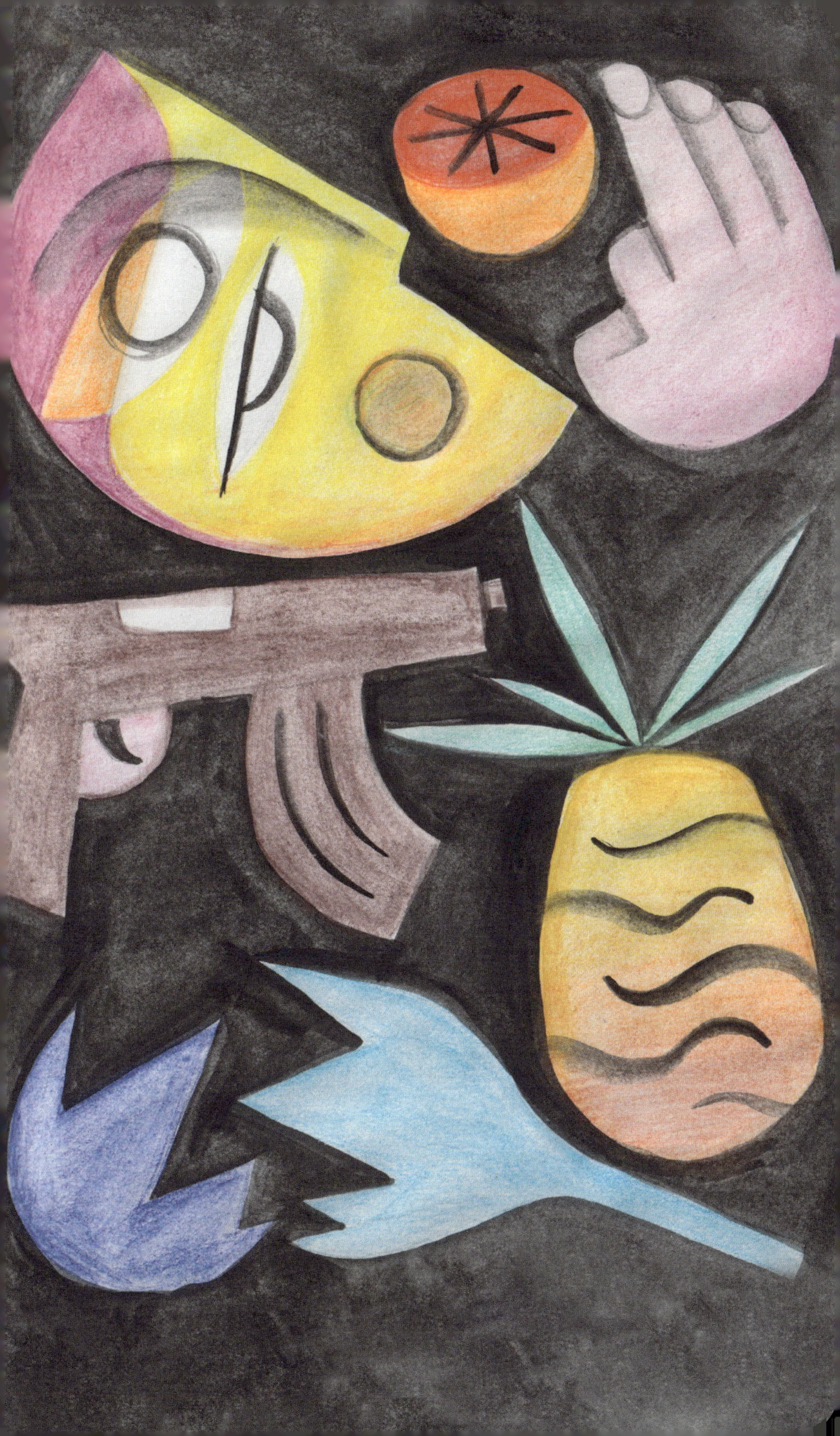

Thanks to:
All the people who supported this project, for making it happen.
Anna, my family, skateboarding.
Lars for his help and patience.
In loving memory of Luis Lucas.

Imprint

© Slanted Publishers, Karlsruhe, 2020
© for all artworks by Rubén Sánchez, Badalona
© for book design by Lars Harmsen, Munich

Rubén Sánchez
Badalona, Spain
iamrubensanchez.com

Slanted Publishers UG
(haftungsbeschränkt)
Nebeniusstraße 10
76137 Karlsruhe
Germany
T +49 (0) 721 85148268
info@slanted.de
slanted.de

Artwork: Rubén Sánchez
Editorial direction & design: Lars Harmsen
Publishing direction: Lars Harmsen, Julia Kahl
Production management: Julia Kahl
Retouching: Laura Nádvornik, Cihan Tamti
Printing and binding: TBB, a.s., Banská Bystrica
Paper: Munken Lynx, Munken Pure

The publisher assumes no responsibility for the accuracy of all information.
Publisher and editor assume that material that was made available for
publishing, is free of third party rights. Reproduction and storage require
the permission of the publisher.
    The German National Library lists this publication in the German
National Bibliography; detailed bibliographic data is available on the
Internet at dnb.d-nb.de.

ISBN 978-3-948440-10-7